The Emergence of Ethnicity

The Emergence of Ethnicity
Cultural Groups and Social Conflict in Israel

Eliezer Ben-Rafael

CONTRIBUTIONS IN ETHNIC STUDIES, NUMBER 7

Greenwood Press
WESTPORT, CONNECTICUT • LONDON, ENGLAND

Library of Congress Cataloging in Publication Data

Ben-Rafael, Eliezer.
    The emergence of ethnicity.

    (Contributions in ethnic studies, ISSN 0196-7088;
no. 7)
      Bibliography: p.
      Includes index.
      1. Israel—Ethnic relations.   2. Ethnicity.
3. Social conflict.   I. Title.   II. Series.
DS113.2.B46   1982   305.8′0095694   ·81-17131
ISBN 0-313-23088-9 (lib. bdg.)   AACR2

Library of Congress Catalog Card Number: 81-17131
ISBN: 0-313-23088-9
ISSN: 0196-7088

First published in 1982

Greenwood Press
A division of Congressional Information Service, Inc.
88 Post Road West, Westport, Connecticut 06881

Printed in the United States of America

10 9 8 7 6 5 4 3 2 1

For my wife Miriam
and our daughters Segal and Lior

Contents

Part IV Ethnicity and Society

Figures and Tables

Figures

Series Foreword

"Contributions in Ethnic Studies" focuses upon the problems that arise when peoples with different cultures and goals come together and interact productively or tragically. The modes of adjustment or conflict are various, but usually one group dominates or attempts to dominate the other. Eventually some accommodation is reached: the process is likely to be long and, for the weaker group, painful. No one scholarly discipline monopolizes the research necessary to comprehend these intergroup relations. The emerging analysis, consequently, inevitably is of interest to historians, social scientists, psychologists, and psychiatrists.

"Israeli society has become ethnically pluralistic," Dr. Ben-Rafael demonstrates in this volume, for reasons the Israelis themselves more or less fully appreciate. The main emphasis is upon two so-called Oriental groups, originally from Yemen and Morocco, who compose, respectively, approximately 6 and 14 percent of the Jewish population. They are only two of the many minority groups who, with few exceptions, have occupied positions subservient to 45 percent of that population, the Jews who have migrated from Europe and America (the Ashkenazi) . Arabs constitute 15 percent of the total population; yet, as one of them has said with only slight hyperbole, "My people are at war with my country."

The book is divided into four parts. The first section is devoted to a history of modern Israel and to presenting a theory of ethnicity. The theory is a general one and hence applicable outside of Israel. It may well constitute a scholarly landmark not only for sociologists, psychologists, and historians but also for decision makers and leaders who are trying to inject more sanity into the conflicts among groups that pervade our unhappy era virtually everywhere. Relevant, modern social science literature is summarized as well as Israeli studies, including research heretofore unavailable to those without a knowledge of Hebrew. Elaborate figures (diagrams) block out the parameters of the subject, which is thus made more easily intelligible.

The second section is devoted to "the objective side" of the "ethnic encounter" between the Yemenites and the Moroccans on the one hand and the dominant Ashkenazi on the other hand. The migrants brought their own culture and way of life with them into the land of honey. Although their ancestors for many generations and they themselves had been devout Jews, they were confronted with difficult, puzzling challenges as they tried to forget the experiences of the Diaspora and settle down in an already well-structured society.

In the third section, "the subjective side," the author presents data he himself has gathered from samples of these oriental citizens of Israel. The people report how they feel about themselves, their traditional culture, their identifications, other Jewish groups, and their present and future status within the greater society. By and large, let the secret be communicated here, they retain fierce loyalty to their own ethnicity.

But Israel, the final section emphatically suggests, inescapably is changing. The children of the oriental groups who have been born in Israel, nevertheless, learn significant aspects of the Yemenite and Moroccan culture of their parents from those parents and from the segregated communities within which most of them live. The principal sources facilitating but not ensuring change are contacts with the dominant Israeli culture in integrated schools, during compulsory military service of both sexes, and as a result of the increasing number of mixed marriages. Will or should Israel achieve a melting pot of its disparate ethnic Jewish groups and its Arabs whose positions within Israel are also analyzed in these pages? As bravely and as objectively as possible, Dr. Ben-Rafael tosses this perennial conundrum about and provides new and sensitive insight by way of his theory and its accompanying data.

Leonard W. Doob
May 6, 1981

Preface

Ethnic studies devoted to Jewish groups in Israel include hundreds of items and cover a wide range of interests. To mention but the major trends, many researchers have concentrated on modernization of traditional groups, sociocultural developments of rural communities, questions pertaining to social stratifications, politics or education, and intergroup relations.

Despite this profusion, however, up to now no attempt has been made to draw out a *comprehensive* picture of the Israeli case that might reveal features unexamined by researchers concerned with specific issues. This is the aim of this book, an aim that could be achieved only after confronting two major problems. The first concerned the elaboration of a consistent conceptual framework and the second, the undertaking of empirical research into essential questions left uninvestigated by previous studies.

As for the theoretical problems, it was my privilege to discuss many issues with Seymour M. Lipset, George C. Homans and Orlando Patterson during my stay at Harvard University as a research fellow. I am also much indebted to Shmuel N. Eisenstadt, Moshe Lissak, and Erik Cohen of the Hebrew University of Jerusalem who read parts of earlier drafts and made most useful comments. I benefitted from the suggestions of Emmanuel Marx, Yonathan Shapiro, Moseh Shokeid, Sacha Weitman, Yochanan Peres, Ephraim Yaar and Hanna Herzog from Tel Aviv University, and Alex Weingrod and Steve Sharot of Ben Gurion University. I also have had the opportunity to present the theses of this book to colloquia of the Department of Sociology and Anthropology of Tel Aviv University and of the Department of Behavioral Sciences of Ben Gurion University, to the yearly Conference of the Eshkol Institute of the Hebrew University of Jerusalem, and to the Conference on Ethnicity in Israel held at Ben Gurion University. On all these occasions I received important comments. The empirical research was financed by the Eshkol Institute and the Ben-Zvi Institute and carried out with the help of my assistants, Avital Mizrahi, Eli Lazare, and Sheryl Maliki. I would also like to thank Victor Blau, Debbie Golden, and Tamar Berkowicz for their work on the manuscript.

Last, but not least, my wife Miriam and our daughters Segal and Lior have demonstrated patience which alone made this book possible.

PART I

THEORY AND REALITY

Introduction

1

The Jewish population of Israel is surely one of the most heterogeneous and recent in the world today. Besides non-Jewish citizens (15 percent of the whole) no single ethnic group accounts for more than one-seventh of the total (see Appendix 1). From 650,000 in 1948, this number increased to 1.4 million in 1951 and 2.3 million in 1965. In 1972 immigrants still comprised 53 percent of Jewish citizens and Israeli-born were thus a minority.

The differences among various groups are numerous and pertain to customs and physical traits as well as language of origin. All, however, share the same religious background and several historical experiences entailed by their common Jewish identity. But in the Israeli reality, a broad differentiation is made between Jews of Euro-American extraction (The "Ashkenazi")—45 percent of Israel's Jewish population in the 1980s—and those who come from North African and Middle Eastern countries (the "Orientals")—55 percent. The major differences between them lies in socioeconomic cleavages that often blur the distinction between specific origins.

Social gaps (see Appendix 2) between the two major categories are quite large, indeed, and shrink only slowly during the years. The general distribution of Israelis shows an over representation of Ashkenazi in bigger cities (mainly Tel Aviv and Haifa) and, to a lesser extent, in the central area of Israel (Tel Aviv and its periphery).[1] Orientals are more numerous in older towns on the outskirts of larger urban centers (half their total population) and even more so in farther areas like the Negev or Galilee, where they inhabit new agricultural settlements and "development towns." In other words, Orientals are underrepresented in those parts of the country that include two-thirds of Israelis (Haifa, Tel Aviv, and the central area) and overrepresented elsewhere.[2] In the big cities themselves,[3] they form the vast majority of lower-class neighborhoods.

Let us remember, however, that Euro-Americans have, as a whole, been in residence longer than Orientals: up to 1947, 227,814 of them arrived as immigrants, as compared to only 39,254 Middle Easterners and other people of Asian countries and 7,234 North Africans. In 1948 they were still 55 percent of the population while Orientals were only 10 percent, and 35 percent of native born Israelis were mostly of Euro-American parents. This picture changed significantly between 1948-54, when along with 258,545 Euro-American *olim*, (Jewish immigrants to Israel), 206,138 Asians and 100,562 North Africans arrived. Immigration of Asians then largely stopped, but 263,027 Westerners came during the next two decades, and North Africa contributed a further 241,054 citizens.[4]

It is in this context of pronounced differences in veteranship, socio-economic position, and geographic location that problems of social integration have arisen. One sign among others: in development towns as well as in lower-class urban neighborhoods, deviant subcultures were soon to develop,[5] and up until today juvenile delinquency is far more common among Orientals than Euro-Americans (the ratio was 6:1 in 1956).[6] Concurrently an impressive list of books has depicted Oriental Jews as relegated to a condition of inferiority and as resenting an assumed negative attitude toward themselves on the part of the "domineering" Ashkenazi. As late as 1979, a member of Parliament of Oriental origin, despite his affiliation to the governing coalition, did not hesitate to declare:

It may be said that the system (of absorption) made impossible any substantial improvement. The establishment has neglected the correct way of integrating hundreds of thousands of immigrants. There has been no planning nor, in fact, any absorption. The system is not designed to solve the problems created from the start.[7]

Such views express a strong feeling of deprivation; it is no wonder that in a national survey no less than four-fifths of Oriental respondents declared that discrimination by Ashkenazi effectively existed.[8] In return, many Orientals show less willingness than Euro-Americans to accept sacrifices required by the Government under difficult circumstances.[9] Blunt accusations are frequently voiced, and the following quote from an ethnic paper is but one instance:

For many years an unforgivable sin has been committed by the Jewish Agency. No competent and devoted emissaries were sent out to our brothers in the Iranian Exile to propagate the News of Salvation and to prepare them for the Return. . . . The only emissaries sent were chosen on the basis of party allegiance as a reward for their contribution to electoral campaigns unrelated to their abilities or education. . . . Some were concerned only with their personal enrichment.[10]

In the same vein, the relative absence of Orientals in prominent positions nourishes polemics, and one of the most acute disputes of this sort has concerned the TV and radio channels:

At the steering committee of the Broadcasting Authority [the roof organization of the TV network and official radio stations] which numbers seven members, . . . six are Ashkenazim and the seventh, . . . though of Bulgarian origin, lacks any awareness or motivation regarding the ethnic issue; he is only concerned with his role of "politruk" on behalf of the right wing of the political map.[11]

Another topic raised in recent years by ethnic activists is their feeble participation in the delegations to the peace talks with Egypt:

No newspaper in Israel has insisted on this [the absence of Orientals in the Israeli delegation at the peace talks with Egypt]. No spokesman of the free press in the country has objected to the composition of the delegation in Washington. Seemingly, everyone agrees that Ashkenazim and non-Ashkenazim are equal as far as war is concerned but, regarding peace, Ashkenazim are more equal.[12]

Yet it would be a mistake to conclude hastily that the break in the national consensus is deep. Protest, it must be noted, has been weakly concretized in ethnic political action: at the first general election in 1949, one person was elected on a Yemenite list and four on another Oriental list, at the second Knesset (Israeli Parliament) in 1959, only two Orientals were elected in addition to the one Yemenite and, from then on, despite the efforts of various lists and the spectacular growth of the Oriental population in Israel, no member of an ethnic group entered Parliament as an independent until 1981. It is only in the 1981 elections that one finds again three Orientals elected on an ethnic ticket, while at the same time Oriental masses, more than ever, bring their support to nonethnic parties.

In general, a firm conviction exists among all groups, including the Orientals, that a bond of solidarity and common values unify all Israeli Jews[13] and that ethnic identity will gradually disappear over time. Among Orientals, there is a high degree of readiness to accept new behavior patterns in order to diminish their particularism, which is a frequent object of self-criticism.[14] Yet, from this viewpoint, objective reality develops at a slower pace than conciousness. Much research indicates attitudes enduring among Orientals that are evidence of their particular personality: education is often perceived differently and of less centrality than among Euro-Americans;[15] religious practices, though changing their character over time, remain anchored in the community;[16] and many Orientals have a strong tendency to voluntarily concentrate among themselves[17]. Last but not least, research has shown that many Orientals share many attitudes regarding the social order which are characteristic of a traditional premodern background.[18]

The center is not indifferent to the complexity of the ethnic situation and it invests much in what it calls the "encouragement of the underprivileged." Frequently, however, these efforts hurt the sensitive. Under the aggressive title "A Cancer in the Social Body," an Oriental activist, for instance, complained that:

A short time ago, the television showed students who volunteered to help underprivileged and *discriminated* [my italics] families, to teach them and to raise their intellectual standard. In all these cases, the picture was quite clear: First Israel [the Ashkenazi] carries the burden of Second Israel [the Orientals]. . . [and] this is the image broadcast by television.[19]

It is in this uneasy context that the following study is aimed at investigating Israeli ethnic reality. By means of the analysis of two groups that differ widely from each other—though both belonging to the Oriental category—we hope to reach generalizations that will enable us to outline the model of ethnicity exemplified by the Israeli Jewish setting. The first group under study is the Yemenites, who originate from far southwest Arabia and who, though accounting for but 6 percent of the population, make up the most veteran Oriental stock. They are representative of other groups such as the Kurds or the Libyans, who were also isolated, and of traditional communities transplanted almost entirely to Israel. The second group consists of the "Frenchized" Moroccans who, on the contrary, are both the largest, 14 percent of Israeli Jews and more than one-fourth of the Orientals, and one of the most recent entities in the human mosaic of the country.

To be sure, ethnicity is by no means a topic of minor importance in present sociology. Countless ethnic conflicts in many Western countries during the last few decades have been among its major concerns, while several contemporary factors, such as the structure of global communications, the attraction by prosperous nations for poorer countries and the ideological or political challenges of certain states have created a wide diversity of new Diasporas. Several theoretical approaches have been suggested which emphasize social processes leading either to the gradual disappearance of ethnic groups or, on the contrary, to the emergence of ethnic conflicts. Some theories focus on given aspects of the social setting, others on the ethnics' own attributes and perspectives. Moreover, various models give different weight to each of the three major dimensions of the social endeavor; namely, the cultural, socioeconomic and political.

Sociologists such as Parsons or Shils[20] point out a growing assimilation of ethnic minorities into the mainstream of society through ethnic desocialization and the appearance of interest groups crosscutting ethnic entities; they view the saliency of ethnicity as transitional and of only minor significance in the long run. Others, such as Bell[21] consider the maintenance of ethnic solidarity as "functional" from the ethnics' viewpoint: through it they attain political and economic achievements in a democratic society where organizational resources are always available and the political scene is very sensitive to pressure groups. Ethnicity, furthermore, with its symbols and emotional involvements, is also viewed as fulfilling an important role in the crystallization of communities in a setting characterized by the "mass society" model. Still other scholars consider ethnic survival as related to the stratification system which often connotes ethnic origin and class position. This fact is explained by Lenski[22] by such factors as differential predispositions of groups to adjust successfully to the rules of the social "game" or by Simpson and Yinger[23] by the growth of prejudices retarding integrative processes. Van den Berghe[24] focuses, in his work, upon structural features of Western society, such as economic competition, which create objective conflicts among groups.

In sum, the sociological approach in this field is quite unsystematic; in fact, the major difficulties confronting sociologists reside in the twofold enigma inherent in ethnicity in contemporary societies. On the one hand the question arises as to those "objective" elements, that is, elements pertaining to the social order *per se*, which can explain the fact that the same ethnic group meets a different fate in societies that are similar with regard to their stratificational, economic or political structures. Hoetinck,[25] for instance finds in several Caribbean settings a substantial variance in the plight of blacks with respect to the degree, nature, and conflictual aspect of their interaction with whites. On the other hand, an additional issue refers to those factors—whether "objective" and related to ethnic participation in social spheres or "subjective" and referring to self-images and perceptions—which clarify how various ethnic groups evolve differently in the same setting. Studies like Glazer and Moynihan's[26] vivid comparisons between Puerto Ricans and blacks, or Italians and Irishmen in New York provide evidence of substantial variations.

Our own contention regarding this twofold viewpoint is that the problem of ethnicity is best viewed as an encounter between a setting and a group, an encounter whose evolving and shaping are explained (beyond the impact of conjunctural circumstances such as demographic features, specific problems at given periods, and the like) by the setting's culture as represented by its center, and the sociocultural features of ethnics, insofar as these can both be analyzed *before the encounter or, at least, outside its context*. There is good reason for underlining these words, since ethnic phenomena *in* the context of the encounter itself already express the latter's dynamism and therefore neither explain the nexi of problems inherent in it and nor, hence, both its objective and subjective characteristics.

NOTES

1. A. Berler, *Arim Hadashot Beisrael* [New towns in Israel] (Jerusalem: Israel Universities Press, 1970), pp. 64-69.

2. Israel Central Bureau of Statistics (ICBS), *Thunot Demografiot Shel Haohlosiah—Helek Beit* [Demographic characteristics of the population—Part

Two] (Jerusalem: Population and Housing Census 1972, Series No. 10, 1976), pp. 38-54; Vivian Klaff, "Ethnic Segregation in Urban Israel," *Demography* 10, no. 2 (May 1973): 161-82.

3. See Y. Peres, "Politika Veedatiut Beshalosh Shhunot Oni" [Politics and ethnicity in three slums], in *Israeli Society 1967-1973*, ed. R. Kehana and S. Kopstein (Jerusalem: Academon, 1974), pp. 175-90.

4. Israeli Central Bureau of Statistics (ICBS), *Statistical Abstract of Israel 1975* (Jerusalem, 1975), p. 6.

5. R. Bar-Yosef, "Absorption versus Modernization," in *Israeli Society, 1967-1973*, ed. R. Kehana and S. Kopstein (Jerusalem: Academon, 1974), pp. 8-43.

6. Committee of Investigation of Delinquent Youth in Israel, "Prakim Mitoh Hadoh" [Chapters from the report], *Megamot* 7, no. 4 (October 1956): 377-89.

7. I. Ketsef, "Riayun Hahodesh" [Monthly interview] *Bamaaraha* 219 (March 1979): 14.

8. Y. Peres, "Politika Veedatiut Beshalosh Shhunot Oni" [Politics and ethnicity in three slums] pp. 175-99.

9. S. Levy and L. Guttman, *Indikatorim Hevratiim Leisrael-22 Beianuar-12 Bemers 1974* [Social indicators for Israel: January 22-March 12, 1974] (Jerusalem: Institute for Applied Social Research and Institute for Communication, Hebrew University 1974), pp. 1-14.

10. Ben-Zion Cohen, "Hahet Hakaved Shel Hasohnut Klapei Yehadut Paras" [The grave sin of the Jewish agency toward Persian Jewry], *Bamaaraha* 219 (March 1979): 7-8.

11. H. Mizrahi, "Guf Tsiburi Lereshut Hashedur Blee Netzig Sfaradi" [A public body to the broadcasting authority without sephardic representation], *Bamaaraha* 219 (March 1979): 9.

12. E. Nissan, "Mekoman Shel Lo-Ashkenazim Bamasa Umatan" [The place of non-Ashkenazim in the negotiations], *Bamaaraha* 215 (November 1978): 7.

13. R. Bar-Yosef, "Absorption versus Modernization," pp. 8-43.

14. Y. Peres, "Zehut Edatit Veyahasim Bein Edatiim Beisrael" [Ethnic identity and inter-group relations] in *Mizug Galuyot*, ed. O. Cohen (Jerusalem: Magnes Press, 1969), pp. 74-87.

15. J. Shuval, "Value Orientations of Immigrants in Israel," *Sociometry*, 26 June 1963, pp. 247-57.

16. S. Deshen, "Dfusei Hishtanut Shel Masoret Datit: Beit Haknesset Haedati" [Patterns of change in religious tradition: the ethnic synagogue] in *Mizug Galuyot* ed. O. Cohen (Jerusalem, Magnes Press, 1969), pp. 66-73; E. Cohen and J. Katan, *Kehilah Ktanah Bemerhav Metropolitani* [A Small

Community in a Metropolitan Area] (Jerusalem: Mehkarim Besotsiologia Hebrew University, 1966), p. 40.

17. A. Weingrod, "Mehagrim (olim) Lokalism Veshilton Politi" [Immigrants, localism and political power], *Amot* 10 no. 4 (February-March 1964): 15-28.

18. H. Rosenfeld, "Eer Olim: Kiryat Shmoneh" [An immigrant town, Kiryat Shmoneh] , *Mibifnim* 20, nos. 1-2 (May 1958): 87-95.

19. J. Orientali, "Mahalah Memaeret Mekarsemet Beguf Hahevrah" [A cancer in the social body], *Bamaaraha* 217 (January 1978): 5.

20. T. Parsons, "Some Theoretical Considerations on the Nature and Trends of Change of Ethnicity," in *Ethnicity*, ed. N. Glazer and D. Moynihan (Cambridge, Mass.: Harvard University Press, 1975), pp. 53-83; E. Shils, *The Torment of Secrecy* (London: Heinemann, 1956).

21. D. Bell, "Ethnicity and Social Change," in *Ethnicity*, ed. N. Glazer and D. Moynihan (Cambridge, Mass.: Harvard University Press, 1975), pp. 141-74.

22. G. Lenski, "Group Involvement, Religious Orientations and Economic Behavior," in *Racial and Ethnic Relations*, ed. B. E. Segal (New York: Crowell, 1972), pp. 154-68.

23. G. E. Simpson and J. M. Yinger, *Racial and Cultural Minorities* (New York: Harper & Row, 1958), pp. 103-10.

24. P. L. Van den Berghe, *Race and Ethnicity* (New York: Basic Books, 1970), pp. 21-41.

25. H. Hoetinck, "National Identity, Culture and Race in the Caribbean," in *Racial Tensions and National Identity*, ed. E. Q. Campbell (Nashville: Vanderbilt University Press, 1972), pp. 57-61.

26. N. Glazer and D. Moynihan, *Beyond the Melting Pot* (Cambridge, Mass.: MIT Press, 1974), see particularly pp. 294-310.

The Rules of the Ethnic Encounter in Israel

2

THE THEORETICAL STARTING-POINT

Turning first to the question of that which is unique to particular societies (and which could explain the special fate of ethnics in a given setting), useful insights are provided by theories that go beyond the Parsonian paradigm of universal modernity and rediscover, in a Weberian vein, the importance of historical culture in the evolution of these societies. Approaches such as Lipset's, Eisenstadt's, Almond and Verba's, or Znaniecki's[1] suggest that the dynamics of any particular setting depend primarily on what we will call *foci of cultural development*, which consist of bodies of beliefs, values, and outlooks widespread in society and rooted in social history. Those foci explain both the setting's resemblance to other settings with regard to some aspects of its culture and its uniqueness with regard to others. Diversely relevant to different areas of social participation, they may be seen—in the same vein as Eisenstadt's concepts of "codes" and "ground rules"—as molding the *cultural orientations* pertaining to those areas. In turn, these orientations codify the more specific *rules* which outline precise patterns of activity and social interaction with respect to definite social issues.

This view is highly significant as regards ethnic study, since this cultural stock—the foci of cultural development, orientations referring to spheres of activity, and rules defining practical arrangements—explains, beyond conjunctural circumstances, the setting's approach to new candidates and its response to questions posed by their very presence and integration.

The first of these questions is, of course, how far these new candidates are entitled to membership. In different societies, even those equally modern and liberal, diverse beliefs, values, and outlooks may stress the exclusiveness of membership differently. Accordingly, access of candidates depends not only on economic or other interests of the absorptive setting in the group but also on the nature of images of itself. It is in relation to these images that it perceives the cultural character of the candidates and the "if" and "how"—from a cultural viewpoint—by which such candidates may become members.

Acceptance into membership—if it is endowed—means a whole new set of rights in other spheres and, mainly, in socioeconomic markets and the polity. The question here is, how do these rights effect the fate of new members in these dimensions of the social endeavor? More specifically, the problem now is to what extent does the scope of these rights permit the group's participation in these spheres as indistinct from other people? In modern liberal societies, it is true, sociopolitical ideologies allow egalitarian orientations to be reflected in the fact that any member enjoys equality on numerous issues, from access to social services to political privileges intrinsic to citizenship. Yet, even in such settings, status and power are by no means unimportant differentiations. As regards the stratificational problem, the greater the endorsement of hierarchal principles as such, the less does mere membership actually entail equal participation of all in various social rewards. Moreover, and whatever the stress on status differences, the nature of an ethos justifying hierarchical concepts may also require meeting definite demands with regard to participation in certain kinds of activity. Rights of participation, their scope, and the specific demands conditioning their use define status opportunities available to new members and as such, constitute the rules of the stratificational dimension of the encounter.

Additional bases of inequality, however, also legitimized by certain widespread beliefs and value orientations, may also exist in the setting which, unlike the above, do not pertain to criteria defining similar conditions for all, but rather to special facilities of access to prominent positions for a particular group. Such a group, insofar as criteria of its formation are beyond the reach of "outs," that is people who do not belong to the group, appears to the latter to enjoy privileges and to represent the limits of their own potential achievements. Furthermore, if such a group expresses its eminence by a special status not only on the public scene in general, but also more particularly, in the polity and the hierarchy of authority, it then becomes for the "outs" what may be called a *dominant stock*. In sum, both the patterns of political elite recruitment—mainly the degree of their "monopolization" by exclusive circles—and the general rights of political participation as defined by the regime, comprise the absorptive setting's contribution to the location of newcomers within this regime. Thus, we suggest that on the whole, the setting's response to questions posed by the problems arising from integration of candidates into major social areas may be seen as rules of the ethnic encounter. These are widely dictated by its cultural orientations, which crystallize the working of these spheres and which are themselves diffused by the setting's foci of cultural development. In accordance with this formulation, moreover, it is also evident that the rules, orientations, and foci, though central components of the setting's culture, are not necessarily equally internalized or even accepted by all. At least in the occurrence of the encounter, and because of the very presence of outsiders—the candidates for membership—they make up but a *dominant culture* which explains the actions of only one partner in this occurrence, the absorptive setting itself as represented by its center.

THE ISRAELI VERSION OF DOMINANT CULTURE

The description of the dominant culture in Israel offers a fairly well-defined, though contradictory picture. The people who elaborated this culture, and whose work is still significant in contemporary Israel, originally transferred values acquired in a totally ·different environment, that of the Diaspora. Diaspora, of course, does not refer to a uniform reality; yet, beyond the disparities, at the heart of Judaism there is the solemn Covenant between God and His people which binds all Jews to a belief in a common fate, sustained by a wide range of religious-national symbols. One of the most eminent of these is the spiritual tie with the Holy Land, a concept which defines the very condition of Diaspora ("Disperson" in Greek) as a Galut ("Exile" in Hebrew).

The crisis experienced by the East European Jewish communities in the nineteenth and early twentieth centuries formed the background of the growth of revolutionary currents there. Zionism, influenced as it was by the wave of nationalism in Europe, drew much of its impetus from the fact that it proposed new solutions in secular terms to problems which had always been a part of these communities' life: it presented the problem of Exile with a practical answer, the creation of a secular Jewish state in Israel, and it pointed to the means to be used, the resettling of Jews to be implemented by a political movement. In Palestine itself, the Zionists attached themselves to a "cultural revolution" which was to create a national and secularizd framework of cultural reference for all, and represented a transformation of a legacy rather than a creation *ex nihilo*. As described by Deshen:

> While the early nationalist pioneers who settled in Palestine were in many ways radically heterodox, they nevertheless transplanted many practices from their traditional Diaspora homes. . . Thus, the Jewish calendar with its cycle of festivals and Sabbath days. . . . [M]any religious practices such as circumcision . . . stayed in force. Through the use of the Hebrew language, numerous traditional symbols, sentiments, and associations survived though the symbols often underwent change and profanation. . . . [Yet] it is the Jewish "national spirit" that moves [now] the people's view of its unique elected destiny, creates its lofty moral teaching, and nurtures the attachment to the historical homeland. . . . The way was thus cleared for the development of secularism which, however, paradoxically is couched in traditional symbols and language.[2]

By planting such seeds, Zionism has up to now maintained the principle of Jewish solidarity within the Israeli ideology and culture, and has made the Israeli state its most prominent contemporary symbol. The ingathering of Jews from all over the world, the central goal of Zionism, was further sustained by the state of belligerency with the neighboring Arabs, as the number of Jewish defenders became a measure of national security for the disputed state. This strengthened the solidaristic orientation toward all Jewish immigrants, regardless of origin; hence the fully open and direct concept of membership orienting their acceptance.

By the same token, however, the cultural shade of each "returning" group, though seen as an enrichment of Jewish civilization worthy of inclusion in the general culture, is also considered an obstacle to the "melting of all exiles into one nation" (*mizug galuyot*) if it remains the patrimonium of a single group. By its insistence on a national and cultural identity of all Jews prior to their immigration, this "melting" perspective presents the fusion of groups as the accomplishment of a culture and reconstruction of a historical entity. This idea, let us add, is accompanied by a certain desire on the part of the founding European establishment to prevent "Levantization" of society. This term reflects their fear that integration of the Jews from North African and Middle Eastern countries might bring a blurring of norms of civility, disciplined public behavior, and integrity in personal interactions, characteristics associated with the social life of Mediterranean countries.

However, by definition, *mizug galuyot* is not meant, in theory, to break the cultural identity of the groups, but rather to extend it in order to embrace all of them.[3] Thus, symbols of ethnic integration are much emphasized and in 1968, for instance, an Oriental was elected Speaker of Parliament, while in 1978 another became president of the state. On the other hand, this melting perspective cannot but demonstrate permissiveness toward temporary particularism of various groups since the more they show a specific *Jewish* culture, the more explicit their right to full membership. It is no wonder, therefore, that regarding religious rituals, particularism is accepted, *volens nolens*, as legitimate. Until this day there is a diarchy of the rabbinate, and Ashkenazi and Oriental rabbis share responsibility for rabbinical functions.

To what extent, however, is membership as such a sufficient condition of equal social status in Israel? In this respect, the solidaristic orientation inherent in Zionism is again relevant and, more particularly, the strength of socialism in the Zionist movement. Originally, this trend represented that pole of Zionism most opposed to the traditional Galut setting, which achieved dominance in the pre-1948 Jewish community in the country. After the "making of the revolution" and the establishing of the state, socialist Zionism was "routinized" into the detailing of practical obligations of the center towards the periphery and the maintenance, with other forms, of socialist structures. Moreover, the trade unions, the Histadrut, have retained much of their power, and wide social gaps between social classes receive only restricted legitimacy. This egalitarian perspective explains the setting's "generosity" toward the underprivileged in general, and it is expressed in the allocation of ecological resources, the redistributive aspect of social policies and the amplitude of welfare services.

However, this "generosity" does not exhaust the setting's approach to class differentiation. Israel today is very far from the egalitarian setting of its past, and stratificational features have grown much more complex. This may be explained by the strengthening of another focus of cultural development, the modern ethos or, more accurately, the Western perspective, which shapes the dominant view of technological standards, economic growth and consumption styles. This focus has legitimized the expansion of private enterprise and the principle of economic competition. New cultural bearings insist on individual achievement, and the wide scope of rights that express the "generosity" of the setting no longer prevents the emergence of substantial social distances; criteria of socioeconomic status are now much like those of Western societies in general, such as professional competence, formal education, and an entrepreneurial spirit. As seen below in more detail, these requirements especially act to hinder those groups which originated from nonmodern societies and which are still influenced by traditional outlooks. For them, and in contrast with the former "rules" of solidarity and equality, these mean the need to resocialize, to abandon parochial behavior, and primarily, to accept the culture of other groups as a referent.

Yet another focus of cultural development is the cultural impact of recent history on the setting. The main factors here include the growth of the Jewish population through immigration in a geographical area of impoverishment and semi-desert, and the permanent state of belligerency with neighboring states. Until 1948, besides the ideological commitments (such as participation in collective or cooperative settlements and in political parties), the dominant behavioral model insisted on productive work (mainly agricultural, in a period when land was the chief asset available for economic development), and military imperatives (i.e. sharing defensive responsibilities). This model was also imbued, concurrently with its anti-Galut mood (to repeat, Zionism was a revolt against the Diaspora), with a pragmatic outlook toward problems, roughness and exaggerated frankness in human relations, and a willingness to anchor oneself in Middle Eastern culture and landscape. The social evolution has weakened this model by strengthening cosmopolitan outlooks and deepening the reference to Western civilization, but this model has not fully disappeared, and life-styles are often opposed to non-Israeli Jewishness or even to those shown by new immigrants.

This ethos is mainly relevant to the public stage, where it is principally personified by those people who settled or were born in the country before the mass waves of immigration (1948-52). As in any society of immigrants, veteranship is a basis of prestige and authority associated with the evaluation of one's contribution to the fostering of the setting while a special aura also surrounds the "generation of continuity," that is, the founders' offspring who, by their being "natural" to the reality created by their parents, give it its fullest legitimacy. This aura is even more brilliant since this second generation also carried the burden of crucial national challenges. This "generation of continuity," together with the "Founders," make up a *dominant stock* which clearly distinguishes itself from the rest of society. Homogeneous in origin,[4] this stock, which is not to be confused with the whole of the European groups, emerges at the major points of public responsibility, from state bureaucracy and the army to political parties, and constitutes the present-day upper stratum of society.

In the context of solidaristic and egalitarian orientations entailed by the other foci of cultural development, and of the democratic rights pertaining to citizenship, this dominant stock, to be sure, is unable to become a hermetic caste. On the one hand, it accepts individuals of "special merit," and these, as seen further, include people who, by their very inclusion in the dominant stock, are to symbolize the social and national integration of new groups. On the other hand, it grounds its prominence on a strong feeling of special civic responsibility. But, as described by Ben-David,

Israel is a society wherein a minority thinks itself and sees itself, since the very beginning, as the legate over all others. There is an elite which says what is to be done and how to behave in every respect. This elite is involved in the life of every person, determines his earnings, the contents of education of his children, and does not consider any aspect of social life outside its authority.[5]

More particularly, the patronizing of North African and Middle Eastern groups of immigrants, who represent an element quite alien to the culture of the absorptive setting, is implemented through temporary, *ad hoc* institutions intended to provide them with "guidance" in their first steps in the setting. In some cases, ethnic elites are even coopted into the stock itself. A typical expression of such an attitude is

Table 2.1 Foci of Cultural Development, Cultural Orientations and Rules of the Ethnic Encounter

Spheres of Social participation	Foci of cultural development	Cultural orientations relevant to the ethnic encounter	Rules of ethnic encounter as defined by the absorptive setting (arrangements dictated by "rules")
Membership and culture	Zionism and secularized national Judaism	Strong solidaristic perspective referring to all groups—aspiration to *Mizug*	Open concept of membership for Jews of any group (citizenship accorded on arrival), in the frame of a melting perspective and a secularized national frame of cultural reference
Stratification	Socialist ethos and impact of Zionism as a social philosophy	Egalitarian perspective and weak emphasis on social hierarchies	"generosity" of the setting expressed in a wide scope of educational and economic rights for all groups of citizens (including, for instance, rights to lodging or exemption from income tax for several years for new immigrants)
	Modern ethos	Justification of inequality on the basis of differential individual achievements	Requirement to "modernize" referring primarily to occupation, and indirectly to many spheres of social life (importance of formal education for jobs)
Polity	Democratic philosophy	Formal egalitarianism	Endowment of formal privileges of citizenship; but existence of a dominant stock limits potential achievements of others; principle of "guidance" exerted by this stock over underprivileged and the setting up of numerous buffering institutions of a more or less temporary character (welfare agencies, absorption workers, party structures)
	Cultural impact on society of immigrant endeavors, wars, and urgent national challenges	Importance conferred on veteranship, participation in national tasks and descent from "founders"	

reflected in the following passage from a novel which describes a union "boss" speaking of the possibility of allowing Oriental workers at a quarry to elect their own foreman:

. . . [W]e have to go the hard way and demand more work for more rights. . . to hold the rights in a closed hand and make the workers fight for them. . . . What are rights worth if you don't exact anything in return?. . . First work and afterwards you concede rights, bit by bit. . . . One must be patient, this is a hard and dirty job.[6]

The various foci of cultural development, shaping the personality of Israeli society as an absorptive setting, their related orientations relevant to the ethnic encounter at its several institutional levels, and the subsequent "rules" of this encounter are summarized in Table 2.1, where some institutional arrangements inspired by the "rules" are also given.

On the whole, the Israeli version of dominant culture insists on the "melting" perspective and on the transitional character of differences, while at the same time and notwithstanding its "generosity," it emphasizes the need to modernize and to accept the "guidance" of a dominant stock. If the picture drawn in the introductory chapter contrasts sharply with these expectations, the reason resides in the nature of the ethnic encounter which is shaped by the ethnics to no less an extent than by the dominant culture.

NOTES

1. S. M. Lipset, *The First New Nation* (New York: Anchor Books, 1967), pp. 1-13; S. N. Eisenstadt, with M. Curelaru, *The Forms of Sociology—Paradigms and Crisis* (New York: John Wiley & Sons, 1976), pp. 347-73; G. Almond and S. Verba, *The Civic Culture* (Princeton: Princeton University Press, 1963), pp. 307-36; F. Znaniecki, *Modern Nationalities: A Sociological Study* (Westport, Connecticut: Greenwood Press Publishers, 1973), pp. 57-79.

2. S. Deshen, quote from an earlier draft of "Israeli Judaism: Introduction to the Major Patterns," *International Journal of Middle East Studies*, 9, February 1978, pp. 141-69.

3. S. Deshen, "Political Ethnicity and Cultural Ethnicity in Israel during the 1960's," in *Urban Ethnicity*, ASA Monographs (London, N.Y.: Tavistock Publications, 1974), p. 284.

4. A. Elon, *The Israelis: Founders and Sons* (London: Wiedenfeld &

Nicholson 1971), pp. 41-56; for an analysis of the growth of Israel's political elite, see Y. Shapiro, *Hademokratiah Beisrael* [Democracy in Israel] (Ramat-Gan Massadah, 1977), pp. 158-65.

5. J. Ben-David, "Dyun" [Discussion] in *Mizug Galuyot*, ed. O. Cohen (Jerusalem: Magnes Press, 1969), p. 91.

6. E. Ben-Ezer, *Hamahzevah* [The Quarry] (Tel Aviv: Am Oved, 1963), pp. 63-64.

The Israeli Edot

3

DEFINING AN ETHNIC GROUP

An ethnic group[1] is usually defined as a collective entity, the members of which share in common: (1) some primordial attributes such as religion, origin or history, language or "race"; (2) particular sociocultural features; and (3) a consciousness of constituting a group different from others belonging to the same setting. This definition, however, though it insists on specific criteria—primordial attributes, sociocultural particularism, and awareness of kind—includes collectivities that may widely differ from each other: it refers to groups located in a given territory (such as "national minorities") as well as to others which originate in a foreign land; it comprises groups which by their models of behavior, class and political attributes contrast with the rest of society and others much less noticed; it includes entities aspiring to a recognition of collective rights (such as religious groups) and also those ready to integrate into society without any "preconditions." Beyond this diversity, which is the very characteristic of this field, a closer look at the definition of an ethnic group raises several difficulties. To begin with, the role of "primordial attributes" must be clearly understood. According to Geertz:

By a primordial attachment is meant one that stems from the "givens"—or, more precisely, as culture is inevitably involved in such matters, the "assumed" givens—of social existence: immediate contiguity and kin connection mainly, but beyond them the givenness that stems from being born into a particular religious community, speaking a particular language, or even a dialect of a language, and following particular social practices. These congruities of blood, speech, custom, and so on, are seen to have an ineffable, and at times overpowering, coerciveness in and of themselves. One is bound to one's kinsman, one's neighbor, one's fellow-believer, *ipso facto*; as the result not merely of personal affection, practical necessity, common interest, or incurred obligation, but at least in great part by virtue of some unaccountable absolute import attributed to the very tie itself.[2]

This definition, however, should be reassessed on one point. Certainly, in no few cases, primordial attributes effectively create, or are at least related to, special feelings of identification and given sociocultural endeavors. But one may also easily point to examples in which they have lost their appeal.[3] "Race," religion, language, or origin bear a sociological significance only if accounting for some particular reality. From this viewpoint, an ethnic group is but representative of a situation where, in a given social context, primordial attributes do contribute to peoples' awareness of kind and are connected to some sociocultural particularism.

Yet the definition of both awareness of kind and sociocultural particularism in the delineating of an ethnic group is also problematic. Thus, sociocultural particularism refers to those features appearing in a given setting, as especially pertaining to the group's participation in the various spheres of social activity, from culture to status and power. These behavioral patterns and symbols, community endeavors, family models, and occupational or political structures, which are more or less characteristic of the group, however, are in fact the outcome of the encounter between the groups' value orientations, predispositions, and resources by which it was characterized outside this context, with the practical conditions, exigencies, and influences of its actual environment. These contours of the ethnic group in the setting, which constitute, as such, an objective reality, should be seen therefore, as an *occurrence* to be accounted for by underlying processes involving the group's original starting-points as well as the additional factors, depending on the absorbtive setting, that have already been outlined in Chapter 2 where the concept of dominant culture is discussed.

In the same manner, awareness of kind actually shared by ethnics in a given social situation may also be seen as a *product* of the latter rather than its explanation. When keeping this in mind, awareness of kind which, as indicated by the term itself, represents a subjective phenomenon, refers to at least four different questions. Above all, this notion implies the conceptualization of the group's primordial attributes into a *primordial identity* indicating the group's self-perceived concept of collective distinctiveness from the "outs." This is not necessarily the case, and primordial attributes may be considered, if at all, more as individual "givens" (such as date of birth or physical stature) than as entailing special feelings of belonging—let alone of pride of belonging—to a definite collectivity. One may be of Czech origin in Canada or an offspring of a Protestant family in France without much concern for others around who share the same attribute. Thus, to speak of an awareness of kind is appropriate only if, in a precise social context, primordial attributes create boundaries of an entity, which is not merely a statistical category but at least a normative phenomenon, if not a real grouping. This primordial identity varies, of course, from one case to another, not only according to the very primordial attributes on which it is grounded, but also according to the terms in which it is formulated and which reflect the group's own general perspective on its encounter with a given dominant culture.

Whatever the manner in which it is defined, however, this primordial identity delineating boundaries of a given collectivity takes on a significance that goes beyond its starting-point. Indeed, once a concept of distinctiveness between people is forged, it enables a perception of the members' endeavors in the various aspects of their social life in terms of social distances between "ins" and "outs." These images of social distance regarding issues such as status, power, culture, or intergroup social intercourse represent, in fact, the manner in which the ethnics subjectively view their location inside the social setting; by insisting according to the case, on broader or narrower gaps between the groups and the "outs," they elaborate the *practical meanings* endowed by the former to their "being different"—in whatever respect—from the latter.

However, the significance of a primordial identity is by no means exhausted by these practical meanings. A primordial identity may be conceived as bearing an intrinsic value only if it is understood as indicative of a "collective personality," that is, of cultural contents such as value orientations, outlooks on life and society, or justifications of certain styles of behavior. These may either emphasize a sharp difference from, or even attitudes bluntly opposed to, given contents of the dominant culture, or, on the contrary, represent only a variance from the latter and an eclectic amalgamation of diverse influences perceived as *relatively* peculiar to the group.

From these contents, as well as from the expectations intrinsic to the group's self-definition as a collectivity follows, furthermore, an additional view on its distinctiveness in the setting, a view which interprets reality in terms of a "collective plight" and questions the extent to which the group's objective particularism—as it sees it—appears to it as a faithful fulfillment of its "personality" and aspirations or, opposedly, as contradicting, nay even alienating them. In other words, in what measure and in what respects are the ethnics conscious of a collective condition in which they are ready to "recognize themselves" and/or perceive deprivation and conflict?

In a general manner, these *four* aspects, that is, primordial identity, practical meanings endowed to the ethnic cleavage, self-perceived cultural uniqueness, and the overall interpretation of a "collective plight" in society, specify the group's awareness of kind. This awareness refers, let us remember, to people who, by their very participation in a setting which includes them as well as others, are also bound by more comprehensive allegiances and commitments.

In view of these considerations, a more accurate definition of an ethnic group would focus both on elements that make it a particular entity and on elements that underlie the occurrence of the phenomenon. From this outlook, *an ethnic group is a group of people sharing a priori primordial attributes*—race, origin, religion, or other—*and cultural features*—mainly value orientations, concepts, and predispositions inherited from another context—*and who, when confronted with a given dominant culture, appear as characterized in the society by some sociocultural particularism*—in whatever aspects of its social endeavor—*and an awareness of kind* expressing itself in a consciousness of a primordial identity and a related collective personality, as well as in images of distances from "outs" and a given understanding of a collective condition in society.

This definition, in fact, requires starting the analysis of ethnicity with descriptions of the dominant culture on the one hand, and of the sociocultural syndromes of the ethnics prior to the encounter on the other hand. This, it is true, has already been concluded in Chapter 1 and led (in the framework of our present purpose) to the focusing of Chapter 2 on the Israeli version of dominant culture. The discussion of the definition of an ethnic group, however, was necessary at this point, before turning to the groups that are here under study. This definition, it must also be said here, cannot be analytically applied with the same ease to every case. The study of groups which have been a part of their setting for a long time raises many difficulties in distinguishing *a priori* features from current characteristics. Yet it is also implicit in this definition that ethnicity in modern and contemporary settings represents a specific category of ethnic occurrences. Up to the modern era, indeed, people seen as "different" from others with respect to primordial attributes most often constituted enclaves whose relationships with the dominant culture were clearly defined and localized by the very rationale of the social order. Today however, the "heart" of ethnic problems in the nation-state resides, most frequently, in the ambiguities inherent in the *direct* confrontation of people with a dominant culture aspiring, at least in some respects, to comprehend them despite, and concomitant with, the existence of such differences. From this viewpoint, immigrants who attempt to integrate into a new society, or territorial, linguistic, or religious minorities pulled out of isolation by the internal expansion of a national culture, basically illustrate the same general type of issue.

At all events, with regard to the Israeli case, this question is much less complex since it concerns groups which have immigrated at definite periods and the descriptions of which, outside the context of the encounter, are relatively easy to obtain, in the very same manner in which the setting's culture could also be analyzed independently. Thus, the following brief description of the backgrounds of the Yemenite and Moroccan Jews is primarily intended to throw some light on one of the two major starting-points of the Israeli model of ethnicity, that is, the *a priori* features originally "brought" to their environment by the groups under study. These groups were already particular entities in their countries of origin and made up national-religious enclaves, but our present purpose, it should be emphasized, is not to analyze the occurrence of ethnicity there, but only to draw a general picture of these groups as it transpires from historical material. This material, which is the only kind available, though hardly concerned with the variables discussed above, is indicative of the value orientations and outlooks on life and society, as well as the predispositions and expectations which were the lot of Yemenite and Moroccan Jews and which were at the root of their confrontation with the Israeli dominant culture.

THE JEWS IN YEMEN: A QUASI-CASTE

THE JEWS IN A MUSLIM SOCIETY

Local legends date the early settlement of Jews in Yemen during the first Commonwealth. More recently, it has been asserted that Jewish tribes lived there in the first centuries of the Christian Era and some sources report the existence in this period of an embryonic Jewish Kingdom.[4] The Quran concedes the importance of Jewish support in Medina for Muhammed, though Islam soon reduced the Jews to the condition of *dhimmis* (i.e. a subordinate, protected "People of the Book"). The expansion of a rigorist Shi'ite movement was another hardship for the Jews in Yemen, and in 1171 Maimonides sent them a message ("Igeret Teiman") to sustain their spirit. Yet, besides temporary expulsion from large parts of Yemen between 1678-1681,[5] no severe persecutions were faced. In the eighteenth century, a Jew was even appointed minister of finance by Imam Al-Makdi.

In fact, the Jews suffered mainly from strife among the Muslims themselves, and their attempts to encourage one side or the other so as to improve their own lot frequently turned against them. In 1872, for instance, they welcomed Ottoman rule, but when in 1904 a revolt weakened the hold of the Turks, harsher discriminatory laws were enacted against them.

In Muslim eyes the Jews were to remain a low-status caste, strictly discriminated. A Jew was forbidden to carry weapons and to ride a horse or camel; orphans were, by law, converted to Islam; synagogues were dug into the ground to make them lower than mosques;[6] Jews had to wear special clothes and Muslims had priority over them in every public place. A Jew attacked by an Arab child was forbidden to raise a hand and had to ask an Arab adult for help. As "guests," Jews were even exempted from the usual taxes imposed on Muslims; they had to pay instead for their "protection" (the *Jizyah*).

This caste condition was also expressed in the narrow and precise boundaries of their physical location. Jews—54,000 in 1947[7]— were dispersed all over Yemen, but in every settlement there was a "Street of Jews."[8] An estimate of the average community size was fifty-six persons in the late 1940's[9] and only five communities counted from 1,800 to 3,000 Jews. Thus about 80 percent of Yemenite Jews were scattered in hundreds of places quite isolated from each other. Yet in their socioeconomic life a great similarity existed among all communities:[10] the largest occupational group was comprised of artisans (about 45 percent), followed by traders and peddlers (34 percent) and (mainly in the remote areas) farmers (12 percent). A small minority was employed in construction (5 percent), a few held clerical jobs (3 percent). The Jews, in fact, had a "monopoly" over craftmanship, a branch divided into a great number of specialized trades transmitted from father to sons over generations, and they were called "specialists" (Utztah) by the Arabs.[11] Their living conditions were very poor[12] and they were the first struck by famine when the fragile economy of Yemen knew periodic setbacks. Despite their importance on the lower steps of commerce, they never achieved any solid position in the international trade of the country, and only in San'a was there a handful of wealthy Jews.

Because of their great poverty, the death rate was very high[13] and some girls were even reported as being prostitutes. Regular institutions of religious learning (Yeshivot) were out of the question, and at the several which did exist in San'a, students learned in the early morning before going to work. Community life centered on the synagogue, run by elected people including the rabbi, the ritual cantor, and the keeper (gabai), all of them unpaid jobs. In each town or village the rabbi or teacher (mari) also held the position of judge, and in cities three rabbis made up the higher court. The Supreme Court was at San'a.[14]

Hamid Al-Din and Yahiah, the Imams (rulers) during the first decades of this century, were known as quite tolerant towards Jews[15] and even nominated a central leadership to represent all Jews at court. At traditional feasts an ox was ritually slaughtered by the Jews of San'a and presented to the Imam as a gift; on these occasions, written blessings were also exchanged between the Chief Rabbi of San'a and the Imam.[16] It is within this general enforced order of the millet that the Jews of Yemen elaborated their national-religious identity and developed their own legacy.

THE QUASI-CASTE PRINCIPLE AND CULTURAL ORIENTATIONS

The Jews of Yemen, in fact, were not a caste in the full sense of the word. Their own awareness of kind did not accept the assumptions of the dominant culture, and on the basis of their own beliefs they rejected both any aspiration to mix with Muslims and the principle of their inferiority, considering their situation as opposed to the "real order of things." Confident in the biblical and Talmudic theogony, they prayed for salvation to come in this world, through God's Own Will and the intermediary of His emissary. This apocalyptic view, inherent in the Jews' resignation to their condition as *dhimmis*, explains the appearance, at various periods, of men who believed in their holy mission and called for the return of the exiled to the land of Israel.

In the meantime, Jews were characterized by value orientations which, in the absence of direct enquiries, may be read in the descriptions of education, family, community, and cult. Education, for instance, followed two principles: first was the early involvement of children in the life of adults, and second the sacred learning for boys which prepared them to be full adult members of the synagogue. Close contact between sons and fathers and between mothers and daughters inculcated "good manners," politeness, respect for others, and tolerance among children. Sacred studies took place in a small hut under the supervision of a teacher; pupils of all ages learned together and success was tested at the synagogue when the student was given a text to translate. A poor teacher would lose his "clients" and get a bad name in the community.[17] At the age of twelve, a boy went out for work together with his father; at the same age, a girl was already an experienced house worker.

The marrying age arrived soon: between sixteen and nineteen for boys and eleven and fifteen for girls.[18] Choice of a partner was a family matter while community notables might serve as intermediaries. A payment by the groom's family to the bride's provided the latter with money for her needs. The new couple was expected to settle with the help of the husband's father. In the family itself, the importance of each role was emphasized and the wife was especially respected. Though she could neither read nor pray, she enjoyed a high moral status, sustained by religious values.[19]

Beyond the family circle, there were quite strong relationships binding members of the community as a whole. On some festivals, for instance,[20] the poor received gifts from the community in the synagogue, paid by taxes imposed on wealthier members; also, people in trouble received loans without interest. Furthermore, on any important occasion, everyone attended synagogue and special prayers were recited. In this atmosphere, the functions of cult were no secret and just as any literate male could become a teacher, anyone familiar with ritual slaughtering could practice it for himself or others.

The emphasis upon well-defined norms was a binding thread throughout all aspects of Jewish life in Yemen. Special signs were employed for greeting people; table manners were prescribed; speech was much characterized by hints rather than blunt statements, with finger and facial gestures sometimes even substitutes for words.[21] All of these were expressed in synagogue in the style of prayers, at market in the way of bargaining, and in conjugal relations. These were also the rule in the workshop of the jeweller or blacksmith.

Thus, the strict regulations controlling relations between Jews and Muslims were duplicated in clear, well-defined norms inside the Jewish community; but, while the former were imposed by a ruler, the latter were sustained by faith and tradition. Tension between the *dhimmis'* condition and belief in one's unique calling produced mystic attempts to understand the "veiled reality," a trend influenced by the Shi'ist emphasis on religious secrets and esoteric interpretations of sacred texts. Like the Arab, the Jew was a "*homo religiosus*,"[22] anxious about the fate of his soul who accorded a central place in his life to prayers and incantations. The contents of these, of course, differed from those of Muslims. For the Jews, spiritual life meant, first and foremost, attendance at synagogue where the Bible was learned and recited, generally in quite a superficial manner ("as the whistling bird").[23] Yet in the Yeshivot, interested people studied Rabbinic literature, Hebrew grammar, Jewish history, the poems of Yehuda Halevy, and the writings of Maimonides. The synagogues and Yeshivot in San'a were open to students almost every day and circles met around the Zohar, the book of the mystics.[24] It was the custom in Charab and Aden to spend a night learning the Zohar after a circumcision. Yet most people did not attend these circles and when they had a religious or personal problem they turned to their rabbi, who delivered a brief answer without any explanation.

In fact, while the scholars delved into books, the common man was far more inclined to believe in formulae, signs, and keywords, which eased the hardships of life. Superstition among Jews was commonplace and they were devoted clients of sorcerers, whether Jewish or not. The various names of God and the angels were written on amulets or whispered in certain circumstances.[25] It was only in the first years of this century that a small group in San'a surrounding a scholar named Kafih opposed learning the Zohar and Kabbalah (the mystic teachings of Judaism) and the diffusion of superstitions. However, they soon aroused sharp attacks. In 1909 the Turks opened a new Jewish school (*Mahtav*) and appointed Kafih as its director. He made some effort to introduce secular matters along with religious teaching; this provoked a wave of protest among the rabbis, who did not hesitate to accuse him of being a British spy. As a result the school was closed in 1913.[26] This obscurantism however, is explicable in view of the longstanding isolation of Jews in Yemen who had lost most contact with the outside world, since the Hidjaz was not allowed to be traversed by non-Muslims.

THE CONTEXT OF IMMIGRATION

The foregoing, which reveals the nature of Jewish value orientations and predispositions on the eve of immigration to Israel, was also the background to the sporadic resettlement in the Land of Israel from the late nineteenth century on when the Turks conquered Yemen and it became part of an empire which included the Land of Israel. Once the trail was blazed, groups started on their way even after Yemen recovered its independence; then the insecurity which had reigned for decades was an added incentive. A Zionist emissary who arrived there before World War I was received as a prophet despite his own denials.[27] In 1948, when news reached Yemen of the creation of an independent Israel, enthusiasm among Yemenite Jewry was enormous. They arose from every remote hamlet, formed caravans, and moved toward gathering places.

Tens of thousands were flown to Israel from Aden, after agreement with the Imam. In no case were Jews ready to miss the opportunity of the return to the Holy Land though, it is true, their enthusiasm was further encouraged by Arab hostility which grew ever more intense with the development of the Middle East conflict.

As for the figures involved,[28] the first group which arrived in 1881 numbered only 150, but they were continuously joined by others and in 1908 there were already 2,500 immigrants. Large waves began only in 1947 when 12,575 arrived to be followed by 43,619 more from 1948 to 1954,[29] by which time nearly all Jews had left Yemen. In 1972, they numbered 153,142 persons (i.e. 5.7 percent of the total Jewish Israeli population), about 63 percent of whom had been born in the country.

In the context of the above, it is no wonder that Jews originating from Yemen were willing to belong totally to a Zionist Jewish state. Their deep religiosity interpreted its creation as the start of the Era of Salvation and immigration to Israel was to solve the contradiction of the Galut. They expected complete integration in their new environment and no group was more eager to endorse the "fusion of exiles" perspective.

In fact, when faced with the dominant culture in Israel, they were soon to perceive the significance of the "messianic age" in more realistic terms. Both the modern ethos of Israel and the specific characteristics of the "new Israelis" were not only almost wholly strange to them, but were also opposed to their own understanding of the social order. The fundamentally traditional education of the Jew from Yemen, his long isolation from the outside world, his familistic values, his often superstitious beliefs, his severe and dogmatic ways of life and, not least, the modesty which had been inculcated in him by strict discriminatory practices, were all to impede his steps into Israeli society.

It is true that Jews from Yemen had some advantages which could ease their "way in": as former craftsmen and tradesmen, they were familiar with concepts such as the economic market or job specialization. Furthermore, as the most veteran group among the Orientals (about 20 percent arrived before 1948), their "anchorage" in Israeli culture was to be deepest among them.

However, immigration from Yemen to Israel was primarily motivated by a devotion to traditional values and settlement in the Land of Israel was considered its own fulfillment. The ground was therefore weak for a drastic change of outlook and behavior; on the contrary, the initial aspiration was to continue a given way of life. The problems arising from the above, on examining the encounter of these Jews with Israeli reality, quite closely resemble those awaiting the immigrants from Morocco, though the latter's historical and sociocultural experience in no way duplicates that of the Yemenite.

THE JEWS AS INTERMEDIARY: THE CASE OF MOROCCO

THE JEWS UNDER THE SULTAN AND THE CAIDS

Though also originating in a Muslim country, Jews in Morocco made up a very different group indeed. The main distinction, however, appeared after the establishment of a French Protectorate over most of Morocco in 1912. Historians date the first settling of Jews in Northwest Africa to the Phoenician conquest.[30] A holy site for both Muslims and Jews, assumed to be the tomb of Joshua, exists in Tlemcen, Algeria. There is even strong evidence that several Berber tribes converted to Judaism in the Roman era. At all events, prosperous Jewish and Judeo-Berber communities were growing along Northwest Africa's shores (and inland) until the Christianization of Rome caused their decline. Difficulties persisted through the Visigothic occupation and the period of Byzantine power, up to the Islamic conquest of the area in the eighth century, c.e. From then on, Muslim tolerance of the Jews permitted them to win back their affluence and large communities appeared in Kairouan (Tunisia), Fez (Morocco), and many other cities. Yet, in the twelfth century, the Almohades (Islamic fundamentalists) obliged the Jews to reside in special neighborhoods, the *mellah*, and they were reduced to the condition of *dhimmis*, enjoying the protection of the ruler, but despised by their environment; as in Yemen, the *Jizyah* expressed this millet situation.[31]

With the arrival of thousands of Jews expelled from Christian Spain during the Inquisition (late fifteenth and early sixteenth centuries), Judaism again flourished with renewed social, economic, and spiritual vigor. However, Morocco's isolation from the Ottoman Empire and the internal division between the Bled-el-Makhzan and the Bled-es-Siba entailed a fresh decline while a distinction developed between the urbanites of the Makhzan and villagers in the periphery. These latter were considered the property of local caids and their life was quite miserable.

Both the Jews living in cities and those in villages were mostly artisans and peddlers; only a small stratum of rich and influential merchant families, mainly of Spanish origin (Sephardi) provided leadership to communities in the cities. The Sephardi, originating from Iberia, quite easily amalgamated with the local Jews and helped to maintain among them an orientation toward the outside world. Several Sephardic families played an important role in commerce and diplomacy, which strengthened relations between Morocco and its Christian neighbors.

In the framework of the vicissitudes of the Sultanate and the caid regimes, the scattered Jewish communities remained enclaves that saw in their religious faith and legacy not only the "proof" of the injustice done to them but also their solace. As in Yemen, the Jewish patrimonium emerged around the synagogue. Rabbis and other notables constituted the community's leadership, and in each *mellah* a juridical court brought together recognized rabbis. (With the establishment of French Protectorate, a *Conseil des Communautés* made up a unified representative organ of Moroccan Jewry.)

The community funds for mutual aid and the school (the *Kuttab*) were also provided through the Synagogue. Hebrew and Bible were taught to boys from a very early age (sometimes from the age of two) up to thirteen, the year of the bar mitzvah. Afterwards, a youngster was generally expected to start working, though the more gifted were often sent to a Yeshivah.

The Yeshivah was a time-honored institution. Some Yeshivot had existed in Morocco since the ninth century. They had developed near the centers of Islamic studies and eventually entertained close relations with the great Yeshivot of Babylonia, Palestine, and Spain. Jacob ibn Nissim, Joseph Ben-Berachia, Huchiel Ben-Elchanan and El-Fassi were all important figures in the growth of Jewish thought and of Moroccan-born scientists. This cultural dynamism, however, fluctuated over the centuries in relation to social, economic, and political circumstances.

Besides the Spanish emigration, which brought a large group of learned aristocrats, a main contribution to Jewish scholarship from outside deserves mention: from the sixteenth century on, emissaries of the Palestinian Yeshivot of Safed made periodic visits of a few months each for the sake of collecting money and of teaching. As a result of their orientation and that of the Spaniards the learning of the Hidden Truth was well established, and Morocco's rabbinate turned toward the study of the Zohar and the Kabbalah. The Zohar achieved a status almost equal to the Bible, and in the synagogue its place was next to the Holy Scrolls. Confreries of Zohar readers existed all over Morocco and performed ritual functions at ceremonies such as circumcision, bar mitzvah or funeral.[32]

This mystic element in the Jewish cultural life of Morocco was much influenced by a parallel growth of maraboutism among Muslims. Tombs of "saints" became holy sites for them as well; often the same tomb was sacred to Jews and Muslims alike. Furthermore, mysticism among the learned was able to accommodate the popular religiosity of the masses with its superstitions and fears of the "hidden reality." Magic symbols, talismans, and formulae were retailed from one to the other. There are instances of rabbis fighting the wizards' influence and sentencing them to imprisonment; yet, when Jews met them in the street most did not refrain from kissing their hand or touching their clothes.[33] Rabbis, however, were not far from the masses either and their audience was large. The death of one in Fez as late as 1923 was still a dramatic event, and the entire Jewish population assembled in intense mourning ceremonies.[34]

Social distances between the poor and more prosperous, and between the unlearned and rabbis, were quite narrow,[35] while the huge majority of all Jews, including rabbis, confronted precarious living conditions. This reality was perceived by a French officer on a secret mission to Morocco in 1883, who noted their misery, superstitions, and "indecency."[36] He also found Jewish religious life rigorously following the prescribed rituals, but not the moral commands, of the faith. This derogatory account does not do justice to a certain quality of life exemplified, for instance, by the respect accorded women.

THE COLONIAL REGIME AND THE EMERGENCE OF AN INTERMEDIARY

The French, however, were heartily welcomed by the inhabitants of the *mellahs*, who were sometimes severely punished for this by Muslims (as in 1912 when the *mellah* of Fez was sacked). Undoubtedly, the French met many expectations of the local Jewish population, for they turned a new page in their history to no less an extent than in that of Morocco at large. They revoked discriminatory laws and allowed Jews to settle outside the *mellahs*; they opened their administrative ranks to Jewish clerks and promoted modern education;[37] they developed commerce and industry, creating fresh economic opportunities. Hence Jews rapidly concentrated in cities (80 percent by 1953[38]); in Casablanca alone their number rose from 50,000 in 1945 to 80,000 three years later,[39] 30,000 of whom lived outside the *mellah*. The Jewish population totalled 225,000 in 1951, more than 2 percent of the whole.

The new "rules" implemented by European colonialism were to have a tremendous impact on the Jews of Morocco in terms of their awareness of kind and sociocultural particularism. To begin with the latter, migration to cities overcrowded the *mellahs*—the cheapest places to settle—and two square meters per person was the average population density.[40] This new urban element was absorbed into commerce, industry, hostels, and textile factories. By 1947, half of all Jewish male workers in Moroccan cities had become wage earners. Yet a large group remained in more traditional occupations, such as peddlers and artisans, and their conditions of life were as miserable as ever. In fact, this misery was probably even more deeply resented now, in a period of general improvement, when numerous Jews succeeded in escaping from the *mellah* and achieved a new respectability. For those left behind, social problems accumulated; small children were sent out to work, many as boot-blacks; beggars multiplied and alcoholism, as well as prostitution, reached unprecedented rates.[41] Dirt in the *mellah* caused infectious diseases to spread. In the face of all this, Jewish community organizations were often slow to help. To leave the *mellah* and settle among Europeans was the very height of social success.

The picture regarding education, however, was somewhat different. Already in 1862, fifty years before the French conquest of Morocco, the first school of the Alliance Israelite Universelle (AIU, an institution of French Jewry) was set up in Tetuan; another was created in 1865 in Tangier, in 1888 in Fez and in 1900 in Casablanca. When the French troops arrived, 4,500 pupils were already learning their language; in 1951, 25,000 were enrolled in sixty-nine schools. Apart from the AIU, other institutions were active, such as the vocational training frameworks of ORT and the Hebrew Teachers College of Casablanca.[42] Some 50 percent of the children attended AIU and vocational schools and those still learning in the *Kuttab* were now a minority of about

15%. AIU education, it is true, was quite rudimentary and most teachers poorly trained. Nevertheless, its emphasis on the study of French and of secular as well as Jewish subjects, made an important contribution to the promotion of modern orientations among the Jews. However, as late as 1951, 37 percent of Jewish youth were completely uneducated, and of those registered only 66 percent attended school regularly. Most pupils started working after completing their elementary education.[43]

As is evident above, while the French regime and the modernizing processes it set in motion effectively contributed to a cultural and social transformation of Jewry, at the same time they created much confusion regarding their collective conscience.[44] Conflict arose not only between strata and segments, but also among the new intellectuals confronted with conflicting perspectives. There were, for instance, those who identified totally with France and considered themselves candidates for the status of French Jews, with the emphasis on French; in 1932, a periodical, *L'Union Marocaine*, was first published in Casablanca and upheld this outlook. Others, aspiring to a universalistic orientation couched in revolutionary terms, joined leftist parties, while another group actively sustained Moroccan efforts to achieve independence and saw itself as part of the country. Finally, there were the Zionists who viewed the creation of a free, modern Jewish society as a possible synthesis of the opposed perspectives; already in 1926 *L'Avenir Illustré* was published in Morocco with the support of a pro-Zionist philanthropist, Benazaref.[45]

As a matter of course, Jewry as a whole was now subject to powerful and contradictory pressures exerted from both inside and outside the community. On the inside there was the ever stronger preeminence of the new bourgeoisie, the materialistic character of which has been so bluntly drawn by Memmi (whose description of Jews in Tunisia fits Jews in Morocco as well). In the following passage, Memmi recalls an interview with his uncle, a prosperous pharmacist who had summoned him for a "serious" talk:

"If you keep on studying, you will be a pharmacist."... I was not courageous enough to tell him that I preferred to be a physician. He was the one who paid.... [He said:] "A man must earn a good living. This is very important. You will see." For whom this disdain? For those who do not earn enough for a living or toward this conception of profit? At this moment it seemed to me that it was turned to the small earners. As a whole I agreed with him. Money was the honor I wanted to achieve for myself. In the city it was much spoken about, that medicine was overgrown. Young physicians found it harder and harder to establish a practice. Pharmacy, on the contrary, was still a good business. Our bourgeoisie was too recent to have much respect for professional values or callings.[46]

This new bourgeoisie contrasted with the *mellah* population and the villages, and contributed to the Jewish identity crisis. In the meanwhile, however, there were the special features of the political regime that gave the Jews their overall character of an in-between ethnic minority.

Many discriminatory laws, it is true, had been abolished by the Protectorate, including the *Jizyah*. The French, however, did not implement total legal emancipation; the fiction of the Sultanate was maintained and the Jews remained subjects of the traditional authority. They were still considered *dhimmis*, despite the fact that the practical conditions of this status had been abrogated.[47] This juridical vacuum obliged the Jews to bargain incessantly with both the Sultan and the French General Resident over collective practical rights. This deinstitutionalization of the position of Jews in society endured until Morocco's independence, that is, about forty-four years. During this period of time many conflicts placed Jews, Frenchmen and Muslims in opposition to each other, and, on the whole, contributed to a wide confusion regarding their mutual relations. A serious crisis broke out in the late 1940s, for instance, when the Muslim authorities in Meknes decided to build a new *mellah* for Jews and to restrict their rights to settle in other parts of the city; the vehement opposition of the Jews failed while the French remained uninvolved.[48] It is against this general contradictory background that the divergences between cultural orientations inside the Jewish community were sharpened, while at the same time and as depicted by Doris Bensimon-Donath:

In the colonial society, each ethnic group formed a close society. To be sure, the Jews had professional relations with Europeans and Muslims but almost never as friends. . . . Only the young seemed somewhat more inclined than adults to choose friends indifferent to ethnic criteria.[49]

Common to all, in fact, were the collective feelings of insecurity of status, inherent in the very definition of the Jewish condition in French Morocco.

THE CONTEXT OF IMMIGRATION

In 1948 the independent State of Israel was created. To the masses of the *mellah* as well as to the remote rural communities the news seemed to announce the opening of the messianic age. Also, and more concretely, relations between Jews and Muslims in Morocco deteriorated as a result of Middle Eastern events (anti-Jewish riots, for instance, took place at Oujda), and many decided to emigrate to Israel. Jewry as a whole now entered a period of high instability. Yet thousands of Jews who decided to leave the country, many of them of middle-class background, arrived in France rather than Israel. Furthermore, a large number of the emigrants to Israel were hard welfare cases, induced to go by the insistence of the Moroccan communities. Thus emigration to Israel was frequently motivated by factors related to the Jewish condition in Morocco and not only by a deep affinity to the Zionist endeavor *per se*. The fact is that the majority of Jews who finally arrived from Morocco in Israel did so principally on the eve or in the aftermath of Morocco's accession to independence (in the mid- and late-1950's) in provision of, or in reaction to, a new "revolution" in Jewish-Muslim relationships.

In 1972, Jews from Morocco numbered 378,825 (14.1 percent of the Jewish Israeli population), 12 percent of whom had been born in the country. Morroccan immigrants, it is true, were better "armed" than the Yemenites to confront the Israeli setting. As transpires from the above, many had known French culture and colonial concepts of modernity conveyed by the French to Morroco. Many had known big-city life and had been employed in factories or administrative services. Yet their education was frequently rudimentary and traditional outlooks regarding family, religion, or polity were still influential. The motivation underlying the immigration of this heterogeneous group, uncertain of its own partimonium, was both the will to join the new Jewish nation and the aspiration to erase all prior signs of inferiority and insecurity.

TOWARD THE TRANSFORMATION INTO EDOT

The respective Diasporan experiences of Yemenite and Moroccan Jews confirm Orans' thesis on the impact of socioeconomic opportunities upon structures of deprived ethnic entities.[50] Unlike Jews in Yemen, Jews in Morocco who had been accorded new possibilities of educational and economic improvement by the French—notwithstanding political ambiguities and social rejection—were to loosen their compactness and become culturally heterogeneous. Obviously, these differences between the groups would be of some impact on their respective settling in Israel.

Yet in many other respects, similarities in their *a priori* value orientations have also emerged between them which, more importantly than the dissimilarities, concern their very contribution to the premises of the ethnic encounter in Israel. What must be stressed at this point is their common previous formation of discrete entities in their countries of origin. Among the Jews in Morocco, it is true, collective identity and boundaries were less unanimously defined, but they were never ignored, even when moving outside the *mellah* was allowed. Moreover, and again common to both groups, commitments to collective identity and boundaries were formulated in terms of faithfulness to religious traditions and parochial customs. Upon joining a setting which shares their national-religious identity, each new group will now appear distinct in its particular version of Judaism. Paradoxically, this feature symbolizes their country of origin, to which they never *really* belonged.

By the same token, these groups which perceived themselves as "guests" in "host countries" and committed to their self-perpetuation, now in Israel exemplify a new profile, rooted in the concepts of identification with a larger "whole" (the Jewish nation) inherent in their parochial culture itself, independent of the act of immigration. This notion of prior belongingness made them representative of what may be termed an *edah* (pl. *edot*), literally in modern Hebrew a "community of Israel." Edah may refer more generally to any group originating from the outside which sees itself bound to the nation by its perennial self-definition. Cases of "returning Diasporas" are infrequent in the world today but there still are some examples, such as East Germans fleeing to West Germany or European Algerians to France. These groups, too, shared an assumption that they had always belonged to their new society.

This concept of edah refers of course to every Jewish group of origin in Israel. Yet from the above account, it is also evident that edah bears more real, effective meaning for groups like Jews from Yemen or

Morocco than for Jews from Germany, Russia, or America. For the former, due to their non secularized outlooks, the act of immigration primarily represented—despite the uncertainties of many—a fulfillment of commitments to norms, customs, and rituals implied by their definition of Jewish identity and directly transpiring in community institutions. For them, immigration was in no way a "denying of history," as with Zionists in the Yishuv period, nor the expression of a personal attachment to an abstract national aspiration, as with many Jewish Western immigrants. Thus, by virtue of the ascriptive bond defining it, the very notion of edah, which belongs to the universe of traditional community concepts, as such is closer to the world of the Jews from Yemen and Morocco in Israel who, though constituting "edot among edot," are in fact more representative of these.

If we now remember the Israeli version of dominant culture and at the same time generalize from those background features common to Jews from Yemen and Morocco to refer to Israel's Oriental groups in general, it is now possible to outline the main features of the Jewish Israeli case of ethnic encounter.

NOTES

1. See especially P. L. Van den Berghe, *Race and Racism* (New York: John Wiley & Sons, 1967), pp. 9-10; T. Shibutani and K. M. Kwan, *Ethnic Stratification, A Comparative Approach* (London: MacMillan, 1965), p. 572.

2. C. Geertz, "The Integrative Revolution," in *Old Societies and New States*, ed. C. Geertz (New York: Free Press, 1965), pp. 109-40.

3. See especially Mason's outline of acculturation and integrative models in P. Mason, *Patterns of Dominance* (London: Oxford University Press, 1970), p. 59.

4. I. Kafih, *Hilhot Teiman, Haie Hayehudim Betsana Ubnoteah* [The ways of the Yemenites, the life of Jews in San'a and her daughters] (Jerusalem: Ben-Zvi Institute, Hebrew University, 1961), pp. 1-20.

5. H. J. Cohen, *Yehudei Asia Veafrika Bamizrah Hatihon* [The Jews of Asia and Africa in the Middle East] (Tel Aviv: Hakibbutz Hameuad Publishing House, 1972), pp. 13-14.

6. Kafih, *Hilhot Teiman* [The ways of the Yemenites], pp. 105-7.

7. Cohen, *Yehudei Asia Veafrika* [The Jews of Asia and Africa], p. 40.

8. Kafih, *Hilhot Teiman* [The ways of the Yemenites], p. 9.

9. Cohen, *Yehudei Asia Veafrika* [The Jews of Asia and Africa], p. 83.

10. Ibid., p. 101.
11. Kafih, *Hilhot Teiman* [The ways of the Yemenites], p. 227.
12. Cohen, *Yehudei Asia Veafrika* [The Jews of Asia and Africa], p. 100.
13. Ibid., p. 70.
14. Kafih, *Hilhot Teiman* [The ways of the Yemenites], p. 70.
15. Cohen, *Yehudei Asia Veafrika* [The Jews of Asia and Africa], p. 63.
16. Kafih, *Hilhot Teiman* [The ways of the Yemenites], p. 290.
17. Ibid., p. 53.
18. Ibid., p. 107.
19. S. D. Goitein, "Hahinuh Hayehudi Beeretz Teiman Ketipus Shel Hinuh Yehudi Mekori" [Jewish education in Yemen as a type of original Jewish education], *Megamot* 2, no. 2 (January 1950): 152-80.
20. Kafih, *Hilhot Teiman* [The ways of the Yemenites], p. 14.
21. Ibid., p. 265.
22. Goitein, "Hahinuh Hayehudi" [Jewish education], pp. 152-80.
23. Kafih *Hilhot Teiman* [The ways of the Yemenites], p. XII.
24. Ibid., p. 4.
25. Ibid., pp. 267-74.
26. Cohen, *Yehudei Asia Veafrika* [The Jews of Asia and Africa], p. 147.
27. M. Tsadok, *Yehudei Teiman, Toldoteihem Veorhot Hayeihem* [Yemenite Jews, their history and ways of life] (Tel Aviv: Am Oved, 1967), pp. 99-100.
28. H. Tahon, *Edot Beisrael* [Jewish groups in Israel] (Jerusalem: Reuven Mass, 1957), pp. 118-29.
29. Israeli Central Bureau of Statistics (ICBS), *Thunot Demografiot Shel Haohlosiah—Helek Beit* [Demographic characteristics of the population—part two] (Jerusalem: Population and Housing Census 1972, Series No. 10, 1976), pp. 306-7.
30. A. Chouraqui, *Les Juifs d'Afrique de Nord* (Paris: Presses Universitaires de France, 1952), pp. 16-18.
31. Ibid., pp. 62-63.
32. Ibid., pp. 276-84.
33. C. De Nesry, *Le Juif de Tanger et le Maroc* (Tanger: Editions Internationales, 1956), pp. 106-7.
34. P. Saisset, *Heures Juives au Maroc* (Paris: Reider, 1930), pp. 37-41.
35. Ibid., p. 49.
36. Quoted in Chouraqui, *Les Juifs d'Afrique du Nord*, pp. 94-96.
37. Ibid., p. 227.
38. M. Confino, "Nigudim Vetmurot Betsfon Afrika" [Conflicts and changes in Northern Africa], *Mibifnim* 16, no. 2 (November 1953), pp. 566-80.
39. Chouraqui, *Les Juifs d'Afrique du Nord* pp. 164-69.
40. Confino, "Nigudim Vetmurot" [Conflicts and changes] pp. 566-80.

41. Chouraqui, *Les Juifs d'Afrique du Nord*, pp. 192-96.

42. Ibid, pp. 218-22.

43. R. Fuerstein and M. Rishel, *Yaldei Hamellah—Pigur Tarbuti Etsel Yaldei Maroko Umashmauto Hahinuhit* [The children of the Mellah—cultural backwardness among Moroccan children and its educational significance] (Jerusalem, Henrietta Szold Institute, the Jewish Agency, 1964).

44. Confino, "Nigudim Vetmurot" [Conflicts and changes], pp. 566-80.

45. E. Eilon, *Les Juifs en Afrique du Nord, Une Chronologie* (Jerusalem: Departement de la jeunesse et du Hechaloutz, Agence Juive, 1975), pp. 50-60.

46. A. Memmi, *Netsiv Hamelah* [The statute of salt] (Tel Aviv: Am Oved, 1960), pp. 61-62.

47. A. Chouraqui, *La Condition Juridique de l'Israelite Marocain* (Paris: Presse du Livre Francais, 1945), pp. 15-25.

48. Chouraqui, *Les Juifs d'Afrique du Nord*, p. 187.

49. D. Bensimon-Donath, *L'Integration des Juifs Nord-Africains en France* (Paris, La Haye: Mouton, 1977), pp. 60-61.

50. M. Orans, "Caste and Race Conflict in Cross-Cultural Perspective," in *Race, Change and Urban Society*, ed. P. Orleans and E. Russell (Beverly Hills, California: Sage Publications, 1971), p. 94.

The Ethnic Encounter:
Basic Characteristics

4

INTRODUCTION

When considering both the rules of the dominant culture—and following them up at the various spheres to which they refer—and the groups' *a priori* features—insofar as they too are relevant to the various spheres—convergences as well as divergences appear, which circumscribe nexi of problems and delineate in each sphere what we will call the "basic characteristics" of the encounter. In each sphere, that is, culture and membership, stratification, and polity, however, the encounter engenders, in view of our definition of an ethnic group (see chapter 3), two distinct sets of phenomena. Sociocultural particularism, accounted for by the group's location in the setting—and which is expressed by indicators such as ecological data, frequencies of given behavioral models, occupational structures or political allegiances—constitutes the *objective side* of ethnicity. On the other hand, ethnicity is also a *subjective phenomenon.* One is an ethnic not only by exhibiting certain kinds of behavior, objectively observable. This label also implies a feeling of belonging to a group which defines itself by some primordial identity and collective personality and which, by its self-perceived distinctiveness from "outs" in whatever respects of the social arena, appears as representing a particular plight for its members.

In a general manner, and when focusing on whatever level of either objective or subjective issues, the major question of interest for students of ethnicity is universal: By what means and to what extent has the encounter "forged" an entity that remains *distinct* in the setting?

In turning first to the objective side, this question relates to the eventuality of *ethnic pluralism*. This concept means that *society has become characterized by an enduring specific location of a group in the social order.* If such particular location is not only a *de facto* reality but has also been overtly and "officially" recognized as legitimate, it illustrates what may be labelled *institutionalized pluralism*.

However, the question of pluralism—if such exists at all, and if so whether as a *de facto* or a recognized situation—may be answered differently in each sphere. Thus, for instance, regarding the sphere of membership and culture, institutionalized pluralism means that cultural features and symbols pertaining to the dominant culture remain overtly and lastingly unshared by the group, and vice versa. Such an eventuality, if it concretizes through the group's maintenance as a particular community, may be termed *sociocultural pluralism*. As for the socioeconomic dimension, the same problem of distinctiveness concerns the place of the group in the setting's stratification system. *Stratificational pluralism* meaning a persisting and well-recognized correlation between belongingness to the group and socioeconomic status. Finally, with respect to the third sphere, one may speak of *political pluralism* to the extent that the group appears as clearly located in the political system, and its interests as a manifest political cleavage. In sum, and according to the characteristics of the encounter, pluralism may emerge at diverse degrees and show a specific profile according to the spheres wherein it is most salient.

On the other hand, the interest of the subjective side resides in the manner in, and the extent to which the people concerned become aware of themselves as a *distinct* entity. This awareness of kind also represents the outcome of the ethnic encounter; the emergence of each of its four components may be related to different domains of occurrences most relevant to it. Thus, both the formulation of a primordial identity circumscribing a restrictive concept of membership inside the social whole, and the crystallization of the group's self-perceived cultural personality, though by no means unrelated to processes taking place in other spheres, are, by their very nature, primarily bound to problems characterizing the ethnic encounter in the sphere of membership and culture. Similarly, status and power phenomena will inevitably have a major impact on the group's perceptions of practical distances between it and "outs." Finally, it is the interaction between the group's self-definition as such and its self-perceived personality with its perceptions of concrete realities that bring about the extent to which, and the manner in which the group interprets its actual plight in conflictual terms.

From the viewpoint of the group's *distinctiveness*, the meaning of this awareness of kind is obviously crucial and consists of its expressing the very "ethnicization" of a given group of people which is both a reflection of, and gives shape to, their interacting with the other participants in the social setting. Accordingly, the most extreme case of an ethnic group is the one characterized by: (1) a primordial identity defined in terms legitimizing a definitive maintenance of the group; (2) a self-perceived collective personality well crystallized and "closed" to change: (3) perceptions of a wide practical distinctiveness from the "outs" in all respects of the social order; and (4) a highly conflictual interpretation of one's collective plight in society. At the other end, there is, of course, the case sharing opposed characteristics. The more a case resembles the first extreme the more does it constitute a *real grouping*, since its objective particularism—whatever its saliency—is grounded on a compact web of commitments of the members to the group. The closer it is to the second possibility, the more it illustrates merely a *normative phenomenon*, the objective features of which— even if such are salient—are but weakly related to commitments.

On the whole, spheres or facets of social reality are not isolated from each other and, to the extent that occurrences in one sphere may be influenced by occurrences pertaining to others, objective and subjective phenomena interact also with each other. More particularly, awareness of kind is necessarily a function of objective reality in the same manner as the social location of people is not unrelated to self-images and aspirations. At all events, both the subjective and objective sides of ethnicity as "supplied" by the various and interrelated areas of the encounter, accumulate in the ethnics' contribution to the molding of society wherein they constitute, in turn, a "transformational agent" altering its "physiognomy." In each respect, and viewed from the angle of *society as a whole*, this question concerns the *discontinuities* which now characterize the society because of the encounter; that is, the extent to which different cultures or cultural variants cut across certain spheres of social activity, together with their "fermenting" group-formation processes that discontinue webs and currents of social interactions. Thus, if the encounter starts with the defining of a frame of absorption by the dominant culture to which the group must necessarily adjust, it leads to their own involvement in the reshaping of society. The equation device may be used to clarify this line of argument. (See Fig. 4.1).

The nexi of problems, which are at the root of the "configuration" of the Israeli case, are considered below. Our discussion draws heavily from the terms and contentions characteristic of the debates not only among Israeli scholars and writers, but also among militants and publicists. The structure of this discussion, however, follows the guiding principles of our theoretical approach, which has been gradually presented in the foregoing chapters and which will be further detailed in the following.

CULTURAL PLURALISM

In the sphere of membership and culture as asserted in Chapter 2, it is the dominant culture's perception of the group's *a priori* features which accounts for its specific application of the rules of membership. On the other hand, however, the approach of the dominant culture is confronted by the group's own perceptions of the concept of membership in the setting and its cultural corollaries which, of course, depend mainly on the nature of its primordial attributes and *a priori* value orientations, including its own expectations from the ethnic encounter.

As a matter of fact, in viewing the ethnic encounter as a process of "ethnicization," occurrences in this area of membership and culture are most significant and mainly concern the subjective side of ethnicity as a whole. Indeed, ethnicity here refers precisely to the emergence of a sense of belongingness to a group that is a segment of the society at large, and a self-affirmation of "uniqueness," whatever the framework of more comprehensive allegiances maybe offered in the context of a definite dominant culture. Thus, "ethnicization" signifies first the group's subjective confrontation with given criteria of membership and cultural contents, through which it becomes aware of itself, that is, perceives its primordial attributes as a particular and meaningful identity and its own cultural "uniqueness"—whether drawn from a "legacy" or acquired in actual endeavors—as a collective personality.

Figure 4.1 The General Outline of the Ethnic Encounter

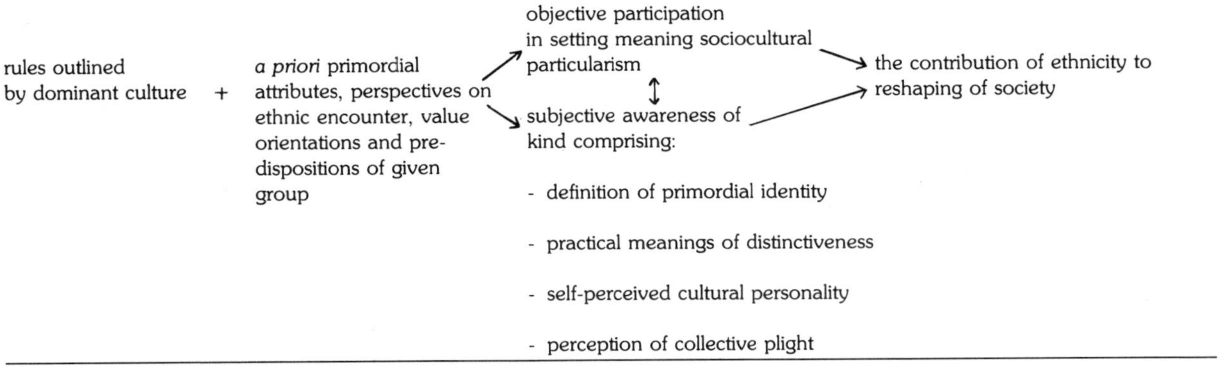

rules outlined
by dominant culture   +

a priori primordial
attributes, perspectives on
ethnic encounter, value
orientations and pre-
dispositions of given
group

objective participation
in setting meaning sociocultural
particularism

subjective awareness of
kind comprising:

- definition of primordial identity

- practical meanings of distinctiveness

- self-perceived cultural personality

- perception of collective plight

the contribution of ethnicity to
reshaping of society

From this viewpoint—and this conclusion was implicit in Chapters 2 and 3—objective and subjective processes pertaining to the group in the additional spheres of stratification and the polity, though interacting with it, contribute but complementary characteristics to a model of ethnic encounter, the starting-point of which is to be found primarily in the area of membership and culture. In this area, the subjective side of ethnicity is of particular importance, and, if vigorously affirmative of the group's existence, may constitute the ground for ethnic communities voluntarily turning in toward themselves. The behavioral models and symbols eventually exhibited by such communities represent—as distinct from value orientations and identities that are essentially subjective phenomena—the sociocultural particularism of the group. These, in turn, further influence the group's images of its cultural distinctiveness from "outs." Figure 4.2 summarizes the above in the form of an equation.

When turning to the Israeli case, this area of the encounter shows, in brief, a situation where a dominant culture is ready to confer membership unconditionally, though it aspires to the future total disappearance of the groups through the latter accepting its own secularized cultural references; these rules are confronted by people who go through a radical transformation of their primordial identity as a result of the encounter, that is, from Jews *in* given places to Jews *from* given origins. These groups are ready in principle to melt into a whole of which they defined themselves beforehand as an integral part. On the other hand, by their traditional or quasi-traditional value orientations, they cannot but endorse sacred meaning to "legacies." Both the contradictions existing between the dominant culture and the ethnics' attitudes, and the inconsistencies in each one's approach, account for the appearance of the edah concept of ethnic entity, together with an enduring and partially institutionalized sociocultural pluralism.

To specify further, notwithstanding the convergences existing at first glance between the groups of immigrants and the absorptive setting on the question of membership and the ultimate goal of the fusion of exiles (*mizug galuyot*), demographic concentrations homogeneous from the viewpoint of origins were soon to appear and became a permanent feature of Israeli reality. Though these "dispersed concentrations," with a wide range of parochial symbols and models, may easily be understood at the first steps into the country—immigrants to

Figure 4.2 The Ethnic Encounter in the Sphere of Membership and Culture

rules of membership
and related cultural   +
reference

a priori features of the group
(mainly primordial attributes
given value orientations and
the perspective over the encounter) →

objective characteristics
sociocultural particularism
of the ethnic group within
the context of its status vis-à-vis
membership in the setting
↕

subjective characteristics
formulation of the ethnics' awareness
of kind regarding

- primordial identity

- collective personality

- perceptions of cultural difference from "outs"

Israel, as to anywhere, saw in their proximity to people of their own stock a means of smoothing the hardships inherent in resettling—the essential fact here is that for *certain* groups, closer than others to a traditional outlook, this pattern was not to remain a mere episode.

According to Chapter 2, a partial explanation of this phenomenon is to be found in the dominant culture's ambiguities. The *a priori* features of traditional groups are entitled to tolerance, as a tribute to Jewish civilization in general. However, the dominant culture, imbued as it is with Eastern European Jewish legacies, is also basically alien to what is specifically Yemenite or Moroccan in these groups' cultures and, let us repeat, frankly hostile to any obstacle to full acceptance of its own cultural references, acceptance which, in its view, is the precondition for the total implementation of *mizug*. At most, it is ready to absorb some symbols of these groups and to officialize differences of cult.

For traditional or quasi-traditional groups, such rules were to create a paradoxical situation as explained by Deshen:

Immigrants from the Near East. . .came to a society whose institutions were already formed and were manned by immigrants from the earlier waves. Therefore, they had to adapt per force, whether to a greater or lesser extent, to the institutions and norms, which they found in the new country.[1]

On the other hand, many of the cultural features and orientations toward life and society shared by the groups represented their basic notion of Judaism as imprinted by their experience in the Diaspora. By symbolizing particular origins—a like religious and national identity being common to all—they contributed to the above-mentioned inversion of identity, from Jews in Yemen or in Morocco to "Yemenites" or "Moroccans" in Israel. This inversion could not but be followed by a partial de-legitimization of culture, since primordial identities labelled by territorial concepts do not have for those involved the same sacred significance as "Jewishness." Moreover, many of the value orientations themselves underlying the behavioral models always thought of as inherent in the religious faith were now seen by other Israeli Jews as merely pertaining to them. This crisis—which as such is quite favorable to cultural changes—was all the more acute for these groups, since immigration to Israel was justified by loyalty to traditions. This latter point, in fact, sets some limits to their readiness to waive, even for the sake of *mizug*, any outlook or symbol comprising what they *now* perceive as their own personality *inside* the nation. One touches here upon the dilemma at the root of the traditional edah-type of ethnic group which points to a subdivision of the nation insisting alike on inseparability from the "whole" and on the—"temporary"—distinctiveness of the group. Yet, by the very conviction explicit in this concept of prior belongingness to the whole *by right*, we can explain why these edot which are remote from the Eastern European legacies also regard the latter's conspicuousness in the dominant culture as discriminatory. The following is but one voice among many:

At last, television has started producing something about Zionism. The Zionism of television, however, is, in a word, the Zionism of the Ashkenazim. It forgets all about the other edot of Israel. As understood by the producer, the national movement of the Jewish People is an Ashkenazi movement only, the history of the Russian and Polish Jew. What of the other Jews? Had they community organizations, a national life? That is, seemingly, without any importance.[2]

These contentions reveal that while both the dominant culture and the Oriental edot include the whole nation in their religious and national labels of identity, and neither excludes anyone from "Jewishness" or "Israeliness," each side has a different interpretation of these notions. Thus the secular dominant culture views religion and its multivariate customary expressions as a mere reflection—and not a necessary one—of a national principle to be stated in universal terms. Among Ashkenazi, it should be emphasized, Zionism has emerged as the fruit of impressive theoretical efforts to justify Jewish national aspirations on the grounds of general theories of nationalism. In contrast, for the traditional or quasi-traditional edah which interprets its immigration as the direct fulfillment of its perennial calling, "Jewish Nation" is primarily conceived in religious and customary terms requiring an adherence to models consecrated by history. Each edah illustrates a particular version of this adherence; though it "understands" that differences may exist between groups and schools, it finds it difficult to envisage Judaism for itself outside its own cultural context, despite the latter's contemporary crisis. According to Banton's pertinent remark:

Any host society demands certain standards of newcomers before it accepts them. If the standards are set too high, the newcomers do not try to meet them. If they are set too low, the newcomers do not place much value upon the acceptance accorded them.[3]

The reason for the low standards in this case resides in the weakness of the ground for heightening them in the eyes of the dominant culture as well as the edot considering the importance both accord the latter's very presence in the setting, beyond the differences between respective interpretations of the fact itself. In this context, moreover, Israel illustrates a case where the low standards required are concomitant with a relatively low readiness for thorough cultural changes, which for the traditional or quasi-traditional group takes the form of a rhetorical question: "Israel" being theirs as Jews, what might justify, in the Land of the Jew, the abandonment of attributes which were adhered to while among the Gentile?

In sum, the edah concept of an ethnic group, defining origin in terms of a primordial identity, as well as the perception of values and life-patterns as worthy of lasting commitments and as representing a collective personality, shape an awareness of kind which gives an impulse to the maintenance of ethnic communities, notwithstanding the edah's constituting a "temporary reality waiting for melting." The cultural and symbolic expressions of these are numerous; they run from edah-based synagogues and styles of prayer to community festivals, patterns of leisure activity, and customary cooking. Some patterns, in fact, tend to be amplified over time rather than deserted. This is the case, for instance, for the *hillulot* described for the Tunisians by Deshen:

Judaeo-Tunisian rites. . .initially centered around the death of pious men, which was conceived as a mystical marriage of their souls with God: hence the term *hillulah* (literally "feast" or "wedding feast") for memorial rites. . . .In popular sentiments and customs these commemorations became joyful and happy celebrations. . . . The current popularity of Tunisian celebrations throughout Israel. . .is manifest in several ways. Completely new *hillulot* are those in honor of Rabbi Hayim Huri, who died in the town of Beersheva in 1957, and of Rabbi Hvita Cohen, who died in the village of Berekhya. . .in 1958.

The new *hillulot* started on a very small scale. At first, only local people, relatives and persons who had known the deceased personally attended. Over the years, however, more and more persons thronged to these *hillulot*, which in some cases came to attract thousands from distant localities all over the country.[4]

This perpetuation of legacies in ethnic communities represents the impact of subjective phenomena on the emergence of objective socio-cultural realities. On the other hand, and by the same token, they strengthen the perception of a cultural distance between "ins" and "outs" and, as a corollary, self-segregative tendencies and reciprocal prejudices. "Israeli" behavioral values (see Chapter 2) more particu-larly, are quite remote from the mind of Oriental groups, and intergroup face-to-face relationships are frequently fraught with uneasiness, mis-understandings and prejudices:

[Rabinowicz asks:] "Moshe, . . . we are friends. Our relationship is not only like between a foreman and his worker. If there is something, . . . [S]ay 'dugri' [frankly] what is going on with you!"
 Moshe David thinks: Dugri! Dugri! That is your word, you the Ashkenazi, . . . It is impossible at all to speak to you . . . and when you say "dugri!" you spoil everything. Your words are only a trap. . . . You know that there are things it is impossible to speak out on—in this way you can get rid of them. A good invention: "dugri!". . . He says to Rabinowicz: "Everything is OK. You are a kind man, God help you!"[5]

On the other side of the barrier, obviously, prejudices are also the lot of many an Ashkenazi's image of Orientals, which is also frequently witnessed by literature:

Leizer-Yankel did not pay much attention to his "strange" Moroccan neigh-bor. He gave him some respect because of the gold and silver coins he saw in his shop (Daoud even lent him some coins, once . . .), but besides this he had no interest in thinking about him. It seemed somehow to Leizer-Yankel that . . . his neighbor's home was under a bad influence . . . but was he not Sephardic?[6]

The extent to which all of the above applies more specifically to Yemenites and Moroccans is to be a major topic of the following chapters. It is, however, implicit from the foregoing definition of the problem of ethnicity in the sphere of membership and culture that it does not affect every group in the same measure, even groups which by their recent arrival in Israel have barely participated in the emer-gence of the dominant culture. Indeed, the less tradition-minded the group, the more they should be able to accept the concept of mem-bership as formulated by the absorptive setting. By the same token, and let us repeat, as the setting is homogeneous not only with respect to nation but also to religion and race (except, from the latter view-point, small groups of black Jewish Indians and Ethiopians), the less such groups consider their *a priori* sociocultural features a sacred legacy, the less can they "look back" to their past as commanding enduring commitments, and the more they are prepared for cultural change, thus diminishing the contrast existing between them and the cultural stereotypes of the dominant culture.

To be sure, groups such as recent West European or American immigrants may feel estranged from several national symbols drawn directly from Eastern European cultures—from Hassidic music which plays a role in Israel's "official" folklore to Hebrew-translated Yiddish literature, which constitutes a central part of school curricula. On the other hand, their secular concept of nationhood and often nontraditional style of religious practice enables them to accept the referring of these symbols to the nation as a whole and to minimize the impact of their own *a priori* attributes pertaining to their "Americanness," "Frenchness," or whatever. Groups of this kind contribute concretely to the emergence of a *nonethnic stock* wherein the offspring, at least, of *all* secular groups effectively disappear as ethnics without leaving any trace. The symbols of this stock, it should be emphasized, are drawn directly from the dominant culture, and whatever their closeness to particular legacies, are intended to comprehend every segment of the social whole they define. It is in the context of these considerations that throughout the following, a distinction will be made between "others" and "outs." "Others" will be used only to designate this nonethnic stock; "outs" will refer to all people who do not belong to the group specifically discussed, whether belonging to other edot or to "others."

At this point, however, we might also deduce that the process of "desacralization" of the Oriental edot's legacies in a Jewish country should also lead unavoidably to their "de-ethnicization." This would find its strongest expression in the new generations born in Israel, which have known its system of education, including military service, and an overall involvement in a non-Diasporan environment. Secularization, if meaning de-ethnicization, should contribute to the weakening, or even the dissolution, of ethnic communities. Thus what has happened to Ashkenazi should, seemingly, also apply to the Oriental edot in the long run. To speculate on the distant future is hazardous, but what must be emphasized with regard to *present* reality is that contrary to the former, secularization among the latter was to occur *after* the emergence in Israel of compact communities; indeed their faithfulness to traditional ways was even strengthened initially by the very fact of immigration to the Land of the Jews. In this context, the process of desacralization of traditions, engendered by the confrontation with alternative versions of Judaism, a secular-minded dominant culture and new, unforeseen, social endeavors, was to take place inside communities already well crystallized and whose overt symbols and life-styles were heavily grounded in the Diasporan past. Thus the "buying" of fresh norms as well as the deletion of many a rite and custom contribute to the *"eclecticization"* of the culture of communities, which by their very existence—still strengthened by the fact that the edot were particular groupings in their countries of origin—maintain some power of attraction over many of their members. Hence, these communities, though developing new forms over time, cannot be seen as negating their original ethnic character despite the heteroclitic contents of their present cultural features. This is conveniently summarized in Figure 4.3 which specifies the terms of Figure 4.2. These subjective and objective characteristics of the encounter in the sphere of membership and culture are to be kept in mind when turning to occurrences pertaining to the other spheres.

THE STRATIFICATIONAL DIMENSION

The confrontation in the sphere of stratification of given rules of participation—depending on both the rationale of the socioeconomic markets and rights of participation correlated to the question of membership—with relevant *a priori* features of the ethnics, that is, predispositions and resources accounting for capabilities to meet the requirements of markets, signifies (at least in the long run) a transformation of the group's characteristics regarding occupations, standards of living, education, or styles of life. On the other hand, this confrontation may also represent a meaningful change in the setting's general status map. The more so the case, the more are definite stratificational features salient in the group's particularism. It may also be assumed that from the subjective viewpoint, the more so the case, the more should the group share resulting perceptions of status distances from the "outs." These, to be sure, should be interpreted through the

Figure 4.3 The Emergence of the Edah

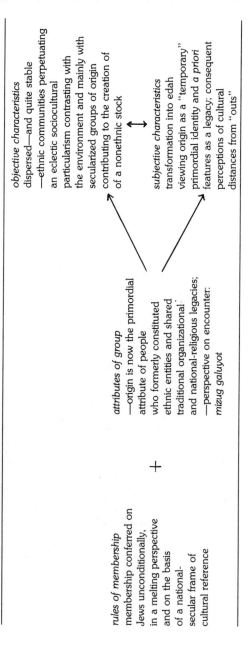

rules of membership
membership conferred on
Jews unconditionally,
in a melting perspective
and on the basis
of a national-
secular frame of
cultural reference

+

attributes of group
—origin is now the primordial
attribute of people
who formerly constituted
ethnic entities and shared
traditional organizational
and national-religious legacies;
—perspective on encounter:
mizug galuyot

objective characteristics
dispersed—and quite stable
—ethnic communities perpetuating
an eclectic sociocultural
particularism contrasting with
the environment and mainly with
secularized groups of origin
contributing to the creation of
of a nonethnic stock

subjective characteristics
transformation into edah
viewing origin as a "temporary"
primordial identity and *a priori*
features as a legacy; consequent
perceptions of cultural
distances from "outs"

expectations and aspirations in this concern and account for either integrative images of one's part in the setting or, on the contrary, feelings of alienation and conflict.

By using again an equation to clarify the argument, and in the context of the encounter in the area of culture and membership, one may draw out Figure 4.4.

In this sphere, the Israeli case illustrates a situation where the setting appears quite "generous" in the rights and services provided to any groups of immigrants, though social status remains to be acquired through competition by individual achievement. With regard to the generosity of the setting, the dominant culture converges with the ethnics' *a priori* expectations, but as far as social status is concerned this is not the case. For the edot, immigration from nonmodern (or partially modern) countries and settling in Israel signified a radical change in all aspects of occupational life; yet by the same token, they were to meet countless difficulties in competing with "others" and many of their people were soon reduced to lower positions. To the extent that skills relevant to a modern economy had been learned in the past, they were mostly attached to jobs that are of a low status in Israel. In this context, given origins were to become broadly correlated with socioeconomic inferiority and the edot were to crystallize as *ethnoclasses*, that is, groups of people sharing not only sociocultural features as ethnic entities but also underprivileged class positions. This evolution is especially conspicuous since in view of their numerical importance, the edot originating from non-Western countries were soon to "monopolize" most inferior positions, thus creating a clear and well-perceived overlapping between categories of origin and class cleavages.

All this, in fact, is sustained by the data overviewed in Chapter 1 which express eloquently the hardships experienced by the ethnics in meeting status requirements. The impact of additional circumstances, however, cannot be denied in this concern; besides the demographic concentration, which as such weakens the influence of the environment, the ambiguous attitudes (also discussed in the former section) of both the dominant culture and the edot toward parochialism soften the rigor of processes of resocialization. At the same time, let us add, the "generosity" of the setting, anchored in the egalitarian emphasis of Israeli social philosophy, also diminishes the price of nonmobility.

Figure 4.4 Ethnicity and Status

rules of socioeconomic participation, including rights and requirements

+

a priori relevant sociocultural features (mainly predispositions and resources) of a given group of people

→

objective characteristics: location of the group on status map

→

subjective characteristics: status distance from "outs" as an object of the group's perceptions of distinctiveness and interpretation of its plight

A direct consequence of "ethnoclassization" is the ethnics' resentment of what they perceive, against the background of their expectations as an edah, as a collective deprivation accompanying their efforts to adjust to Israeli society. Thus, sharp feelings of alienation are prevalent (see Chapter 1) and are expressed in acerbic criticism of the "establishment"; poverty, which as everywhere is correlated with prostitution, begging, and juvenile delinquency, has also caused the "others" to associate moral deprivation with Oriental origins. This attitude is expressed frequently in the media as well as by novelists, and the following quotation from a popular novel is but one instance among many:

Again Sasson David [an unemployed Indian immigrant married to a Persian and addicted to gambling] visited the employment office. He was sitting there waiting and in the meantime was telling his usual stories. People were listening. In the evenings he was in the gambling house. One night he went home with a man. The man was fat and held a package. "This is my friend, Shimon the fisherman" he told his wife. "He has brought some fish and we will eat together. . . . " The woman was very happy as food had been very scarce in the house for the last fortnight and her feet were swollen. After the meal, Sasson David said: "This man has brought us food and he is even ready to give us some money, and all these only for sleeping with you in my place."[7]

In this context of economic hardship, marginal status, and social vicissitudes, the claims of ethnic activists are most often turned toward material problems:[8] "Notwithstanding the importance of culture and legacies which increase the pride of people . . . these will not solve the problems of the Orientals: the main problem is the poverty of development towns and of the slums of the big cities."

Unavoidably, stratificational pluralism, which blatantly differentiates on a more or less permanent basis between Oriental ethnoclasses and a nonethnic stock predominant in middle and higher strata, gradually becomes recognized and reflected in the appearance of new tokens in daily speech and official policies. "Edot Mizrah," (literally, the "Oriental-groups-as-a-whole," but used in the sense of "Orientals as a whole") and "Ashkenazi" are among the most widespread of these and they connote socioeconomic inferiority with given cultural entities. This recognition of socioethnic cleavages, however, does not mean a shrewder perception of their contents; in fact, the use of such tokens, in an ethnic sense, represents in itself a major fallacy in the interpretation of Israeli ethnic reality.

As the *de facto* pluralism is in sharp dissonance with the *mizug* perspective, it is seen by many—politicians or public servants as well as sociologists and statisticians—as a transitional stage not only *toward mizug* but also *of mizug*. At this stage, assumedly, people first assimilate with those who are closer to themselves both socially and culturally, creating new, broader ethnic groups which substitute the more restrictive identities. This "submelting of edot" assessment, whatever its attractiveness from the viewpoint of the *mizug* ideology when confronted with a pluralistic reality, does not, however, stand up to a closer look at its two key concepts—Edot Mizrach and Ashkenazi. About these it may be said that they merely point to sociocultural categories, that is, nominal classes of people differing from each other by given broad, cultural and/or social features.

The majority of Ashkenazi, indeed, have had contact with Yiddish culture and been influenced by Christian civilization; in Israel they mostly belong to the prosperous strata of the population. In contrast, the Orientals, who are concentrated in the lower class, have generally had some (though often very light) contact with the Sephardi legacy and have been affected by Islamic culture. It is hazardous, however, to conclude from this characterization that these two entities constitute new ethnic groups as such. As discussed earlier, in a setting dominated by a secular ethos that is homogeneous regarding race, religion, and nation, nontraditionalist Ashkenazi groups demonstrate a strong tendency toward general "de-ethnicization" inside the Israeli Jewish collective. Neither is the "Orientals-as-a-whole" an appropriate token though it refers to people who constitute ethnic groups. As suggested by Ben-David:

We speak of Edot Mizrah. Obviously there is nothing of this kind. Edot Mizrah is not a religious tradition; there is a Yemenite tradition, there is an Iraqi tradition, there is a Moroccan tradition. A person who comes from a given place and has grown up there does share some feelings toward a particular tradition. "Oriental," however, is a generalization which has been created here, in this country. . . . This means that some negative identity has been forged regarding the Oriental edot as a result of a generalization of various phenomena and their relating to a given group of people.[9]

Thus this concept mainly expresses and *recognizes* the broad overlapping of categories of origins with socioeconomic situations and, at the same time, veils the existence of multiple ethnic groups at given points of the setting. More than anything else, it illustrates the lack of accurate perception of ethnicity when viewing it from the peak of social reality, when in fact it takes place chiefly at the bottom. Hence, it is only in the sense of sociocultural *categories* that the terms of "Ashkenazi" and "Orientals" are used throughout these pages.

With the help of Figure 4.4 and in the context of both the edah-type of ethnic group and the Zionist ideology pertaining to the ethnic encounter in the area of membership and culture, the stratificational dimension of the case may be summarized as shown by Figure 4.5.

Thus, as seen in the former section, if sociocultural pluralism in Israel refers to the simultaneous appearance of a nonethnic stock and of edot, stratificational processes add a class dimension to the picture: the nonethnic stock constitutes mainly the middle and upper classes while among the edot many are reduced to the condition of ethnoclasses.

This statement, however, does not exhaust the description of stratificational processes involving ethnicity. As in any democratic and modern country, many socioeconomic markets and paths of mobility in Israel are open to whoever meets their requirements, and these possibilities cannot but permit upward social mobility of those ethnics able to enter meritocratic competition. On the other hand, the greater the contradiction between the situation emerging in the sphere of status and the dominant culture's vision of the fate of ethnic groups in society—and this is especially relevant to the Israeli case—the more should one expect special initiatives from the center to influence the outcome of stratificational rules. Moreover, such an interference with problems pertaining to the area of membership and culture in the sphere of stratification eventually may also be congruent with pressures exerted in the same direction and originating in the political sphere.

These last remarks account for the strong emphasis, observable in the Israeli center's policy, upon educational efforts among ethnics. Thus[10] in Israeli universities in 1964 there were only 237 of various Oriental origins out of 10,000 persons ages twenty to twenty-nine, but the figure was 510 in 1974, an increase of 114 percent; the parallel figures for the Jewish population in general were 379 and 716, which means a rate of increase of only 88 percent. Among the student body itself, Orientals, who accounted for 13 percent in 1969, were 16

Figure 4.5 The Creation of an Ethnoclass

rules regarding status	+	*relevant features of group*	→	*objective characteristics*	→	*subjective characteristics*
—"generosity" of the setting but modern requirements for status achievements		traditional or quasi-traditional orientations toward status, occupations, education, etc.		people of Oriental origins "monopolize" lower positions; the ethnic communities become ethno-classes- recognition of wide overlapping between categories of origins and social status		perceptions among ethnics of distances from "others"; feelings of deprivation; alienation and resentment toward "others"

percent five years later (1974). This progress is due not only to the social improvement of numerous Oriental families and their greater willingness to consider higher education as a natural process for their children, but also, and to a wide extent, to a large variety of special programs for socially underprivileged pupils, whether at high school or university level. It is no longer rare, hence, to read in the newspapers information of the following kind:

From the statistics of the Haifa Technion, it emerges that 80% of students from underprivileged background who had taken special preparatory programs have obtained an average grade of 65 in 1977 . . . while as for the graduates from this group, all but two or three have achieved a grade above 70 which are not lower scores than the average at the institution.[11]

On the whole, and though precise data are not available, many ethnics really do accede to a higher status than the bulk of their edot; it may be estimated (with caution) that about one fourth to one third of Orientals participate in social hierarchies at a level which locate them outside lower or low-middle strata (see Appendix 2). Yet the question which then arises regarding the subjective side of the ethnic encounter is to what extent do these people remain a part of their stocks. To be sure, this question concerns the problem of acceptance by "others" to no less an extent than the mobile ethnics' own velleity, and this part of the question is by no means self-evident. Cases are known, as for example, the blacks in Brazil, where status effectively opens new doors and narrows social distance; by contrast in other instances, as the blacks in the United States a few decades ago, mobility of ethnics may create a reaction of discriminatory self-closure among "outs" who feel threatened.

As a matter of course, discrimination is not unknown in Israel either and practical examples are quite often reported:

When I was working at the Jewish Agency, . . . a man who was 50 years old and father of 10 children was injured in a work accident and applied to us for assistance. . . . He was turned down by the secretary of the department because . . . "there was no money for such purposes." I knew that there still was a budget for cases like this, and I also knew that a Polish immigrant had been assisted recently for similar reasons. . . . When I asked the secretary of the department . . . he answered: "Yeheshkel, this man is an Oriental like you. You have to help him. The budget of the department is for more important purposes. . . . " This incident opened my eyes.[12]

On the other hand, however, segregation practices, social self-closure or even mere prejudice cannot gain any legitimacy in the context of the *mizug* perspective of the dominant culture itself. In fact, experiences of discrimination occur mainly in dealings with lower-class ethnics by "others" of higher status. Among the mobile ethnics, as illustrated by this quotation—the speaker confesses that he had his eyes "opened" by the case of someone else who was in a lower-class position—discrimination is rarely decried.

At the same time, as for the mobiles' own velleities, the edot's own emphasis on *mizug* cannot but encourage them to willingly assimilate among "others" once a distance has been created anyway between themselves and their communities of origin—differences of social status being mostly correlated with education and a greater internalization of the dominant culture. It is the meeting of these orientations and the openness of "others" that account for the low level of ethnic segregation in middle-class neighborhoods and the high rates of exogamous marriages among mobile ethnics.[13] All these also account, of course, for the complaints of ethnic activists who deplore:

A most painful thing is that many among the intellectual stratum of the Orientals ignore the people of their edot and get away from any ethnic activity. They have become successful and prosperous and have left the public stage. . . . There are among them economists and businessmen who could contribute a lot in all domains, but they do that only for themselves.[14]

This deleting of the mobiles' ethnic consciousness may be seen, it is true, as the very working of the melting perspective and as such the fulfillment of a crucial social value accepted by all. Yet, by the same token, this subjective phenomenon, which enables the disappearance of mobiles among "others," also signifies objectively a constant "*truncation*" of active elements from the edah which remains an ethnoclass. By this, ethnic mobility—whatever its amplitude—contributes but minimally to the altering of the basic lines of the Jewish Israeli model of ethnic encounter. This aspect of the stratificational sphere of the ethnic encounter may also be summarized by specifying Figure 4.4 (see Figure 4.6). This picture, in fact, represents a striking confirmation of a situation hypothesized by Banton:

That people climb from one social class to another does not necessarily weaken class differences and may indeed strengthen them, for the socially

Figure 4.6 The Impact of Social Mobility

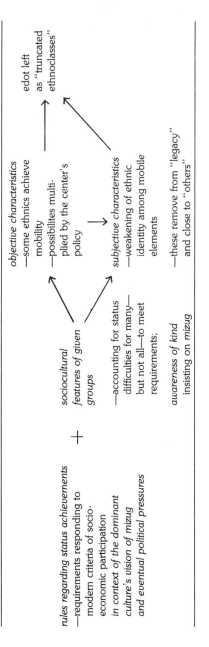

rules regarding status achievements
—requirements responding to modern criteria of socio-economic participation *in context of the dominant culture's vision of mizug and eventual political pressures*

+

sociocultural features of given groups

—accounting for status difficulties for many—but not all—to meet requirements;

awareness of kind insisting on mizug

objective characteristics
—some ethnics achieve mobility
—possibilites multi-plied by the center's policy

subjective characteristics
—weakening of ethnic identity among mobile elements

—these remove from "legacy" and close to "others"

edot left as "truncated ethnoclasses"

ambitious person strives to obtain the distinguishing characteristics of people in the higher class, and when he has "arrived" he is apt to draw the line all the more sharply between those who have those characteristics and those who do not.[15]

ETHNICITY IN POLITY

The polity is the third major dimension of the ethnic encounter. As far as the dominant culture is concerned, the encounter in this sphere depends, in a democratic regime, not only on the formal rights conferred on the ethnics as related to membership, but also on criteria of preeminence—which account for many aspects of the recruitment of the political elites—as well as on the extent of responsibility allowed by the center vis-à-vis the periphery in general. These latter rules, which are significant in the comparative study of democracies,[16] should be reflected in both the political "offers" made to the ethnics and in the scope of the center's dealing with their problems.

Yet in this area too, rules are confronted by given outlooks characterizing the group itself. First, obviously, there are the groups' own views of politics embedded in their a priori cultural features, which imprint themselves in the manner they respond to issues such as the nature of the state or their role as citizens. Second, the polity is an area where one's belongingness to society receives its most ritual expressions, and where patterns of behavior also reveal people's feelings in this concern, which again pertain to the awareness of kind that is crystallized in the sphere of culture and membership. Third, the polity, at least in a democratic regime, is a forum where interests drawn from very diverse spheres may appear and become relevant issues of the game of power; as such, this forum permits the ethnics to put forward problems that preoccupy them and are related to their plight as a whole, including, of course, in the political arena itself.

What emerges from these considerations is that besides those factors which are specific to this sphere—such as patterns of recruitment or the political concepts of the ethnics—all main elements pertaining to other areas are present here too. Thus, a systematic approach has to clearly define the part played by each of them, and to distinguish among those which are primarily relevant, respectively, either to the objective or the subjective sides of the encounter in this sphere.

Regarding the objective aspect, we should remember that the question under review is the extent to which the encounter engenders a situation of *political pluralism*. This question is divisible into two more specific issues, namely: (1) the extent to which the participation of ethnics in political power is clearly and enduringly differentiated, which points to the possibility of *de facto political pluralism*; and (2) the extent to which ethnicity is directly, overtly, and autonomously articulated in polity, which refers to the possibility of *institutionalized political pluralism*.

In the context of the above it may be suggested that regarding the first issue—to the degree that full political rights are conferred on the ethnics—it is the encounter between the rules of political recruitment and the ethnics' *a priori* features which should explain their access to political power.

The question of institutionalized pluralism, however, implies different meanings according to the factor that constitutes in this respect the principal source of ethnic reality. Thus, for instance, an institutionalized ethnic pluralism in polity dictated by the dominant culture means that arrangements initiated by the center encourages a distinct and permanent location of the group in the political system. Such official arrangements are then legitimized by the perspective of the dominant culture on the ethnic encounter leading to some assumption of "separate development" of the group. However, even in the case that the dominant culture endorses, on the contrary, a melting perspective and, consequently, opposes the institutionalization of ethnicity in polity, such a reality may still be imposed "from the bottom" by the ethnic group itself.

An eventual situation of *de facto* pluralism, for instance, mainly if accompanied by inferiority in other spheres, may be a strong incentive for ethnics to set up autonomous lobbies, even political movements or factions. This conclusion, moreover, is reached not necessarily only in a situation of inferiority: political conjunctures, may permit expectations of gain from such efforts even in different circumstances. On the other hand, not every situation of inferiority *must* lead to political reactions, even if advantages can be expected. In fact, what may here be of a determinant weight is the subjective side of ethnicity, which concerns how far the ethnics' awareness of kind comprises an understanding of one's "collective plight" appropriate to the creation of a political entity. Stated in Marxist terminology,[17] the main subjective question is whether ethnics make up a "for-itself" group developing a community of interests and political consciousness or are but an "in-itself" group unready to articulate its various cultural, social, or political concerns on the political stage.

According to our definition of the concept of ethnic awareness of kind, objective circumstances, it is true, account for the ethnics' perceptions of the practical meanings of ethnicity in society and, henceforth, influence their political consciousness. At this point, however, it should be remembered that this concept of ethnic awareness of kind also differentiates between such perceptions and the ethnics' *general understanding* of their "plight" in society. This understanding, it was stated, is to be seen as the outcome of the interaction between the diverse practical meanings and the more basic factor of the ethnics' perspective on the ethnic encounter as reflected in the terms in which they define their boundaries and their "unique" collective personality. This perspective, though interacting with them, integrates the practical meanings into the ethnics' overall understanding of their "plight." Thus, like for the eventuality determined by the dominant culture, the institutionalization of ethnicity in polity depending on the ethnics and their becoming a "for-itself" group, represents the interrelated dependence of objective ethnic political realities on questions involving the group in the sphere of culture and membership. To clarify this line of reasoning, one may again use the equation device [see Figure 4.7].

In brief, and recalling Chapter 2, Israel illustrates in this sphere a situation where the dominant culture defines criteria of elite recruitment barely within reach of the ethnics and endorses the center with a "guiding" mission regarding their *total* integration. On the other hand (see Chapter 3), the ethnics constitute groups of immigrants originating from traditional or quasi-traditional settings and they exhibit in numerous ways sociocultural features—including attitudes toward politics and polity—which remove them from the dominant culture. These gaps entail distinction between their plight and that of "others" in all major spheres of the encounter, including—let us add here—participation in political power.

For most of these groups it is true that becoming full citizens in a democratic country represents quite a radical change from the Diaspora and that from this viewpoint there is a basic convergence of the

Figure 4.7 Ethnicity in Polity

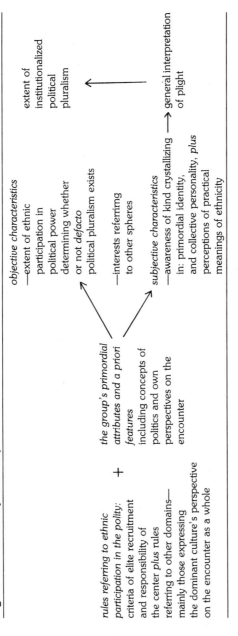

rules referring to ethnic participation in the polity: criteria of elite recruitment and responsibility of the center *plus* rules referring to other domains—mainly those expressing the dominant culture's perspective on the encounter as a whole

+

the group's primordial attributes and a priori features including concepts of politics and own perspectives on the encounter

objective characteristics
—extent of ethnic participation in political power determining whether or not *defacto* political pluralism exists

—interests referring to other spheres

subjective characteristics
—awareness of kind crystallizing in: primordial identity, and collective personality, *plus* perceptions of practical meanings of ethnicity

extent of institutionalized political pluralism

⟶ general interpretation of plight

absorptive setting's approach and the ethnics' expectations. Yet, against the background of the *mizug* perspective, the overall differentiation of the latter from the "others" strengthens the perceptions of marginality among them. On the other hand, the very nature of the aspirations which define them as "temporary" edot explains also the ethnics' reluctance to interpret their plight in a "for-itself" group vein, despite the conflictual images they share of their condition; by their consequent relative muteness and notwithstanding their potential power— that of numbers in a democracy—they avoid the institutionalization of ethnic pluralism in the polity. This attitude is all the more significant in its contrast to the edot's self-affirmation—as discussed earlier in this chapter—as sociocultural collectives loyal to given religious legacies.

To specify these statements further, and turning first to the fact that the polity and the public scene in general are an additional domain of inferiority for the edot, let us remember that criteria of preeminence in Israel are firstly related to veteranship and to major contributions to national life. The edot, for the most part, arrived "late"; because of this as well as their predispositions, they were but minimally involved in setting up institutions or sectors such as the army, the kibbutz movements, the parties, the public service, industrial plants, or the universities which are the principal pillars of Israeli society. Thus, from their viewpoint, those who lead these institutions constitute a *dominant stock* monopolizing preeminence. More particularly in the polity itself this monopoly is sustained by given structures, the most important of which is the electoral system of proportional representation which places "lists," not candidates, in opposition and thus encourages centralism in party organization. This gives much weight to elements solidly anchored in the political apparatus—like the kibbutzim—as well as to prominent leaders who, due to reasons of popularity, frequently coopt dominant personalities from sectors enjoying public prestige. All these refer but to a minority among the Ashkenazi themelves but put particularly the ethnics' position at a disadvantage in central political bodies such as the government, Parliament, or the executive of the powerful Histadrut (General Federation of Trade Unions) (see Appendix 2). As stated bluntly by an ethnic activist,

The "cake" is distributed according to who sits next to the front table. The one who does not worry about himself is discriminated against, and this is the fate of the majority of the Israeli people, the Oriental population. All parties get their power from our support, but we are unable to use this power and receive our part of the cake.[18]

Thus, well-perceived political inferiority widely overlaps social and cultural cleavages and contributes to the conflictual significance of the ethnic encounter as a whole. A situation of this kind could find overt expression in a regime which, despite its centralized structures, permits new forces to emerge, since 1 percent of all votes cast is enough to obtain a first seat in Parliament.

The readiness of the ethnics to fight their own battle is attenuated, it is true, by numerous means used by the center to prevent this eventuality. Most important here are the buffering institutions, from party-sponsored networks to governmental agencies, which attempt to orient them and which frequently appoint active ethnics to minor or middle-range positions, for example, secretary of a union or membership in a town council. In some instances, they are even nominated at higher levels and integrated in the dominant stock itself. For a long period this strategy was appropriate to the patrimonial conception of politics shared by many among the edot. Other means employed to similar effect and reflecting the center's perspective on the ethnic encounter are the articulation of integrative symbols emphasizing the unity of the Nation and the dominance of the theme of social integration in policies regarding matters such as education, taxation, or the construction of dwellings. All of these fully accord with the rules referring to a "responsible dominant stock" and partially account for the neutralization of ethnic power, as decried by ethnic activists:

Again, the slums are "discovered" by politicians on the eve of municipal elections in Haifa. . . . Is this situation new? Is it specific to municipal elections? Are the Haifa candidates different from those in any other electoral campaign? We know the answers; they are well known to the inhabitants of the slums. . . . The slums are a huge reservoir of ballots able to raise up governments, parties and municipalities. The parties know that this reservoir is not organized and they care that it remains so.[19]

Yet, as shown by this quotation, the variety of means utilized by the center is unable to veil the fact that political inferiority coincides with other ethnic cleavages in a general picture leaving much room for conflict and alienation. To interpret the ethnics' political reactions to this, however, requires more than just considering objective reality. Thus, despite their wide participation in lower-strata positions, they are by no means attracted to leftist groups encouraging them to grow "conscious of their proletarian condition." It appears that a lack of class awareness is due precisely to their ethnic consciousness. As already mentioned in Chapter 1, ethnics interpret their social plight in terms of intergroup relations, that is, the "lot reserved to them by the 'others'," rather than through a class-conflict concept.

On the other hand, and despite the compactness of their communities that eases communication among them, neither do ethnics show any real wish to organize independently, which would be beneficial to them in view of their numerical importance and potential voting power (it is only in the 1981 general elections that an ethnic list succeeded to obtain a small representation in Parliament). In earlier sections at least two reasons for this situation were noted: by remaining distinct edot, ethnics of various groups may have difficulty in crystallizing as a unified, meaningful force; on the other hand, by the assimilation of their active elements into new strata, they also remain ethnoclasses truncated from their modern elites. However, as already mentioned, underlying both factors is the ethnics' self-definition as "temporary" edot; by their adherence to the *mizug* perspective they show no eagerness to contribute their support to ethnic tickets. Such a support, if massive, would entail the institutionalization of pluralism in the polity where it would receive its most definitive consecration.

Thus, they become a floating element, which is witnessed on the political scene when, as they achieve stability in the setting, the edot gradually liberate themselves from the control of buffering institutions. To the extent that political preferences are apparent, they have demonstrated that it is toward the nationalist Right or the religious factions that many are led, due to their closeness to traditional values. Moreover, until 1977, the Right was always confined to an opposition role, and support of it presented the added advantage of expressing conflictual feelings against an establishment which had "guided" the first paces and was held responsible not only for the achievements but also for the shortcomings of integration. This turn-about of allegiances was recognized by the principal victims themselves, the left-of-center former regime, as confirmed by its main media outlet, the Histadrut trade union daily:

The 1977 political "revolution" has been caused by a new majority which is not Ashkenazi any more but made up of Orientals born in Muslim countries or in Israel. This non-European majority has made an alliance with the right-wing of East European Zionism and has raised Begin to power.[20]

Yet, in the final analysis and *considering their voluntary muteness*, this kind of political behavior may hardly be labelled irrational. The ethnics' floating between the main parties and their determinant importance today in the "crowning of kings" is bound to increase their bargaining power. On the one hand, their support creates obligations toward them by those they help raise to power; on the other hand, it heightens the "price" of their being "brought back" by those they have unseated.

However, voluntary political muteness, is understandably less the rule as one moves away from the nationwide scene and approaches the local level on the periphery. Here, ethnic communities are dense and numerous, and less normative obstacles hinder direct, overt expression of interethnic antagonisms. But even here ethnic politics are generally still veiled behind nonethnic labels:

For about 10 years, until 1965, the Lamed Aayin, [middle-of-the road liberal party on the national level] branch of Ayara, was virtually a Moroccan ethnic party. . . . [T]he Israeli Labor Alignment. . . also comprised. . . associations of immigrants from Rumania, Tunisia, Morocco. . . . Candidates running for election were selected on the principle of ethnic representation. . . . Mafdal, the national Religious Party, the third major party in Ayara . . ., was originally run mainly by Moroccan politicians.[21]

This description articulates the evolution of the party-linked buffering institutions which, constrained to attract ethnic "clienteles," have changed from networks controlling ethnics from above to channels of expression of ethnic cleavages. Moreover, what is evident here is the discrepancy in the Israeli polity between the place of ethnic politics in peripheral areas and in the center. In this context, the absence of institutionalized political pluralism may appear quite relative and therefore unprotected from eventual crises. As seen in a later chapter, although such crises may break out, even then—and here again the strength of the value premises of the ethnic encounter as a whole is evident—it is by no means possible to observe any expression of either a "proletarian consciousness" or revivalist claims in a "black-is-beautiful" vein. In these cases as well, the perspective remains turned toward the horizon of *mizug* and toward the attainment of material, practical advantages, which are normally expressed in the framework of organizations wherein ethnics participate with "others." The following quotation is typical of this mood, which shows one more paradox in the Israeli case of ethnicity: though the edah phenomenon is essentially cultural, it mainly takes the form of material and practical exigencies on the public scene.

I believe that thanks to the investment of serious resources to close the ethnic gap and liquidate the slums, and of good and competent teachers in development towns—and if opportunities are equal for all—the big turn will come toward the creation of One People with a rich and versatile culture conveying the legacies of all edot.[22]

This background accounts for the main types of ethnic politicians who may be found in Israel. There are the local figures who hold positions at the municipal level and attract the ballots of their ethnic communities; there are the typical ethnoclass leaders who are the "strong men" in lower-class neighborhoods or in the working place; there are also, at another level, those who have been coopted by, and into, the dominant stock and symbolize the edot's "integration" in the political system. These ethnic politicians—including the latter type—can by no means be considered the leaders of their stocks. They may well attempt to strengthen their power on the political scene by developing an ethnic constituency, but as a rule, they can hardly hope to achieve their aim outside national parties which in essence are nonethnic. Moreover, the legitimization of such political ambitions lies in the advancement of the socially underprivileged and not in promotion of ethnic issues as such. Finally, and in the context of the "truncation" of the ethnoclass from its mobile elements, these politicians, even if themselves of middle-class standing, find but a restricted following among those ethnics who have chosen nonpolitical paths to achieve social mobility.

To sum up these considerations by specifying the terms of Figure 4.7, one obtains Figure 4.8.

CONCLUSION: CRYPTO-PLURALISM AND "IN-ITSELF" GROUPINGS

To sum up by turning first to objective aspects which (we recall) question the existence of pluralism and its particular profile, the Israeli

Figure 4.8 The Conflict "In-Itself" Grouping

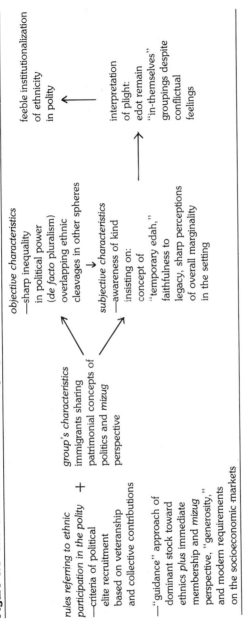

rules referring to ethnic
participation in the polity
—criteria of political
elite recruitment
based on veteranship
and collective contributions

— "guidance" approach of
dominant stock toward
ethnics plus immediate
membership and mizug
perspective, "generosity,"
and modem requirements
on the socioeconomic markets

+

group's characteristics
immigrants sharing
patrimonial concepts of
politics and mizug
perspective

objective characteristics
—sharp inequality
in political power
(de facto pluralism)
overlapping ethnic
cleavages in other spheres
→
subjective characteristics
—awareness of kind
insisting on:
concept of
"temporary edah,"
faithfulness to
legacy, sharp perceptions
of overall marginality
in the setting

feeble institutionalization
of ethnicity
in polity

interpretation
of plight:
edot remain
"in-themselves"
groupings despite
conflictual
feelings

case illustrates a situation where a sharp differentiation distinguishes the edot's location in all major spheres of the encounter. Thus, in the area of membership and culture, though unconditionally accepted, the ethnics remain numerous in distinct sociocultural communities which contrast with their environment; from the viewpoint of social status, despite the "generosity" of the center and opportunities encouraging the social mobility of significant numbers of ethnics, most of the groups have become and remained ethnoclasses; in the polity and notwithstanding the democratic regime, they are still clearly underrepresented in the political elite. All these, it is true, were concomitant with most radical transformation of traditional or quasi-traditional groups that in the past were religious-national enclaves in patrimonial settings. Yet this transformation, rather than deleting the pluralistic principle, has produced a new model, an essential characteristic of which is that the more one moves from the cultural sphere to the political, the weaker its overt and "official" recognition. Thus, if the maintenance of parochial symbols is still quite legitimate even to the dominant culture—though assuredly doomed either to integrate with the national culture or to disappear—class cleavages overlapping ethnic differences are seen as a challenge to be met. At the same time, in the polity—which plays a determinant role in the recognition and legitimization of social reality—ethnicity is refused meaningful independent expression, at least at the countrywide level. This basic contradiction between *de facto* pluralism in all major spheres and the blurring of its overall institutionalization is best defined by the concept of *crypto-pluralism*.

This model, in fact, is widely dependent on the subjective aspect of the encounter. In a general manner, and if we follow the elements of our definition of ethnic awareness of kind (see Chapter 3) and the analysis of the encounter in its various spheres, Israel illustrates a quite particular case. As an outcome of processes pertaining to the endowment of membership and the interpretation of cultural differences in the face of those who, by the secularism of their cultures and the reassessment of collective symbols, merge into a nonethnic stock: (1) traditional or quasi-traditional groups are brought to consider their origin as a focus of identity, delineating temporary collective boundaries inside comprehensive religious and national concepts; (2) underlying this self-defining of the ethnic groups as edot, self-perceived "contents" of their "personalities" are connected to a notion of "legacy," emphasizing— in spite of a partial decentralization—the present continuity of Diasporan values and norms. On the other hand, and as a result of the above, as well as of other "objective" occurrences in the spheres of status and power, (3) the edah concept of distinctiveness receives practical meaning in terms of social distances between "ins" and "outs" in the major contexts of social relationships, and this distance is but feebly attenuated by the raising of some to positions easing assimilation with nonethnic "others" or even with the dominant stock; thus (4) if the ethnic groups may "recognize" their personalities in many "objective" cultural models exhibited by their communities, their *overall image of their "collective plight"*—in view of their expectations as "temporary" edot—is conflictual, nay even alienating, though for the same reason and despite these perceptions, the compactness of their communities, and their potential power, they are unable to crystallize into "for-themselves" groups.

At this point, it is finally possible to summarize all three spheres of the encounter from both the objective and subjective viewpoints, by specifying the general terms of Figure 4.1. This is shown by Figure 4.9.

The last column of Figure 4.1 it is true, has not been specified in Figure 4.9. In fact, these are both the objective and subjective features of the encounter—called *basic characteristics* below—which, when looked at from the viewpoint of society as a whole, represent in themselves as well as in their reciprocal relationship, the very contribution of ethnicity to the molding of the setting. To delve deeper into this sequence at this point, however, cannot be done without raising objections.

All the above indeed was founded only partially on solid evidence, which consisted more often of individual testimonies, or general estimations than empirical data. Therefore, it comprised but an *interpretation* of the case derived from a definite theoretical approach. Accordingly, the "basic characteristics," several of which represent at this stage in fact but an assumed reality, were presented as explicable by the confrontation of given rules with *a priori* features of Oriental groups, generalized from the study of two particular groups. All these signify that our outline of the Israeli model has still to provide a consistent interpretive framework when leaving the level of abstract considerations and entering into concrete social reality, at least as manifest by the two groups that are the direct object of enquiry.

Figure 4.9 The General Outline of the Jewish Israeli Model

rules outlined by dominant culture
—immediate membership for Jewish immigrants
—"generosity" in resources allied with requirements regarding status
—democratic philosophy
—principle of "guidance" by dominant stock

+

Jewish groups of given origins sharing traditional or quasi-traditional value orientations and mizug perspective on the encounter

crypto-pluralistic syndrome referring to communities tributary on Diasporic symbols and behavioral models consisting of "truncated ethnoclasses" politically mute in the face of nonethnic middle-class and dominant stock and raising mainly instrumental exigencies

edah-type of ethnic groups based on origin expressing self-perceived eclectic cultural "personality" in margins of society; interpreting collective plight in terms of deprivation concomitantly with reluctance to become "for-themselves" groups

It is toward this kind of validation that we now turn. However, in order to make explicit the structure of the following it must be emphasized that the dual investigation of objective and subjective features of groups presents a special problem. Each kind of "characteristics," indeed, requires a different methodology: while objective aspects can be delineated by statistical indicators—from demographic patterns to regularities of political behavior—subjective traits can be studied only by investigating the attitudes and feelings of the people involved in the framework of an *overall* description of their self-image as ethnics. This need to switch methodologies demands, for the sake of a fluent and continuous exposition, that we analyze each side separately, despite their interaction. These reciprocal relations, however, will be touched upon wherever necessary and will be at the center of the concluding chapter, where we will more substantially discuss the impact of ethnicity for Israeli society as a whole.

NOTES

1. Quoted from an early draft of S. Deshen, "Israeli Judaism: Introduction to the Major Patterns," *International Journal of Middle-East Studies*, 9 February 1978, pp. 141-69.

2. E. Nissan, "Min Tsionut Mitkahechet Shel Hateleviziah" [The type of ignoring Zionism of the television], *Bamaaraha* 219 (March 1979): 23.

3. M. Banton, *Race Relations* (New York: Basic Books, 1967), pp. 369.

4. S. Deshen, "Political Ethnicity and Cultural Ethnicity in Israel During the 1960's," in *Urban Ethnicity*, ASA Monographs (London, N.Y.: Tavistock Publications, 1974), pp. 296-97.

5. E. Ben-Ezer, *Hamahtzevah* [The quarry] (Tel Aviv: Am Oved, 1963), pp. 8-9.

6. Y. Bourla, *Ishto Hasnuah* [His hated wife] (Tel Aviv: Am Oved, 1959), p. 49.

7. S. Kalo, *Haaremah* [The heap] (Tel Aviv: Am Oved, 1962), p. 116.

8. Y. Masika, "Thiat Hatarbut Shel Edot Hamizrah Adyin Eina Poteret Et Bayat Haedot" [The redemption of the culture and tradition of the Oriental groups does not solve yet the problems of the edot], *Bamaarah* 224 (August 1979): 13.

9. J. Ben-David,"Dyun" [Discussion], *Mizug Galuyot* ed. O. Cohen (Jerusalem: Magnes Press, 1969), pp. 89-90.

10. Council for Higher Education, *Higher Education in Israel—Statistical Abstracts 1977-1978*, (Jerusalem) April 1979, pp. 14-15.

11. *Haaretz*, 18 October 1978.

12. Y. Sofer, "Riayun Beinenu Levein Atsmenu" [Interview between ourselves], *Bamaaraha* 213 (September 1978): 8-9.

13. V. Kraus, "Social Segregation as a Function of Social Class and Ethnic Status," (Jerusalem: Hebrew University, Department of Sociology and Anthropology, 1978) (Mimeograph).

14. Y. Sofer, "Hasera Manhigut Movilah" [There is no leading leadership], *Bamaaraha* 217 (January 1979): 8.

15. Banton, *Race Relations*, p. 370.

16. See S. M. Lipset, *The First New Nation* (New York: Anchor Books, 967), pp.237-83.

17. See K. Marx, "Le 18 Brumaire de Louis Bonaparte" in K. Marx *Les Luttes de Classes en France 1848-1850; Le 18 Brumaire de Louis Bonaparte* (Paris: Editions Sociales, 1949), p. 258.

18. Y. Sofer, "Sheat Heshbon Hanefesh" [The hour of reflection about ourselves], *Bamaaraha* 225 (September 1979): 9.

19. E. Nissan, "Lifnei Habhirot Laeeriot" [Before the municipal elections], *Bamaaraha* 213 (September 1978): 7.

20. *Davar*, 23 November 1978.

21. Deshen, "Political Ethnicity and Cultural Ethnicity" pp. 285-86.

22. Sofer, "Riayun Beinenu Levein Atsmenu" [Interview between ourselves] p. 29.

PART II

THE OBJECTIVE SIDE

Membership Versus Particularism

5

INTRODUCTION

We turn first to the objective side of ethnicity and begin with an analysis of the encounter in the sphere of membership and culture. As suggested by the "objective basic characteristics," the importance of ethnic communities will emerge clearly and, among Yemenites as well as Moroccans will appear heavily dependent on Diasporan cultural models. The respective models account for several substantive differences between the groups. On the other hand,—and this applies similarly to both groups—there is the undeniable influence of the social and cultural environment that imbues their cultures with eclecticism. Against this background, those features which differentiate Yemenites from Moroccans and which are mainly explained by the periods of their immigration or the size of their groups have but a minor impact.

THE YEMENITES AS A CULTURAL COMMUNITY

The Yemenites were the first Oriental group of numerical importance to settle in the country after the start of Zionist immigration, that is, during the 1880s. As such, they prepared the way for recognition by the Ashkenazi of the Oriental edot as an organic part of Judaism—by no means an easy task. Those who especially encouraged Yemenite immigration in the early twentieth century belonged to the labor movement and their main intention was to increase the Jewish working class in Palestine. However, with the arrival of the first Yemenite groups it soon became apparent that they were far from the revolutionary secular culture of the majority of the Yishuv. In fact, many of the Ashkenazi shared negative feelings toward these darker-skinned Arabic speakers and even suspected that their religious practices were unorthodox.[1] Official letters were even sent to Yemen "suggesting" the postponement of further immigration.

It is no wonder, therefore, that Yemenites in Palestine became bitter, and relations deteriorated between them and veteran communities.[2] It was even argued that Ashkenazi treated them as "slaves."[3] These feelings moderated over time as the Yemenites obtained recognition as a part of the Jewish community and their sympathizers increased; positive labels replaced the former ones and they were now depicted as good-hearted, hard working and faithful,[4] terms that are all related to perception of the lower-class condition. Yet many testimonies show[5] that tags such as "primitive" continued to be conferred on the group, even in some cases, after 1948 by government officials. These prejudices were not to prevent the Israeli government from initiating the immigration of almost all Jews who had remained in Yemen after the creation of the state, but "anti establishment" extremism has long characterized numerous Yemenites. In the 1940's they were overrepresented in both the right-wing anti-British underground and, to a lesser extent, in the Communist Party.[6]

Yemenites in the country soon established organizations to represent them before other groups and institutions. Already in 1902 the "Yemenite Jewish Edah" (Edat Yehudei Teiman), was created to deal with Ashkenazi and Sephardi in Jerusalem because of the development of bad relations between them, and it was later succeeded by the national "Union of Yemenite Jews" (Brith Yotze Teiman). Up until this day, there is a Yemenite periodical, Afikim, and it is always filled with readers' complaints about anti-Yemenite feelings among Ashkenazi, and some even decry collective discrimination. Nowadays, however, it should be emphasized, Yemenite organizations are feeble and do not interest the wide majority.[7]

This lack of interest, however, does not mean that the community itself is dissolving. At the first stage, as immigrants who had to adjust to a new environment, the Yemenites concentrated heavily in particular areas and those who arrived later were, for the most part, attracted by the places of settlement of their predecessors. This tendency to residential concentration has not weakened over the years; one still finds the majority of Yemenites in a rather small zone of Israel, the central area around Tel Aviv, which, up to the early 1950s, was by no means as densely populated as today and where many veteran Yemenites had originally settled. Thus, in Rehovot, Petah Tikva, Rosh Haayin, and Tel Aviv proper there are (1972) almost 100,000 Yemenites, 65 percent of the whole group;[8] and if we include all municipalities of the area—which accounts for but 47 percent of the total population—about 77 percent of it. Yet the key fact is that until now the Yemenites have largely remained in this area, concentrated among themselves: in the zone of Petah Tikvah alone, we find about one-fifth of the group; this includes 10 percent of all Yemenites in Israel found in one single, homogeneous town, Rosh Haayin. As for the 25 percent found in Tel Aviv itself, they are mostly housed in two neighborhoods where they make up respectively 14 and 11 percent of the inhabitants, and the same is the rule for fifteen other areas or settlements numbering important Yemenite communities.[9]

Thus, though a majority of the Yemenites lives in the most popu-lated part of the country together with people of a multitude of origins, and notwithstanding their veteranship, they are still characterized by a high degree of residential concentration. This fact can hardly be explained nowadays on the basis of segregation. In their two main concentrations in Tel Aviv, for instance, their neighbors are of very diverse origins: in the first are Iraqis (17 percent), Iranians (12 percent) and Poles (11 percent); and in the second, Poles (25 percent), Rumanians (11 percent) and Russians (10 percent). In Jerusalem, there is only one section where they are more than 10 percent of the population and their neighbors are mainly Moroccans (14 percent), Poles (11 percent) and Central Europeans (9 percent). Thus, urban Yemenites are by no means a segregated group, and their tendency to commu-nity concentration appears rather to be voluntary.

Another index of the Yemenites' tendency to concentration is their marriage patterns (see Table 5.1). Statistics, it is true, reveal that exogamous marriage has increased over the years and that Yemenites, in this concern, show a preference for Oriental rather than Euro-American partners. Yet, as a whole, the Yemenites still display a strong endogamous orientation. An important conclusion that can be drawn here is that community concentration, which originally was but a

Table 5.1 In- and Out-Group Patterns of Marriages of Yemenite Jews in Israel (% of type of Marriages for Selected Years).

Brides & Grooms of Yemenite Origin (Born in Yemen or Father Born there)	Euro-American	Origin of Spouse		
		Oriental (but not Yemenite)	Yemenite	Total
1968				
Brides	14	17	69	100
Grooms	14	22	64	100
1974				
Brides	19	24	57	100
Grooms	14	27	59	100
Brides & Grooms of Yemenite Origin Born in Israel (Father born in Yemen)				
1968				
Brides	20	22	58	100
Grooms	24	30	46	100
1974				
Brides	19	25	56	100
Grooms	15	28	57	100

SOURCE: Unpublished data, Israeli Central Bureau of Statistics.

mode of adjustment to a new and not always friendly environment, now appears as a reflection of a positive preference for one's own stock.

At first glance it seems that a basic contradiction exists between this voluntary concentration and the Yemenites' "unconditional" readiness to integrate into society. One reason for this apparent contradiction is that they are still a particular sociocultural community which, in several respects, remains remote from Israel's dominant culture. Since their arrival in the country, it is true, they have demonstrated an acceptance of many new behavioral models; the Yemenite woman has become more equal to her husband, while daughters are now willingly sent to public schools like their brothers; in the moshav, the Yemenite farmer has successfully adopted new methods of work;[10] while high consumption standards are now the group's lot in the same manner as the Israelis' as a whole. On the other hand, the socialization—or more accurately, resocialization—undergone by Yemenites in Israel has fallen short of erasing all former models. To mention only a few instances, the woman is still, at least partially, bound to her traditional roles, while in the moshav kinship units play a determinant role in the social dynamics.[11] In fact, Yemenites remain respectful of the customary principle of dependency upon their parents, and though, when married, they settle outside the parental home, they look forward to residing close to it.[12] All these, to be sure, are scarcely perceived from the outside, but in the family circle and the neighborhood their impact remains important.

In Israel, the Yemenite who sees some of his most natural customs as a Jew related by others to his ethnicity finds himself facing a sharp dilemma: confronted by many "kinds" of Jews, he must define for himself what is worth keeping in his culture. The religious character of Yemenite customs and the rigor of past life-styles can only cause ambivalent attitudes in this regard.

At all events, during the early stages of Yemenite immigration, important efforts were invested in the elaboration of Yemenite Judaism; prayer books as well as rabbinic works in the Yemenite style were printed in Jerusalem and Yemenite schools and religious academies were set up.[13] Today the synagogue-centered community life has lost much of its strength and the young generations are less observant than the old, yet the synagogue is still a focus of social life if not of a devotional cult. This maintenance of parochial symbols is a phenomenon quite common to all Oriental communities,[14] though seemingly more pronounced among Yemenites than others.[15] In sum, three or four generations after the arrival of the first Yemenites, they still constitute a community strongly concentrated within itself which exhibits a cultural particularism amalgamating modern and traditional norms, and which stresses parochial symbols.

THE CASE OF THE MOROCCANS

The Yemenites exemplify the case of a traditional group transplanted into Israeli reality; as already emphasized, in several ways, their plight is of wider significance since many other edot share these characteristics, such as the Jews from Kurdistan or Libya. Yet the "bulk" of the ethnic situation in Israel primarily refers to Moroccan Jews, who are the largest single group of origin—more than 14 percent of the whole Jewish population and almost 30 percent of all Orientals.

To recall, the Jews in Morocco became an intermediary entity under French colonialism and, as such, were exposed to strong divergent pressures which weakened their homogeneity and the commitment of many to their parochial inheritance. Yet whatever the intensity of this commitment—and it varied from one stratum to another—it was the faithfulness to traditional symbols and myths that constituted the motivating force behind their immigration to Israel. Those for whom this force was meaningless either settled in France or stayed in Morocco. For the others, the path of Oriental communities into membership had been well prepared by the Yemenites; no question ever arose about their acceptance though, at the gravest moment of the economic crisis entailed by mass immigration (1954), a public debate took place concerning the maintenance of unselective criteria—with regard to age and health—vis-à-vis North African immigrants.

Formal acceptance, however, does not mean social acceptance, and this was especially true for the Moroccans. The cultural vacuum of the *mellah*, which found expression in the behavior of many newcomers, aroused mixed feelings and consequently generalizations about all Moroccans were rapidly formulated. Up until today, Moroccans are the least esteemed group in Israel,[16] and are stereotyped by many as temperamental and aggressive, if not "primitive."[17] Research as a whole is quite definitive on the negative feelings toward them among a substantial part of the population (about one-third),[18] and these attitudes are well perceived by those affected, who for a long time tended to introduce their origin as "Southern French." Moreover, researchers have found an inferiority complex and feelings of shame among Moroccan children regarding their parents, while even adults may share the negative tags which are attributed to their neighborhoods.[19]

Up to now, many Moroccans remain convinced of the existence of an unsolved "Moroccan question" in Israel and are inclined to claim the prevalence of discrimination against them.[20] It is true that Orientals in general feel this way, but most Orientals agree that Moroccans are more affected.[21] These anti-Moroccan feeling have helped them to maintain themselves as a community despite the radical revolution they have undergone, like the Yemenites, in all their social endeavors.

Generally speaking, Moroccans have clearly remained demographically distinct though, unlike the Yemenites, they are mostly situated in peripheral areas outside the conurbation of Tel Aviv. In such regions—mainly in the Galilee in the North and the Negev in the South—their share of the population is frequently much higher than the average proportion: they form almost one-third of the whole Negev population and 80 percent or more of several new towns. Even in the large cities they concentrate in neighborhoods where, again, their number is especially high. In Tel Aviv, for instance, they constitute 22 percent of a single quarter though only 5 percent of Tel Aviv at large, and their percentage in other neighborhoods fluctuates from five to 0.5; in Jerusalem, where Moroccans account for 14 percent of the inhabitants, they are 30 percent of a single neighborhood, 19 and 16 percent of two more and 14 to 8 percent of several others; in Haifa they number 10 percent of the population but 37 percent of a single quarter, 16 percent of a second and from 9 to 7 percent of several others.[22]

On the other hand, however, even in those neighborhoods where Moroccans are most numerous, they live in close proximity to people of varied origins. In the Haifa neighborhood where their concentration is highest (37 percent), some 20 percent of the inhabitants are Rumanians, 10 percent Polish and 4 percent Iraqi. The same is true for the Jerusalem quarter with the largest Moroccan population (almost 30 percent), where Rumanians account for 9 percent, Poles 7.5 percent and Iraqis 7 percent. In the most "Moroccan" neighborhood of Tel Aviv (22 percent), Central Europeans are 21 percent, Turks 12 percent and Iraqis 7.6 percent. Thus the picture that emerges is by no means one of externally imposed segregation. Yet the large proportion of Moroccans in certain places obviously accounts for a wide concentration of social relations among themselves: in one case it was found that 53 percent of all such relations took place inside the group and only 21 percent of socially meaningful relations united Moroccans with people of a different background. Quite evidently, the higher the levels of education and income of Moroccans, the more such relations exist because of the widening of interests.[23] Another factor leading to greater contact with "outs" is belonging to the second generation, where peer groups gain in importance and are more often ethnically heterogeneous.[24]

One key index of the existence of a particular community is that of marital patterns. Table 5.2 indicates that cultural and socioeconomic closeness between Moroccans and other Oriental groups, relative to the Euro-Americans, contributes to a larger share of out-group marriage with the former than with the latter.

Table 5.2 In- and Out-Group Patterns of Marriages of Moroccan Jews in Israel (% of Types of Marriages of Moroccans for Given Years)

| Brides and Grooms of Moroccan Origin (Born in Morocco or Father Born there) | Origin of Spouse | | | | |
	Euro-American	Oriental (but not Moroccan)	Moroccan	Total	N
1968					
Brides	17	37	46	100	1654
Grooms	20	31	49	100	1633
1974					
Brides	18	30	52	100	3388
Grooms	16	26	58	100	3652
Brides and Grooms Born in Israel (Father Born in Morocco)					
1968					
Brides	11	49	40	100	161
Grooms	20	31	49	100	46
1974					
Brides	24	37	39	100	1278
Grooms	23	37	40	100	551

SOURCE: Unpublished data, Israeli Central Bureau of Statistics.

Marriages to Euro-Americans, however, are quite frequent among the Israeli-born of Moroccan origin, a majority of whom choose out-group spouses. Though the fact that a large part of the Moroccans immigrated only in the late 1950s accounts for the small number of Israeli-born brides and grooms, Table 5.2 shows that, all else being equal, birth in Israel leads to far closer relations with other groups. The salient finding of Table 5.2, however, is that the amount of exogamous matings by Moroccans decreases over the years. One reason is the increase of Moroccan youngsters of marriageable age between 1968 and 1974: a large number of youth in an ethnic entity enhances the possibility of in-group marriage since marital choices multiply in the group itself.

Anyway, these figures, taken jointly with the demographic concentration of Moroccans shown above, clearly demonstrate that they still constitute a particular community. This community—like the Yemenites and many other Oriental groups—is remote in several respects from certain models of the dominant culture. A widespread disregard, for instance, for interests of determinant importance to the "others" is expressed in the fact that at the same level of income and family size, Moroccans—and they represent here most other Oriental edot—spend only half as much of their means on education, recreation, and other cultural needs as Ashkenazi. In general, according to researchers, they appear more sensitive to economic achievement *per se*, while high status based on professional qualifications is of less appeal.[25]

Such cultural differences, to be sure, do not ease communication. More especially among Moroccans, a deep diffidence is frequently the rule in the individual's approach to governmental bureaucracy, whatever the context of the contact,[26] eventually giving rise to outbursts of violence.[27] Another instance is the contempt shown by inhabitants of a Moroccan development town toward a lecturer invited for an evening to the local cultural center.[28] Remoteness from the dominant culture is also present in an exclusive predilection of many for cheap movies or in the centrality of soccer in the community's recreational life. The high rates of delinquency among Moroccan youth in Israel are an additional element in this picture: in 1974, for instance, there were twenty cases of juvenile delinquency by youngsters of North African origin per 1,000 members of the group, but only seven Middle Eastern or other "Asians" and five Euro-Americans.[29]

A thesis of deculturation could be proposed here according to which Moroccan Jews in Israel are characterized by anomie at both the individual and community levels. Further data, however, gainsay such an explanation: though North Africans account for the largest number of delinquents, their share among suicides—9.3 percent for the years 1962-1966—is relatively the lowest.[30] Since suicide is a typical expression of anomie, this fact would argue against the deculturation thesis. Furthermore, the violence just mentioned as shown occasionally in dealings with officials is also present at an unusual rate among Moroccans themselves, which suggests that if it has become an expression of conflictual feelings among them toward the establishment, at least one reason is that it constitutes a more longstanding cultural feature of a segment of this community. What has been said of the Moroccan *mellah* sustains this assumption and, if generalizing, "deviancies" of Moroccans from the dominant culture should not be interpreted, from this angle, as a sign of dissolution of the community, but rather as one of continuity, in enduring disadvantageous circumstances.

The general picture, however, is changing, and new elements emerge. In the moshav, as well as in other types of settlement, new economic habits are learned; family life becomes more flexible, and ties among siblings are loosened while the number of children per couple has diminished. As a whole, there is a movement toward the "Israeli" style of life[31] and new occupations gain popularity. In the moshav, it is the economically successful who achieves the position of leader, while many Moroccans from development towns or cities become military officers, teachers, social workers, or clerks.

In this context a cultural discontinuity appears between generations, though it must be emphasized that the empirical gap is quite moderate. Many testimonies, indeed[32] point to a persistent attachment among both older and younger people of Moroccan origin to a specific cultural style running from cooking to outlooks toward life and society. More particularly,[33] the style of social relations among Moroccans is still characterized by a high degree of external expressiveness mixing vividness and noise and centering on public places. These "Mediterranean" features, which are quite opposed to the much more disciplined and elaborate style of Yemenite Jews, are supplemented for many by reference to French culture. Knowledge of French has endowed these with a feeling of belonging to Western civilization, and they tend most often to hold apart from other Moroccans, formerly "mountain people" (villagers) whom they label as "primitive."[34]

As a matter of course, cultural continuity of Moroccan Jewry is principally conspicuous in the sphere of religious life and symbols. The rabbis of the community, it is true, have lost much of their former status—this was already the case in many a *mellah* of French Morocco—but by no means have they been totally ejected from all eminence.[35] Moreover, the longstanding special status conferred by Moroccan

Jewish culture on the study of the Hidden Truth has not fully disappeared in Israel either and circles of Moroccan rabbis studying the Zohar are still numerous. In general, synagogues have maintained their centrality in the community and, as for almost every Oriental neighborhood it is a point of honor for Moroccans everywhere to have their own synagogues, often according to city or village of origin, or even family affiliation. Religiosity, it is true, is losing ground, but synagogue attendance on Shabbat and feasts is still popular; this paradox may be accounted for by the increasing importance of the role of the synagogue as an ethnic symbol. It is in the same way, in fact, that Moroccan folklore in Israel has kept alive old customs such as pilgrimages to tombs of saints or the Celebration of Bread (*Mimunah*) at the end of Passover.

CONCLUSIONS

To underline the main points above, it should first be emphasized that despite the difficulties encountered by each group in Israel, both Yemenites and Moroccans were accepted *by right* into full membership, and this fact alone—which was the chief motive of their immigration—constituted a radical change for them. Yet, though becoming "Jews among Jews," the Yemenites, as well as the Moroccans, were to recreate in Israel compact communities whose cultural traits reflect, beyond the unifying influence of a common environment, both the different Diasporan starting-points and the specific circumstances of their settlement in the country. More particularly, the greater cultural homogeneity and cohesion of the present Yemenite communities relates to their long, continuous legacy, while the Moroccans' two-generation period in Morocco of precipitated changes is apparent in their (often effervescent) endeavors.

The confrontation of *a priori* features with "another" culture was to make the Yemenite as well as the Moroccan stocks quite eclectic as regards the models exhibited by them in areas such as education, family life, religious norms, or leisure activities. Cultural eclecticism, however, does not necessarily signify a deletion of parochialism and by this, of ethnic particularism. The Jews in Yemen or Morocco are barely recognizable in contemporary Israelis of Yemenite or Moroccan origin, but these have still remained distinct groups affirming themselves through Diasporan symbols. These symbols are the main means by which sociocultural pluralism becomes overt and recognized, and the paradox they represent resides in their blatant contradiction of both the edot's and the dominant culture's aspirations to promote *mizug*. The "secret" behind this occurrence (unwanted by all) is found in the ethnics' awareness of kind, to be discussed in Part III. Meanwhile, what has to be emphasized at this point is that the sociocultural pluralism described here is by no means weakened or blurred by concomitant processes in the sphere of stratification.

NOTES

1. H. Tahon, *Edot Beisrael* [Jewish groups in Israel] (Jerusalem: Reuven Mass, 1957), pp. 118-29.

2. J. Tobi, "Letoldot Hayahasim Bein Hateimanim Vehasfaradim Birushalayim Bashanim Tarma'b-Tarsa't" [The history of Yemenite-Sephardic relations in Jerusalem from Tarmab to Tarsat], in *Prakim Betoldot Hayishuv Hayehudi Birushalayim* [Chapters in the history of the Jewish settlement in Jerusalem], ed. M. Friedman, B. Yehoshua, and J. Tobi (Jerusalem: Yad Ben-Zvi, 1966), pp. 192-215.

3. M. Tsadok, *Yehudei Teiman, Toldoteihem Veorhot Hayeihem* [Yemenite Jews, their history and ways of life] (Tel Aviv: Am Oved, 1976), pp. 226-30.

4. Y. Peres, *Yahasei Edot Beisrael* [Ethnic relations in Israel] (Tel Aviv: Sifriat Hapoalim, 1977), p.55.

5. P. Cohen, *Kehilah Veyetsivut Beeer Pituach* [Community and stability in a development town] (Jerusalem: Ministry of Welfare, 1959), pp. 6-12.

6. H. Tahon, *Edot Beisrael* [Jewish groups in Israel], pp. 118-29.

7. A. Deutsch, "Dmut Haelitah Beparvar Teimani" [The image of elite in a Yemenite neighborhood], *Megamot 9*, no. 4 (October 1958): 328-37.

8. Israeli Central Bureau of Statistics (ICBS), *Thunot Demografiot Shel Haohlosiah-Helek Beit* [Demographic characteristics of the population-Part Two] (Jerusalem: Population and Housing Census 1972, Series No. 10, 1976), pp. 298-301.

9. Ibid, pp. 310-37.

10. D. Weintraub "Shinui Vehemshehiut Bemoshav Haolim" [Change and continuity in the cooperative village of immigrants], in *Mizug Galuyot*, ed. O. Cohen, (Jerusalem: Magnes Press, 1969), pp. 158-61.

11. M. Shokeid, "Immigration and Factionalism: An Anaylsis of Factions in Rural Israeli Communities of Immigrants" *British Journal of Sociology*, 19, No. 4 (December 1968): 385-406.

12. E. Katz, and A. Zloczower, "Hemshehiutam Shel Dfusim Edatiim Bador Hasheni (Teimanim)" [The continuity of ethnic patterns within the second generation (Yemenites)], in *Hamivneh Hahevrati Shel Israel* [The social structure of Israel], ed. S. N. Eisenstadt, H. Adler, R. Kehana, R. Bar-Yosef, (Jerusalem: Academon, 1966), pp. 319-34.

13. Y. Ratshavi, "Zhor Leavraham, Zihronotav Shel R'Avraham Alnadaf Zt'l-Letoldot Hakehilah Hateimanit Birushalayim" [In memory of Avraham, the dairy of Rabbi Avraham Alnadaf—A history of the Yemenite community in Jerusalem], in *Prakim Betoldot* [Chapters in history], ed. Friedman et al, p. 162.

14. For a Tunisian Group, see S. Deshen, "Dfusei Hishtanut Shel Masoret Datit: Beit Haknesset Haedati" [Patterns of change in religious tradition: The Ethnic Synagogue], in *Mizug Galuyot* ed. O. Cohen, pp. 66-73.

15. Tahon, *Edot Beisrael* [Jewish groups in Israel], pp. 118-29.

16. R. Bar-Yosef, "Hamarokaim, Reka Habayah" [The Moroccans, the context of the problem], *Molad* 17, no. 131 (June 1969): 247-51.

17. Peres, *Yahasei Edot Beisrael* [Ethnic relations in Israel], p. 89.

18. According to J. Shuval "Bayot Hevratiot Bearei Pituah [Social problems in development towns], (Jerusalem: The Institute for Social Applied Research, 1959).

19. From the Report of the Study Committee on Problems of Youth in the Morasha Neighborhood, presented to the Office of the Prime Minister (January, 1965) "Noar Beshhunat Morashah Birushalayim" [Youth in the Morasha neighborhood in Jerusalem], in *Hamivneh Hahevrati Shel Israel* [The social structure of Israel], ed. S. N. Eisenstadt, M. Adler, R. Kehana, R. Bar-Yosef (Jerusalem: Academon, 1966) p. 290.

20. M. Inbar and H. Adler, *Ethnic Integration in Israel*, (New Brunswick: Transaction Books, 1977), pp. 63-69.

21. E. Cohen, L. Shamgar, and J. Levy, *Doh Sikum Mehkar Klitat Olim Beayarot Pituah* [Research report about Integration of immigrants in development towns], vol. 2 (Jerusalem: Hebrew University of Jerusalem, 1962), pp. 36-38.

22. Israel Central Bureau of Statistics (ICBS), *Thunot Demografiot Shel Haohlosiah—Helek Beit* [Demographic characteristics of the population-part two], pp. 310-37.

23. A. Berler and A. Doron, "Ofakim-Hitpathut Hevratit—Kalkalit [Ofakim—economic and social development] (Tel Aviv: Ministry of Housing, 1969), pp. 132-180.

24. Inbar and Adler, *Ethnic Integration in Israel*, pp. 63-69.

25. M. Lissak, "Degamei Ribud Vesheifot Mobiliut: Mekorot Hahanaa Le Mobiliut" [Models of social stratification and aspirations to social mobility], *Megamot* 15, no. 1 (January 1967): 66-82.

26. From the Report of the Study Committee "Noar Beshhunat Morashah" [Youth in the Morashah neighborhood], pp. 285-95.

27. E. Marx, "Alimut Ishit Beayarat Olim" [Individual Violence in an Immigrant Town], *Megamot* 17, no. 1 (January 1970): 61-77.

28. S. Paz *"Dimui Atsmi, Zehut Vehizdahut"* [Self-image, identity and identification] (Jerusalem: Department of Education, Hebrew University of Jerusalem, 1971) p. 24.

29. Ministry of Welfare *Skira Statistit 1965-75* [Statistical report 1965-1975] (Jerusalem: Ministry of Welfare, 1975), pp. 20-35.

30. B. Kimmerling, "Anomiah Veintegratsiah Bahevrah Haisraelit Veboltut Hasihsuh Haisraeli-Aravi" [Anomie and integration in Israeli society and the salience of the Israeli-Arab conflict], *Megamot* 19, no. 4 (September 1973): 349-73.

31. M. Minkowicz, "Mihamulah Leagudah" [From lineage to association] (Jerusalem: Kaplan School, Hebrew University, 1967), pp. 65-73.

32. See Inbar and Adler, *Ethnic Integration in Israel*, pp. 87-104.

33. See, for example, Paz, *Dimui Atsmi, Zehut Vehizdahut* [Self image, identity and identification], pp. 88-89.

34. H. Rosenfeld, "Eer Olim: Kiryat Shmonah" [An immigrant town, Kiryat Shmona] *Mibifnim* 20, nos. 1-2 (May 1958): 87-95.

35. M. Shokeid, "The Decline of Personal Endowment of Atlas Mountain Religious Leaders in Israel," *Anthropological Quarterly* 52, no. 4 (October 1979): 186-96.

Ethnicity and Social Status

6

INTRODUCTION

The socioeconomic dimension of the ethnic encounter concerns, from an objective viewpoint, the place of ethnicity in the stratificational system. This issue depends on both the range of opportunities available to ethnics (including the requirements conditioning their use) and the choices made by them among alternatives, according to predispositions and preferences; it is the eventual emergence of a persistent, well-recognized correlation between ethnicity and socioeconomic status that defines a situation of stratificational (or socioeconomic) pluralism. In this regard, Israel illustrates a case where the setting appears "generous" in the rights and facilities provided immigrants, though the achievement of social status depends on individual competition and the response to definite demands. Thus, ethnics who originate from nonmodern or partially modern countries meet acute difficulties when competing with "others" for higher status, and many are reduced to lower-class positions. As a result, given origins become effectively correlated with socioeconomic inferiority. It is the purpose of what follows to explicate the extent to which these statements are pertinent to the plight of the Yemenites and Moroccans.

THE YEMENITES AS AN ETHNOCLASS

The resources made available by the setting for absorption of the Yemenites were very limited at the beginning. Though bad conditions were the lot of all until the 1930s, the plight of the Yemenites was the worst: they arrived with almost no property and could not integrate with the urban middle class while, at the same time, their traditionalism left them out of the socialist sector too.

The first groups settled in Jerusalem and Jaffa, where many lived in cabins or tents. They tried at first to earn a living by their customary trades (such as jewelwork and other crafts), and even sent their wives into the job market, mainly as servants. Even young girls had to find some kind of employment.[1] Their plight soon aroused the interest of intellectuals and well-settled people in Jerusalem, who created a special league (Ezrat Nidahim) to help them.[2] Under this impulse, other groups and personalities (mainly the Austrian philanthropist de Hirsch) provided aid for setting up new Yemenite neighborhoods. The Jewish National Fund and the Jewish Agency, the official organs of the Zionist movement, finally recognized their right to special attention and bought them land for additional settlement.

This gradual improvement, however, suddenly deteriorated with the waves of mass immigration: soon after 1948 transit camps were the only available locations for receiving immigrants of whatever origin (the country's population more than doubled in four years). Yet prodigious public efforts created new urban neighborhoods and rural settlements, while from the mid-fifties on, Israel started to change its economy from one essentially grounded on agriculture and city-based services to more industrialized structures (parallelling a further expansion of farming). Yemenites were no longer neglected in the allocation of resources. Within a few years, thirty-nine Yemenite moshavim (cooperative agricultural villages) were established, 24 percent of the new colonization, though Yemenites comprised only 6.5 percent of all immigrants after 1948. Hence, more than any other group, they contributed an important contingent to rural settlements (about 17 percent of their population), mainly in moshavim (some 12 percent). It is true that Yemenite moshavim were more frequently situated in the harder mountain areas than were others (40 percent of their settlements, or 44 percent of all highland moshavim[3]), but as we have seen urban Yemenite neighborhoods were allowed to expand and now represent a significant portion of the central area of Israel.

The "generosity" of the setting, however, was not "unlimited." A most conspicuous fact since the mid-1950s has been the growing importance of the competitive principle on the job market. In contrast to the past, differences of income have widened and for people of traditional and nonmodern background this evolution has required drastic changes in occupational perspectives and educational patterns. All these are the key not only to "success" on the social ladder but also, and more simply, to coping and keeping level with the exigencies of daily life.

The immigration of the Yemenites was a transplantation of a traditional community,[4] and the first who arrived soon knew the necessity of switching trades: many quit the jeweller's workshop and turned to stone carrying, road construction, or agriculture. However, as increasing numbers of male Yemenites became factory or farm workers and their wives servants, the more was their plight at the disposal of non-Yemenite officials or proprietors. What was true of individuals was even more so of whole neighborhoods economically reliant on the outside.

If we now look at the achievements of Yemenites during the three decades since their massive arrival in Israel, they might seem quite relative, especially considering their concentration in a zone which is the most dynamic of the country, economically, socially, and demographically. To a large extent, of course, this fact is explained by harsh competition in metropolitan areas which, rather than encouraging weaker groups, maintains their inferiority even in periods of development and growth.[5] This group, which constitutes less than 6 percent of the Jewish Israeli population and about 11 percent of the Orientals, accounts for 27 percent (1969) of families defined by the Bureau of Social Security as living in conditions of poverty; 24 percent of Yemenites and 29 percent of their children belong to this category.[6] On the basis of the 1963-64 data, no less than 60 percent of Yemenites were classified as "poor" or "near poor," while only 40 percent of North Africans, 23 percent of people of Balkan origin and 8 percent of those from East European countries were similarly defined.[7]

Yet there has been a transformation of the Yemenite group into an entity deeply anchored in the occupational structures of the modern setting. Moreover, in the context of data characterizing cleavages between Euro-Americans and Orientals (see Appendix B), special features provide evidence for the personality of this group. The foregoing figures, indeed, are based on income; when turning to wealth the picture is different: while, from this standpoint, 68 percent of North

Africans, 25 percent of Balkans and 9 percent of East Europeans are categorized as poor or near poor, the percentage for Yemenites is 35. Thus while Yemenites are among the poorest Orientals as regards income, they are relatively better off financially. The explanation is twofold: as the most veteran Orientals in Israel, they have accumulated assets over time (mainly in housing) while, on the other hand, they have always shown a high degree of industriousness and frugality. Quite significant here is the fact that there are proportionally less welfare cases among Yemenites than in any other Oriental group.[8]

On the whole, most Yemenites have contributed to Israel's economic growth by massively participating in blue-collar, low-income strata. As most lacked the training required for middle-class jobs, they have concentrated in the urban working class and, for the agriculturalists, in the small landholders stratum. Only a few have reached more prestigious professions. It is this situation of an ethnic group, when most of its members are lower class, that we defined by the concept of *ethnoclass*.

THE PLIGHT OF THE MOROCCANS

The concept of ethnoclass may be applied to Moroccans no less than to Yemenites. The absorptive setting was as "generous" with them, as with other immigrant groups though most Moroccans arrived only in the late 1950s after the mass immigration period, and demographic dispersion was by then considered a challenge of particular importance. Moreover, the absorption policy was now conditioned by the very number of Moroccan immigrants. As already mentioned, Moroccan Jews are the biggest edah in the country: 14 percent of the whole Jewish population, exceeding by 1 percent the next largest, the Poles (see Appendix 1) and by 5 percent the second major group of Oriental origin, the Iraqi. In 1972, Moroccan Jews in Israel numbered 379,123; only 41 percent were Israeli-born, despite their numerous young children, which is a sign of their recent arrival.[9]

Ninety percent of Moroccans live in cities or towns and only 10 percent in rural areas. This fact reflects the change in absorption policy of the 1950s: a shift in emphasis away from agricultural growth toward urban, industrial development in newly settled regions. It is there that almost half the Moroccan immigrants were housed, three-fifths of them in the South (Negev) and the rest in the North (Galilee).[10] Many others were moved to new cities or newly populated veteran settlements less remote from the central area. In Tel Aviv itself, Moroccans are much less represented than their share of the general population: in 1972 they constituted 5 percent of its inhabitants (who, as a whole, are some 15 percent of Israel's population) and 10 percent of the rest of the central area. In Haifa, too, they are underrepresented (10 percent), while in Jerusalem their number is proportional (14 percent).

On the whole, the absorptive setting made demands on the Moroccans which often stood in opposition to their original predispositions and resources. The rudimentary education of numerous Moroccans, their experience of poverty and their superstitious religiosity as well as colonial concepts of modernity and the outlook of a big-city dweller, were all features that contrasted with conditions of success in Israeli society. Hardship, it is true, was not equal for all Moroccans. For those who had a modern education, problems were much fewer; their own resources and governmental aid proved quite sufficient to achieve urban middle-class positions.

The less privileged Moroccans are found in three main kinds of settlement: the moshav, the development town, and the city. In the moshav, all research points to the huge difficulties which awaited the small minority who tried their hand at agriculture; of those who came from an urban background few remained.[11] Those of rural origin were more numerous, and adjusted to their new way of life, though their traditional outlook frequently impeded their success: kinship units rivalling for power, intricacies of cliques, remoteness from economic matters *per se* were the main factors which made several Moroccan moshavim very slow to prosper.[12] Yet a few years were enough to learn new habits, to grasp the sense of long-term investment, or to understand the "secrets" of organized marketing. A deeper interest in financial affairs was to weaken local intrigues and favor the adjustment of traditional concepts of community to a modern agricultural settlement.

However, a much larger group of Moroccans—60 percent of the group—live in development towns and peripheral cities. Many of these towns were planned on the basis of a few industrial plants needing unskilled workers, restricted services, and a small commercial center. The expectation was that in time the town would develop more foci of activity, elaborate fruitful relations with its rural periphery and

diversify its population by attracting officials, teachers and professionals. Two important features of these towns are that they open opportunities for local elements to share responsibilities of municipal
government, and offer a wide field for socioeconomic entrepreneurship
(though restricted to local affairs). A national survey of social stratification[13] has found that people in such towns often achieve status assets
(mainly in income or politics) while the ethnic majority—Moroccans,
in general—tend clearly to monopolize all special facilities. Furthermore, as the development town is considered as contributing importantly
to the national task of populating remote areas, it is also allowed
numerous privileges such as tax exemptions or even the cooptation of
representatives into the central political elite. (In the 1977 Begin
government a Moroccan Jew from one such town was appointed a
minister.)

This type of town, however, remains quite problematic:[14] in 1963
migration from these settlements was about four times that of the
national rate of local movement: among teenagers between fourteen
and seventeen, 26 percent neither worked nor studied, as against 14
percent countrywide; 33 percent worked, as against 18 percent; 41
percent were learning, as against 68 percent; and the development
towns contributed 7 percent of the national manpower but 25 percent
of the unemployed. Though several of them have become a success,
in general the settlement of a new urban center in a region lacking
natural resources is a challenge to be met only in the long term. In
many cases, when entering such a town one wonders if it is really in
Israel: the dominant language in the street is still a mixture of Arabic,
Hebrew, and French, and the dress of older people is reminiscent of a
Moroccan village or *mellah*.

People who leave the moshav or development town mostly move
to the cities. Yet many Moroccans in urban areas are not happy there
either. Research conducted in a Jerusalem neighborhood where
Moroccans are numerous showed 22 percent welfare cases and a high
rate of school dropouts.[15] Urban Moroccan quarters are still characterized by low public esteem and a high level of delinquency. The bulk of
their inhabitants wish to leave.[16]

As a matter of course, the Moroccan city dwellers share common
socioeconomic characteristics with those in development towns. In the
background is the low educational standard of Moroccan Jews in

Israel—6.5 median years of study for men and 2.3 for women in 1961, while for both males and females among all Oriental Jews, the median was 6.9, 9.8 for Euro-American immigrants, and 11.0 for native Israelis. These statistics are of great significance for the occupational profile of Moroccans in Israel:[17] professionals constituted only 4 percent of all Moroccan Jews usefully employed; managers, administrators and clerks, 4.5 percent. In contrast, Moroccans engaged in work in construction, quarries, mines, factories or workshops accounted for 38 percent and those in low-status services for 16 percent. Another 30 percent were in intermediary positions, from agriculture to small trade (7.5 percent were unknown).

This concentration in lower-class jobs has not changed substantially over the years. On the contrary, recent research[18] shows a high degree of stability: after more than two decades in the country, no less than 53 percent of those interviewed have known a stable socioeconomic condition since their arrival; 32 percent have been upwardly mobile since their first job and 15 percent downwardly. Most interestingly the research demonstrates that this pace of mobility was much slower than that of a matched sample of Rumanian Jews in Israel. Others[19] have shown that the greatest achievements of the Moroccans as well as of other Oriental groups refer to income rather than occupational prestige: it is by developing their initiatives in unprestigious but quite profitable domains (such as mechanical services, taxi driving, or partial building tasks) that some of them have accumulated economic assets.

Moroccan Jews still constitute the edah with the largest number of poor and near poor.[20] In 1969, 110,000 families had an income inferior to 40 percent of the average in Israel as a whole, that is, lived under the poverty line; 43,700 more families earned less than half the average national income, and accordingly were defined as near poor. Poors and near poors made up 25 percent of Israeli families and 33 percent of children. Among the poor alone there were 26 percent of all Orientals, but only 13 percent of Euro-American families; for minors the figures were respectively 30 percent and 4.2 percent. Yet among North Africans (and Moroccans are about 80 percent of them) some 34 percent of households and 40 percent of their children belonged to this category.

But regarding Moroccans too, we should stress that they managed, like other Oriental groups, to become a part—and indeed an important one—of the economic and occupational system. Moreover, the statistics also show that the poverty of North Africans mainly resides in lack of wealth rather than low income *per se*; 40 percent of their families in 1963-64 had earnings that classified them as poor or near poor, as against 60 percent of Yemenites. This characteristic may be ascribed to the impact of partial modern education in Morocco, which was an advantage relative to certain other groups. It is chiefly from the viewpoint of wealth that numerous Moroccans belong to the lowest strata, as illustrated by the fact that, in this respect, no less than 68 percent were defined as poor or near poor, as against 35 percent of Yemenites.[21] From 1972, however, a reform in children's allowances had reduced the number of families defined as poor (and they were mainly the large ones) from 25 (1969) to 11 percent (1975). This step eased the plight of North Africans, but their *relative* position in society has been barely affected.

CONCLUSIONS

In sum, the gap between the Jews in Yemen and Morocco and those who came to Israel from these countries is wide as far as occupations, styles of living, and class structures are concerned; undoubtedly, adjustment to Israeli reality was accompanied by a radical transformation. Yet whatever the scope of these changes, neither Yemenites nor Moroccans were to achieve, for the most part, more than a place on the lower steps of the social ladder. This "ethnoclassization," to be sure, is by no means hermetic and more than a few ethnics, as seen in Chapter 4, do succeed in climbing to higher levels due to the very openness of the socioeconomic markets and to the encouragement of special measures sponsored by the center. Unfortunately, only few data exist regarding the two groups under study, while the impact of social mobility on the ethnic situation as a whole belongs to further discussions of the subjective side of the ethnic encounter. The question of whether or not stratificational processes entail the amalgamation of edot into new broader entities falls into the same category. The diffusion, however, of tokens such as "Orientals-as-a-whole" or "Europeans" in daily speech as well as in official policies represents an overt recognition of a given socioeconomic reality, though not necessarily an acceptance of it as definitive. In fact, the legitimization of ethnic pluralism in society depends principally on its "consecration" by definitions, arrangements, and occurrences pertaining to the polity.

NOTES

1. M. Tsadok, *Yehudei Teiman: Toldoteihem Veorhot Hayeihem* [Yemenite Jews: their history and way of Life] (Tel Aviv: Am Oved, 1967), pp. 233.

2. Y. Ratshavi, "Zehor Leavraham, Zihronotav Shel R'Alnadaf Zt'l-Le Toldot Hakehilah Hateimanit Birushalayim [In memory of Avraham, the dairy of Rabbi Avraham Alnadaf—a history of the Yemenite community in Jerusalem], in *Prakim Betoldot Hayishuv Hayehudi Birushalayim* [Chapters in the history of the Jewish community in Jerusalem], ed. M. Friedman et al. (Jerusalem: Yad Ben-Zwi, 1976), pp. 169-73.

3. Y. Koren, *Kibbutz Hagaluyot Behitnahalut* [The settling of the en-gathering of the exiles] (Tel Aviv: Am Oved, 1964), pp. 125-35.

4. Y. Ratshavi, "Zehor Leavraham" [In memory of Avraham] p. 144.

5. J. Matras, and D. Weintraub, "Ethnic and Other Primordial Differentials in Intergenerational Mobility in Israel," *Jerusalem Seminar on Mobility and Social Stratification*, (Jerusalem: The Hebrew University, April 1976) (mimeographed). See also V. Kraus, and D. Weintraub, "Status Attainment and Ethnic Stratification," (Jerusalem: The Department of Sociology and Social Anthropology, the Hebrew University, 1977) (mimeographed).

6. J. Habib, *Haoni Beisrael Leor Hitpathut Hamaarehet Lehavthat Hahahnasah* [Poverty in Israel in the light of the development of the system for the maintenance of income] (Jerusalem: The Agency for Social Security, 1976), pp. 10-17.

7. J. Habib, M. Kohn, and R. Lerman, *The Effect on Poverty Status in Israel of Considering Wealth and Variability of Income* (Jerusalem: Brookdale Institute of Gerontology and Adult Human Development, the Israel-American Joint Distribution Committee, 1976), p.33.

8. H. Tahon, *Edot Beisrael* [Jewish groups in Israel] (Jerusalem: Reuven Mass, 1957), pp. 118-29.

9. Israel Central Bureau of Statistics (ICBS), *Statistical Abstract of Israel-1975* (Jerusalem, 1975), pp. 52-53.

10. Israel Central Bureau of Statistics (ICBS), *Thunot Demografiot Shel Haohlosiah-Helek Beit* [Demographic characteristics of the population—part two] (Jerusalem Population and Housing Census 1972, Series no. 10, 1976), pp. 298-301.

11. A. Weingrod, "Yetsivut Veeeyetsivut Bemoshavei Olim" [Stability and instability in cooperative settlements of immigrants], in *Moshavei Olim Beisrael*

[Cooperative settlements of new immigrants in Israel], ed. O. Shapira (Jerusalem: The Jewish Agency, 1972), pp. 119-30.

12. A. Weingrod, *Reluctant Pioneers, Village Development in Israel*, (Ithaca, N.Y.: Cornell University Press, 1966), pp. 99-120.

13. Kraus and Weintraub, "Status Attainment and Ethnic Stratification" (mimeographed).

14. Ministry of Labor, Authority of Manpower Planning, *Ayarot Hapituah Beisrael* [Israeli development towns] (Jerusalem: The Ministry of Labor, 1964).

15. From the Report of the Study Committee on Problems of Youth in the Morasha Neighborhood presented to the office of the Prime Minister (January 1965). "Noar Beshhunat Morashah Birushalayim" [Youth in the Morashah neighborhood in Jerusalem], in *Hamivneh Hahevrati Shel Israel* [The social structure of Israel], ed. S. N. Eisenstadt et al. (Jerusalem: Academon, 1966), pp. 277-99.

16. Y. Peres, "Politika Veedatiut Beshalosh Shhunot Oni" [Politics and ethnicity in three slums], in *Israeli Society 1967-1973*, ed. R. Kehana and S. Kopstein (Jerusalem: Academon, 1974), pp. 175-90.

17. M. Inbar, and H. Adler, *Ethnic Integration in Israel* (New Brunswick N.J.: Transaction Books, 1977), p. 28.

18. Ibid., pp. 28-30.

19. See M. Lissak, "Megamot Behishtalvut Haolim Bamaarah Haribudi Vehapoliti Shel Israel" [Tendencies in the integration of immigrants in the stratification and political system of Israel], in *Mizug Galuyot*, ed. O. Cohen (Jerusalem: Magnes Press, 1969), pp. 51-65.

20. J. Habib, *Haoni Beisrael* [Poverty in Israel], pp. 65-94.

21. Habib, Kohn, and Lerman, *The Effect of Poverty Status*, pp. 23-35.

Buffering Institutions and Political "Muteness"

7

INTRODUCTION

We have said that the major concern regarding the ethnic encounter in the polity—from an objective viewpoint—resides in the extent to which (1) ethnics are clearly differentiated from other groups in their participation in positions of power, and (2) ethnic interests are promoted by autonomous structures such as special organizations, parties, or pressure groups.

In brief, as was argued in Chapter 4, while the dominant culture in Israel defines criteria of elite recruitment beyond the reach of ethnics, the center is self-endowed with a "guiding" mission regarding their integration into society. As for the ethnics, the very fact that they are now an integral part of the political community is as such a most radical change from the past. On the other hand, their inferior position in the political elite accumulates with their inferiority in other areas and makes them underprivileged, nay even—in view of their expectations—conflictual entities. However, ethnicity, due to the endorsement by both the dominant culture and the ethnics of the *mizug* perspective, is impeded in becoming an overt, recognized and independent cleavage in the polity.

We propose to show how all these are consistent with regularities observable in Yemenite and Moroccan political behavior as it is reflected in public events and statistical data. In view of sharp differences between the groups' respective *a priori* features, a great variance will emerge regarding the intensity of political involvement as well as the readiness to express grievances; the Yemenites' former quasi-caste condition and the messianic impulses that inspired their migration, on the one hand, and the Moroccans' insecure and restless past on the other, which motivated their move to Israel in the context of a community crisis, widely account for contrasting political reactions. Yet, both Yemenites and Moroccans accept the perspective of *mizug*, which is a basic element in their defining of their awareness of kind. It is this that may explain how both groups, notwithstanding the differences, contribute to Israel's illustrating a case of crypto-pluralism, that is, a situation where ethnicity, though socially, culturally, and politically meaningful, does not achieve any firm, unambiguous institutionalization in the polity.

YEMENITES AND POLITICS

The marginalization of Yemenites does not only refer to economic and occupational spheres; in the domain of politics, too, the group is much removed from preeminence. Though in principle all individuals enjoy the same political rights—a totally new situation for the Yemenites—Israeli political concepts, inspired by both Western democracy and the revolutionary culture of the prestate period, were quite foreign to them, at least in their first years in the country. In fact, a communication gap has existed for a long time between the polity and large segments of the population, which justified a patronage-like attitude toward them on the part of the dominant stock (the "founders" and the "generation of continuation"). If the Israeli political scene has been characterized generally by the operation of such ideological cleavages as religiousness versus secularism, Right versus Left, activism versus moderation (with respect to the Israeli-Arab conflict), regarding the Oriental groups the parties have developed special frameworks for political participation that are remote from any ideological tag. Hence, frameworks such as the "Labor Party Yemenite Circle" of a given town, for instance, were primarily expected to coopt active ethnics into the party and to win the support of their groups by promising rewards such as representation in central political bodies or financial aid to the community.[1] Every party recruited its own ethnic clients, and the model as a whole was reminiscent of patrimonialistic rule. To be sure, besides these partisan structures there were also numerous others which played a similar role. Welfare services, representatives of the

Ministry of Education, agricultural advisers, and voluntary civil organizations were all involved, in various degrees, in supplying services in return for permanent ties with given political labels. This model, it is true, was not remote from the way the Yemenites themselves understood politics at the beginning; like many other Oriental Jews[2] they shared almost personal attitudes toward political leaders and frequently perceived the polity as a whole without differentiating much among its various agencies.[3]

In fact, though the model of buffering institutions limited the group's autonomy, it also contributed to establishing direct relations between the group and national organizations. These relations provided precious support for the group during its period of adjustment and encouraged the emergence of new elements in the community. This fresh element was most often characterized by the qualities of political broker, and oriented the edah toward a problem-solving approach, conveying precise demands to the frameworks with which it was bound up.[4] These people assumed menial public functions such as heads of neighborhood committees, representatives at the Town Council or secretary of a local party branch; and they soon assimilated the essentials of Israeli political culture. In many instances, of course, they aroused among the edah accusations of "belonging to the 'other side'," as echoed in the testimony of one of the edah's veteran public figures:

These political bosses of the Yemenite Organization were actually instruments of the Jewish Agency. Their role was to persuade the Yemenites to be happy with a minimum.... These bosses usually called for a general assembly just before prayers so that nobody had the time to speak up after them.... One of them sent me one day to sell newspapers and definitely to accept the job; "It fits you', he said, 'and it's enough for your needs.... Why should you need more?... Was it better for you in Yemen?"[5]

Undoubtedly, the buffering institutions share some responsibility for the fact that Yemenites, as well as other Orientals, are sharply underrepresented in the political sphere. Up to now only a handful of Yemenites have been coopted by the Israeli political elite, and it is difficult to speak about an anchorage of Yemenites on the central political scene, whether as individuals or as a community. Moreover, when in command of municipalities, they are frequently characterized by a lack of political experience. In the main concentration of Yemenites, Rosh Haayin, it was found,[6] for instance, that political cleavages were unstable and that issues were without any ideological or programmatic amplitude. Corruption was not unknown and support for parties was bargained for on the basis of very specific demands.

Yet, the stabilization of the group, the progress of socialization and the accumulation of assets have gradually diminished the Yemenites' dependency on buffering institutions. These institutions, it is true, were conceived from the outset as temporary means of "guidance." However, a paradoxical phenomenon (see Appendix 3) was to occur at this stage as the group that learned rapidly the meaning of political participation in democracy appeared more and more inclined to express its "liberation" from these institutions by sustaining forces opposed to the "establishment." Nowadays, the majority of Yemenites support the right-wing populism—in the opposition until 1977—and (to a lesser extent) the religious parties, a minor factor in government coalitions under the Labor Party; this tendency was to reach its peak in the 1977 elections when it decisively contributed to the fall of the twenty-nine-year-old Labor Party rule. In fact, this political identification which appeared again in the 1981 election is common to most Oriental groups and has created a new political reality in Israel widely characterized by a right-wing working class. To be sure, this is an evident expression of dissent against the former left-of-center "establishment" blamed for a plight, which by connoting origin and inferiority, contradicts the "melting of edot" perspective. Yet, interestingly enough, by the same token Yemenites do not react in any way to their condition by massively supporting a special ethnic ticket. One must go back to the 1951 poll to find two Yemenite members of Parliament elected on an independent list; from then on and despite the fact that a Yemenite party appears in almost every campaign, no one of this origin has been elected on an ethnic ticket. Moreover, and though most Yemenites belong to the "proletariat," their support of factions on the left of the Labor Party is even weaker than among non-Orientals, which shows how far they are from concepts of class struggle.

This picture is consistent with the subjective elements suggested in Chapter 4 in accounting for the edot's political behavior: although the fact that they perceive themselves as conflictual entities in society explains an "antiestablishment" mood, this conflict is interpreted in ethnic terms—as the lot reserved to the group by the "others"—rather than as pertaining to objective class structures, which in turn explains the rejection of leftist alternatives. Furthermore, the issue of the conflict itself is seen in the nonimplementation of *mizug* and, from this point of view, to sustain overt ethnic politics could but institutionalize a pluralistic reality that is the very object of criticism. At the same time, the parochialism of the ethnics is not foreign to their tendency to support parties which by their conservative outlooks emphasize myths and symbols closer to their own. These considerations as a whole may make understandable the popularity—before and after its rise to power—among Yemenites and the edot in general, of a right-wing coalition which until 1977 had occupied the opposition benches of the Knesset, and voting for which satisfied at the same time the expression of dissent and a general tendency toward the political right. The extent to which this interpretation is validated by the contents themselves of the ethnics' awareness of kind will be a focus of Part III. The immediate question which arises at this point is whether or not the same set of behavioral patterns is also exhibited by our second group under study, the Moroccans.

MOROCCANS IN THE LIMELIGHT

The establishment espoused the same methods toward Moroccans just overviewed with regard to the Yemenites, that is, the setting up of buffering institutions that articulated local community interests in the neighborhood, town, or village. It was by action on the part of the establishment that a Union of Moroccan Jews was created, and active personalities of this origin were coopted into parties. As with the Yemenites, the Labor Party (named Mapai until 1969), and other forces developed a wide web of special party circles for the Moroccans on an ethnic basis, the rationale of which was to bind ethnic interests to existing structures.[7]

Beyond the mere political motivation of parties to gain the support of new groups there was also their basic concern to orient social reality along the lines of the dominant model. As a tool for this aspiration, militants were encouraged to place themselves at the head of new settlements or neighborhoods. Despite their non-traditional character they often appeared as representatives of a supreme authority, and more than once were quite prone to behave as charismatic leaders. Yet when the inhabitants grew more aware of the political game, and found their own direct path to higher levels of the establishment, some of these "bosses" became foci of frictions and were later dethroned by the joint action of the central political leadership and local forces.[8] Another pattern of political activation was the integration of ethnics into unions and on the local workers' council (a body representing the Workers Unions at the municipal level). In these bodies Moroccans in particular are frequently numerous and often accede to leading positions.

Yet all these could not entirely erase the feelings of disappointment the Moroccans were to know in Israel. Many of them, let us repeat, had experienced big-city life in Morocco, and were reluctant to settle in peripheral areas; under the French colonial regime, the administrative and commercial posts which some had achieved and to which many aspired were not open to them in Israel and they had to accept blue-collar jobs; because of their partial (and often rudimentary) European education they saw themselves as "Westerners," but were here considered Orientals owing to their origin from a Muslim country. Even more important, due to their longstanding insecurity of status in Morocco they were very sensitive to any inequality in Israel.

It is in this context that one best understands the inefficiency of buffering institutions with regard to this stock. While they involved numerous individuals, the leaders they produced achieved but a small following in their community, characterized as it was by both a weak internal cohesion "imported" from abroad, and deep feelings of dissatisfaction vis-à-vis the "establishment." In fact, no group in Israel has ever shown such intense involvement in the politics of protest, and in two different periods Moroccans were able to arouse waves of unrest and even riots. The first outburst took place in a Haifa slum, Vadi Salib, in 1959 and quickly expanded to other cities. The major demand was for radical measures to improve the economic plight of the poor, and it was only after several weeks that the situation subsided. A dozen years later, the Black Panthers[9] aroused other slum neighborhoods in Jerusalem and again rioting spread. This time it seemed that the movement was encroaching on the general public scene and it is only after about a year of sporadic street demonstrations that it gradually lost its appeal.

A most interesting feature of these events is the type of leader one finds at their head, whom we may call an "ethnoclass leader"; this type also appears, from time to time in factories or corporations' unions and imprints a new style on work disputes by the toughness of its action. In the Ashdod port, for instance, strikes were successful enough to compel the resignation of the director-general of the Ports Authority. The workers' head was a Moroccan, like the other leaders of dissent in Haifa and Jerusalem, while his opponent was a former army chief of staff. The rise of such ethnoclass leaders can be best understood in the sociocultural context of the ethnoclass, and they are mentioned in many descriptions of the edah:

Nissim Levy was the uncrowned leader of the village. . . not only thanks to his physical strength and the money he brought with him from abroad, but mainly because of the cleverness and cunning he was able to mix, occasionally, with politeness. . . . He could wrap himself in good manners, or be ready for a rough fight—up to blows and knives. After the fight he was able to go right back to his normal face-making, to call for a big *sulha* [a reconciliation party] and to squander his money on all sides.[10]

Basically, ethnoclass leaders voice claims pertaining to social and economic matters only, and do not resort to cultural slogans in a "black-is-beautiful" style. Moreover, they also show aloofness from the ideological cleavages of Israeli political culture, and their policies are aimed primarily at the immediate acquisition of practical advantages. This is also true of more moderate forms of ethnic politics in cities or development towns where, thanks to their numerical importance, Moroccans[11] gradually gain control over local politics under a great variety of labels.

However, as regards the allegiance of the Moroccan masses, it must be said that if the buffering institutions have failed to control them, this is also true of politicians who have tried to set up ethnic parties. Even the leaders of the Black Panthers, who had become the very symbols of ethnoclass protest—their public following at the time compelled the government to appoint a public committee to investigate impoverished youth and take practical measures—were to fail totally when running for election. Unable as they were to achieve any permanent support in this matter (they gained less than 1 percent of the votes in the 1973 general election), they did not resist the solicitations of existing parties, from the Right to the extreme Left, and split into numerous rival factions. (One of them reached Parliament with Arab votes on a Communist ticket in 1977.) Similarly, an independent list headed by the Ashdod leader in 1977 was a thorough failure even among the port's workers.

The same fate awaited another attempt of Moroccan leaders, the "Oded" movement, this time mostly constituted by academics. "Oded"[12] set up fifteen offices all over Israel; its declared aims were to improve the material and educational conditions of North Africans as well as to provide them with an organizational framework which, independent of existing parties, would increase their weight on the political scene. If the first purpose encountered a positive echo, the second was not within their reach and support in edah neighborhoods was nil: no cement crystallized between them and the masses and, in the face of politically inexperienced academics, the veteran parties had no trouble maintaining their influence. In order to enter the political arena "Oded" had to join the liberal, middle-class-oriented "Democratic Movement for Change" for a time, which allowed it one seat in Parliament in 1977. In the 1981 elections, this movement which had united in the meantime with one of the former Black Panthers factions was to fail altogether.

In this latter campaign, however, a new organization was to encounter more success, namely the "Movement for Israel's Tradition" (Tami). For the first time since 1952, three MPs were elected—one of them Moroccan—on the behalf of an all Oriental list. This organization, however, which is the object of a special comment in Chapter 10 did not represent a new attempt to draft the overall support of the "Oriental masses," but rather the enterprise of individual veteran politicians. Though quite strong figures in nonethnic parties (the National Religious Party and the Labor Party), they expected to enhance their stand by running by their own—a pattern successfully used by others thanks to Israel's proportional system—on a list that defined itself at the center of the political spectrum. The 2.3 percent of the votes they succeeded in obtaining came almost exclusively from Oriental (and mainly Moroccan) former supporters of the National Religious Party, who constitute a minority in their edot. In the Parliament itself, Tami's representatives constituted but 10 percent of all Oriental MPs. The future may well show that this attempt represents a crisis of the crypto-pluralistic syndrome, though in the aftermath of the 1981 elections it mainly appears as a minor and temporary alteration. In sum, Moroccan ethnic politics are characterized by a set of elements the combination of which is quite particular. Moroccans are much more active on the scene than any other Oriental group. This is expressed in the large number of ethnic political events involving Moroccans and the variety of leaders among them. Yet, though Moroccans as a whole are the largest ethnic group in Israel and highly concentrated geographically and socially, these leaders have not yet succeeded in promoting any well-rooted independent political framework. Moroccan politicans in fact, are widely known for a nonideological orientation and an aloofness from the norms of the national political scene that is reflected in the fluidity of their allegiances. This trait, thought not specific to Moroccans, is more salient among them because of their greater activism. In any case, these activists present only instrumental exigencies and never emphasize the need to maintain the integrity of a given cultural patrimonium; in other words, "Moroccanness" has not become an effective political banner in Israel despite the fact that numerous prominent ethnic politicians are Moroccans.

By their very political activism Moroccans contrast with the Yemenites. This no doubt explains the cooption of two of them to Begin's cabinet while the most prominent Yemenite politician in 1981 was the deputy secretary-general of the Trade Unions Federation. Yet in both cases, it should be emphasized that the "masses," by liberating themselves from the "guidance" of buffering institutions, are reluctant to express their conflictual feelings by supporting an ethnic ticket or leftist opposition. The statistics (see Appendix 3) show, on the contrary, a disproportionate backing of those right-wing nationalists who were the main opposition to the left-of-center establishment for a long period. From this latter viewpoint, and despite the dissimilarities, Moroccans illustrate the same type of political behavior as do Yemenites.

CONCLUSIONS

On the whole, the picture of the ethnic encounter in the polity provided above should not underrate the fact that becoming full citizens of a democratic country constituted for ethnics a most radical break with their past. Notwithstanding their new rights, however, it remains that both the Yemenites and Moroccans are underrepresented in the political elite, although this *de facto* pluralism does not develop, in spite of their potential political power, into a recognized reality.

Still, Yemenites and Moroccans are supporters of nonethnic parties and it is to these that they bring their complaints of political inferiority as well as feelings of inferiority in other social hierarchies. Their "liberation" from buffering institutions has mainly increased their bargaining position and permits them to express more pointedly both their criticisms of the "establishment" and their preference for certain forces on the political spectrum. In the long run, to be sure, this behavior is bound to amplify the "generosity" of the center.

With all these, however, ethnics seemingly do endorse the dominant culture's reticence to recognize, at least *in* and *by* the polity, the pluralism which exists in all spheres of the ethnic encounter. In this respect, they contribute, to no less an extent than the absorptive setting, to the emergence of the *crypto-pluralistic syndrome*. Underlying this syndrome and widely accounting for the role played by ethnics in its crystallization are the "spectacles" through which they see themselves as ethnics and interpret their social fate. It is to this set of problems that we finally turn in the following chapters.

NOTES

1. A. Weingrod, *Israel, Group Relations in a New Society* (London: Pall Mall Press, 1965), pp. 60-65; R. Zamir, "Beer Sheva 1958-1959—Tahalihim Hevratiim Beeer Pituah" [Beer-Sheba 1958-1959—Social processes in a development town], in *Hamivneh Hahevrati Shel Israel* [The social structure of Israel], ed. S. N. Eisenstadt et al., (Jerusalem: Academon, 1967), pp. 335-65.

2. R. Bar-Yosef, "Absorption versus Modernization," in *Israeli Society 1967-1973*, ed. R. Kehana and S. Kopstein (Jerusalem: Academon, 1974), pp. 8-43.

3. H. Riger, "Le bayot Hahitarut Shel Noar Teimani Baaretz" [The problem of integration of Yemenite youth in the country], *Megamot* 12, no. 3 (April 1952): 244-84.

4. A. Deutsch, "Dmut Haelitah Beparvar Teimani" [The image of elite in a Yemenite neighborhood], *Megamot* 9, no. 4 (October 1958): 328-37.

5. M. Al-Pool, "Riyaun Hahodesh" [Monthly interview], *Bamaaraha* 216 (December 1978): 16.

6. P. Cohen, *Kehilah Veyetsivut Beayarat Pituah* [Community and stability in a development town] (Jerusalem: Ministry of Welfare, 1959), pp. 6-24.

7. E. Cohen, and J. Katan, *Kehilah Ktanah Bemerhav Metropolitani* [A small community in a metropolitan area] (Jerusalem: Department of Sociology, Hebrew University of Jerusalem, 1966), pp. 41-52.

8. For the case of Yeruham, see S. Paz, *Dimui Atsmi, Zehut Vehizdahut* [Self-image, identity and identification] (Jerusalem: Department of Education, The Hebrew University of Jerusalem, 1971), pp. 15-22.

9. See E. Cohen, "The Black Panthers and Israeli Society," in *Israeli Society 1967-1973*, ed. R. Kehana and S. Kopstein (Jerusalem: Academon, 1974), pp. 166-74.

10. E. Ben-Ezer, *Hamahzevah* [The quarry] (Tel Aviv: Am Oved, 1963), p. 13.

11. S. Paz, *Dimui Atsmi, Zehut Vehizdahut* [Self-image, identity and identification], pp. 26-31.

12. A. Lef-Gez, "The Oded Movement," (Jerusalem: The Hebrew University, 1976) (mimeographed).

PART III

THE SUBJECTIVE SIDE

Self-Images of Ethnics

8

INTRODUCTION

The foregoing three chapters have shown that Israeli society has become ethnically pluralistic. In this new reality the social order prior to the ethnics' immigration as well as the latter's former status as *dhimmis* are hardly recognizable. However, underlying this reality are the subjective elements which play a role at all stages of the foregoing discussion.

We may recall that awareness of kind primarily indicates the ethnics' attitudes *vis-à-vis* the setting on the ground of those meanings they endow their primordial attributes; these, by becoming a focus of racial, religious, or other self-identification and commitment, create the group's restrictive primordial identity and boundaries; while from this concept of distinctiveness the ethnics perceive and interpret the reality of their relations with "outs" in the various areas of the social endeavor.

Beyond these sets of questions, however, there are also the ethnics' images of their "collective personality" in the setting. This "personality," to be sure may express *both* some continuity of these *a priori* concepts and outlooks that widely determined their role in the encounter as a whole, and the appearance of new attributes acquired through the encounter itself.

Finally, the "spectacles" through which ethnics view social reality and explain their understanding of their general plight in society, account for the extent to which they recognize themselves in the condition which is actually theirs.

Chapter 4 was quite explicit regarding the features of ethnic awareness of kind that are related to the various dimensions of the encounter.

Thus, it was suggested, as a result of problems emerging in the sphere of membership and culture, and while certain groups do effectively melt into a non ethnic stock, that (1) other groups, by virtue of their religious and tradition-inspired understanding of immigration, see themselves as "temporary edot," that is, as groups that make up inalienable subdivisions of the whole, whose distinctiveness grounded on origin is expected to vanish in the future. Behind these identities (2) there are the self-perceived "unique contents" of the edots' "personalities" representing a faithfulness to a *legacy*, notwithstanding the "desacralization" this undergoes in a homogeneous Jewish environment. It is from these components of the ethnics' awareness of kind that the emergence of lasting ethnic communities is accounted for, while this very occurrence as well as additional processes in the areas of social status and politics explain the fact that (3) the *edah concept of distinctiveness* is endowed with practical meanings of social distance in all major categories of the ethnics' social interaction with "outs." Such distance, it was assumed, is but minimally altered by the upward mobility of individuals who tend to "disappear" into the non ethnic stock. Finally, against the twofold background of aspirations instrinsic to the notion of edah and fidelity to a given "personality," the ethnics' interpretation of their collective plight must be ambivalent: that is, (4) if they effectively "recognize themselves" in many features of their objective sociocultural particularism, their perceptions of marginality and inferiority in additional aspects of the social endeavor should reveal conflictual feelings and alienation *vis-à-vis* their "lot." At the same time, by virtue of their very understanding of the ethnic encounter through the concept of *mizug*, they remain, in general, "in-themselves" groups, reluctant to engage in open ethnic activism.

It is in order to validate these "subjective basic characteristics" that the research discussed below was conducted. Before turning to it, however, three more points should be clarified. First, it should be emphasized that investigating ethnic perceptions of distinctiveness from "outs" requires us, in the Israeli context (see Chapter 4), to distinguish between the nonethnic stock (predominantly Ashkenazi), the "others" as uniformly termed here, and Oriental groups in general. Operationally, this consideration demands that the relevant sets of variables be studied concomitantly with regard to each of these entities.

A second remark, of a more general character, pertains to the question of whether or not research into attitudes at a given moment in time only describes a static condition. What may be said here is that changes in the ethnic group were focused on two important aspects. First, in our analyses both of the ethnics' distinctiveness within the setting and of their views of their particularisms, much room was given to questions of time perspective, which at least reflects current images of change. Second, and in our view the major answer, the research as a whole concentrated heavily on one of the most important factors of change in any ethnic model, that is, the impact of social mobility of ethnic individuals in the evolution of the group. This problem was also discussed in Chapter 4 and referred to above in statement (3).

The final point to be stressed is the fact that, similar to the analysis of the objective side of ethnicity, by no means should one expect conformity of findings regarding the two groups under study; to be sure, differences of sociohistorical endeavors prior to immigration as well as conjunctual circumstances would also be influential here. Yet, insofar as these differences do not gainsay the "subjective basic characteristics," we may consider them as variations within the same model.

This research was conducted during 1978-79. It investigated two random samples of the Yemenite and Moroccan upwardly mobile cohorts. The samples were taken from census lists made available by local Yemenite and Moroccan associations in the areas of Jerusalem and Tel Aviv. Out of hundreds of names randomly picked from these lists and contacted by the interviewers, those who entered the samples were all (1) people of middle-class occupations (see Table 8.1) (2) whose fathers were characterized by low-class positions. These proceedings delineated a Yemenite sample of 139 persons and a Moroccan sample of 152 persons.

The sizes of the samples answered the goals of the research, which required personal and quite lengthy interviews on the basis of a questionnaire filled out by interviewers. Table 8.1 shows the samples' background characteristics; these were *not* to correlate significantly with any of the major issues of the research which was another, though *a posteriori*, support of the investigators' decision to accept the sizes of the samples.

The first purpose of this research was the investigation of the ethnic awareness of kind of Yemenite and Moroccan mobile elements. The

Table 8.1 Characteristics of the Two Samples (%)

Background Characteristics	Yemenites (N = 139)	Moroccans (N = 152)
a. *Sex*		
1. Women	27	17
2. Men	73	83
Total	100	100
b. *Age*		
1. 25-39	65	49
2. 40-54	32	48
3. 55+	3	3
Total	100	100
c. *Age at time of immigration to Israel*		
1. born in Israel	61	36
2. immigrated up to age of 11	31	42
3. immigrated after age of 11	8	22
Total	100	100
d. *Education*		
1. primary and partial secondary	4	30
2. secondary	32	33
3. higher	64	37
Total	100	100
e. *Military service*		
1. none	24	9
2. completed with grade up to first class	13	4
3. completed with grade up to sergeant	47	33
4. completed with grade up to lieutenant	14	48
5. completed with higher grade than lieutenant	2	6
Total	100	100
f. *Occupation*		
1. professionals, academics, students	22	19
2. technical, military, teachers	34	22
3. clerks, functionaries	15	30
4. technical trade, middle range businessmen	29	29
Total	100	100

second purpose was the investigation of the samples' images of the ethnic awareness of kind of the edot themselves. Both samples, indeed, consisted of people who despite their social mobility were still close, in terms of time, to the ethnic community. Standing at some distance—and only at *some* distance—from their groups, they were also able to depict their groups more clearly and coherently than others who either belonged totally to the reality investigated or were very far from it. For these reasons, the mobile Yemenite and Moroccan were ideal *informants*.

In a general manner, according to the concept of "awareness of kind" and the twofold purpose of the research, respondents were expected to yield four kinds of data.

1. their perceptions of subjective phenomena involving them (such as their identification with given labels or attitudes toward definite problems);
2. their perceptions of objective phenomena involving them (such as of their relations with "outs" or with the ethnic community);
3. their images of the edot's perceptions of subjective phenomena involving the edot in general (i.e. of the general norm within the edot with respect to subjective phenomena);
4. their images of their edot's perceptions of objective phenomena involving the edot in general.

It is with respect to categories 1 and 2 that respondents were exclusive subjects of the study. The information provided by categories 3 and 4 also permitted the analysis of the data under the heading of the "impact" of social mobility on the mobiles' ethnic awareness of kind (see the next chapter).

On the other hand, with respect to categories (3) and (4) respondents also played the role of informants. Regarding category (4), it must be remarked, the pretesting of the questionnaire showed that our questions were unnecessarily complicated: what informants understood as the perception of their fellow ethnics was, in fact, nearly identical to their own view of their edot's reality. Hence, respondents' own perceptions, in these respects, were accepted as the relevant information.

This latter point inevitably raises, as for any survey based on informants, the question of the credibility of their reports. The fact that respondents differentiated themselves on many other counts than those pertaining to category (4) supports the credibility of the findings as a whole. What is more, the two samples, let us repeat, are random samples of the cohorts of mobile Yemenites and Moroccans. Their images of their stocks, henceforth, are *real* at least as far as the images of these cohorts are concerned. This considerably enhances the reliabilty of the data. This is even more the case when a high degree of unanimity also transpires among informants; this, it has turned out, was frequent among both Yemenite and Moroccan respondents.

Thus, in a strict methodological sense, the hypotheses, the samples' distributions, and the statistics presented below refer to, and are representative of, the stratum of mobile ethnics and their images of their respective groups. Yet, for this very reason, it is also our contention that the data, if confirming the hypotheses, are also widely informative of the edot themselves.

From all these considerations, however, it follows that caution is required in our interpretation of the findings, particularly since this project is a first attempt at a comparative investigation of edot in Israel. This is its main merit but also its weakness, as no other comparative work done in Israel was available that could constitute a starting point.

THE CONCEPT OF "TEMPORARY EDAH"

THE HYPOTHESES

The first questions we addressed to our informants concerned the groups' concept of distinctiveness *vis-à-vis* "outs." The "subjective basic characteristcis" suggested here that the groups define themselves as temporary edot. "Translated" into more precise hypotheses, (1) informants would confirm that one's origin from a given country is generally perceived in the edot as an important focus of collective identification; (2) this focus is formulated in terms of "subdivision" of the more comprehensive labels of "Jewishness" and "Israeliness"; (3) despite processes of melting with "outs," such processes are seen on the whole as minimally affecting the group's existence; at the same time (4) the perspective on the encounter at large makes conspicuous a general expectation of total melting in the future.

All these should first apply to the edot's self-images *vis-à-vis* "others." Our main contention in Chapter 4 was that it is the ethnic encounter in the area of membership and culture between the *a priori* features of *given* groups with the dominant culture embodied by "others" that creates ethnic communities enduringly reliant on Diasporan endeavors.

Israeli society, however, is highly disparate and besides "others" —the predominantly Ashkenazi and nonethnic middle and upper classes—there is also (let us repeat) a great variety of groups which share in common for the most part, many episodes of a past in a Muslim country, some influence of the Sephardic legacy, and, more concretely, wide participation in lower social strata. The question which then arises is to what extent are the shortcomings of a general "melting of edot" in the short or middle runs—if such are effectively the rule—simply explained by the "submeltings" of groups relatively closer to each other by culture and status?

If this is the case, we may suggest that tens of different origins hardly correspond to the concept of a "common" primordial attribute leading to one particular awareness of kind. Hence, such an evolution of ethnic relations would mean a de-ethnicization of Israeli society, and the vanishing of ethnic cleavages as such. This eventuality was sustained by the discussion in Chapter 4 regarding the non-Oriental stock, but it remains quite doubtful as far as the edot are concerned, despite the wide use, in Israel, of the concept of *Edot Mizrah* (the Orientals-as-a-whole). This concept, it was argued, represents but the interpretation by the dominant culture of a *de facto* pluralism contradicting its expectations.

It is in this context that our research also hypothesized that (5) informants will support the statement according to which "Orientals-as-a-whole" is *not*, in the edot, a major focus of ethnic self-identification—a token entirely alien to the sphere of phenomena of ascriptive identities and by no means an intermediary concept of belongingness linking the edah and the Nation; (6) similarly, melting among the edot is *not* viewed as much more overwhelming than between edot and "others" despite the greater objective, socioeconomic closeness (ascertained earlier) and consequent higher rates of intermarriage; and (7) the edot's perspective, it should be reported, on the past as well as the future does *not* reveal among them any attraction toward such an Oriental submelting.

EDOT VERSUS "OTHERS"

Ethnics in Israel bear several labels of identity simultaneously: they are Jews by national-religious concepts, Israeli citizens by nationality, Orientals by continent of birth, and Yemenites or Moroccans by country of origin.

Table 8.2   The Relative Importance of Various Identities in the Edot as Reported by Informants (%)

a. Identities graded by choices	Yemenites (N = 139)	Moroccans (N = 152)
1. Jewish identity as first choice (out of 100% 1st choice)	71	84
2. Israeli identity as second choice (out of 100% 2nd choice)	60	82
3. Group of origin as third choice (out of 100% 3rd choice)	52	63
4. "Oriental" as third choice (out of 100% 3rd choice)	12	8
χ^2 on basis of distributions of all three choices =	324.21; p<0.005	606.12; p<0.005
b. Identities as source of pride		
1. Jewish identity		
(a) restricted source of pride	11	55
(b) important source of pride	10	36
(c) very important source of pride	79	9
Total	100	100
2. Israeli identity		
(a) restricted source of pride	14	21
(b) important source of pride	32	47
(c) very important source of pride	54	32
Total	100	100
3. Identity of group of origin		
(a) restricted source of pride	22	59
(b) important source of pride	33	31
(c) very important source of pride	45	10
Total	100	100
χ^2 of (3) versus (2) =	4.11; p = 0.10	50.52; p<0.005
χ^2 of (3) versus (1) =	36.00; p<0.005	0.76; p>0.10

Table 8.2 shows, in accordance with hypothesis (1) that origin as such is reported as a focus of identification that is not less important than "Israeliness" (for the Yemenites), or "Jewishness" (for the Moroccans). On the other hand, however, our informants are also convinced that "Jewishness" and "Israeliness" are more dominant sets of identities for the people of their stocks and more meaningful criteria of belongingness. Hence, on removing the "Oriental" label, to be discussed further on, we obtain from Table 8.2 a concept of ranking order consistent with hypothesis (2) according to which the more comprehensive the label, the greater its importance, that is, a ranking order that goes from "Jewishness" referring to a world community to "Israeliness," which points to more restricted boundaries and, finally, to the group of origin in Israel.

This emphasis on comprehensive labels, however—and in accordance with hypothesis (3)—does not mean in any way that origin is reported as but a feeble criterion of distinctiveness: convinced of speaking on behalf of their groups in general, only one-third of Yemenites and none of the Moroccans consider that their respective stocks have "melted" to a high degree with Ashkenazi; 23 percent of the Yemenites and 6 percent of the Moroccans answered "to some extent" and all others (40 percent of Yemenites and 94 percent of Moroccans) depicted the degree of "melting" as at best restricted.

The difference between Yemenites and Moroccans may be explained by veteranship in the country which (as seen later) is positively correlated with contacts with "others." Yet both groups of informants are quite unanimous on other points, namely the continuity of ethnic identity despite veteranship: a wide majority of Yemenites (77 percent) and of Moroccans (88 percent) think that a third-generation Israeli offspring of one's group remains, in general, a part of it. Only a small minority (4 percent of Yemenites and 3 percent of Moroccans) is convinced that such people are not labelled in ethnic terms any more. A major factor "dissolving" this label is to be born of a "mixed" marriage (see Table 8.3), though even here many informants still think a particular ethnic identity persists according to that of one of the parents.

Thus, in a general way, it is by no means possible to conclude that a strong emphasis on comprehensive labels, including "others," is associated with a deletion of ethnic identities. In fact, what is reported

**Table 8.3 Ethnic Identity of Offsprings of Mixed Marriages
(as seen by the people of the edot[a]) (%)**

(a) - Father Ashkenazi, mother from the edah	Yemenite Informants (N = 139)	Moroccan Informants (N = 152)
Ethnic identity of offspring in eyes of most people of edah:		
1. edah	22	13
2. "Oriental"	31	6
3. Ashkenazi	11	17
4. Israeli Jew without label	36	64
Total	100	100
(b) - Mother Ashkenazi, father from the edah Ethnic identity of offspring in eyes of most people of edah		
1. edah	37	29
2. "Oriental"	3	1
3. Ashkenazi	10	10
4. Israeli Jew without label	50	60
Total	100	100

[a]The term "edah" was used throughout the interviews as it is by this token that people generally designate their group of origin.

here is the very appearance of such identities as meaningful concepts of distinctiveness *inside* wider frameworks of reference. These comprise not only the fact of nationality, as in the case of any ethnic group, but also a concept which transcends it, namely the national-religious notion of "Jewishness," which, by expressing an unconditional belongingness to a given whole, makes the particular group of origin the edah-type of entity. By the same token, the edot—it was suggested by hypothesis (4)—should be reported as accepting the principle of *mizug* and seeing themselves as temporary groupings.

This self-image as temporary groupings, one will recall, is directly related to the very concept of a traditional or quasi-traditional edah: the group remains a distinct entity because it cannot envisage belonging to the greater whole outside of its own legacy, yet at the same time it fully endorses the imperative of contributing to the unification of this whole of which it sees itself an integral part. This sense, one may add, represents the essential difference between the edah-type of ethnic groups in Israel and other groups such as the Jews in contemporary Diaspora. For the latter, primordial identity constitutes a concept of group definition, *independent* of, and which *must accommodate* with, the wider allegiances of the dominant culture. This accommodation will, in turn, determine the commitment required of the group members in order to maintain its self-perceived "uniqueness." In other words, for the Jews in Diaspora, the major ethnic problem is "how to remain a distinct group"; for the edah, the problem is: "How is it conceivable not to remain so *despite* one's aspiration to 'disappear'?"

Accordingly, our research at this point turns to the question: To what extent do Yemenites and Moroccans really aspire to "disappear" as special separate entities? To answer, it is enough to consider the perspectives shared by the informants about the evolution of their groups' "distinctiveness" from "others" and (in this regard) their expectation of the future. From both these viewpoints, and whatever their precise positions—in fact, on most following items they are widely unanimous—Yemenites as well as Moroccans are mostly convinced of an identity between their own feelings and those dominant in their respective edot. Thus concerning both the past and future, and though Moroccans are less optimistic in general, the two groups of informants are convinced of a constant weakening of their edot's overall saliency in the social setting. As for socioeconomic realities, for instance, about two-thirds of both groups of respondents feel there has been great improvement during the last several decades; the wide majority of both samples (about 80 percent) believes that social mobility in the future (twenty years) will raise large numbers of their groups to a higher status. Regarding power, it is true, both images of the past and expectations of the future are more reserved: only one-fourth of Yemenites and almost none among Moroccans feel there has been great improvement in the representation of their groups in the polity, while about half of both samples (43 percent of Yemenites and 56 percent of Moroccans) think there has been but slight improvement, if any. For the future, not less than 45 percent of Yemenites do not foresee a substantial change, but on this point Moroccans are more optimistic—only 21 percent share this view—a finding which may be related to their higher degree of political activism.

Regarding cultural gaps too—and this point is especially crucial here—informants appear quite convinced of the narrowing of distance and, again, it is the Moroccans who are more extremist. From Table 8.4 it emerges that (according to informants) the main "agents" preserving customs and traditions of the group are those who lack secondary education and were born abroad, two criteria that are gradually vanishing among the edot. The weakening—or more accurately, the changing—of cultural particularism, however, is much stronger among Moroccans than Yemenites, and this fact is consistent with former descriptions (see Chapter 3).

Finally, regarding social interaction, the most striking datum of Table 8.5 is the informants' unanimous belief in the future restricted importance of the edah as a factor of social proximity, and which contrasts with their report of present preferences (see Table 8.8). A difference does appear, however, between Yemenites and Moroccans with respect to the groups or categories with which social "melting" is

Table 8.4 "Who Preserves the Edah's Customs and Culture?" (%)

Groups in the edah		Among Yemenites (N = 136)	Among Moroccans (N = 150)
a. Educated people born in Israel			
1. at least "to some extent"		50	10
2. to a small extent, if any		50	90
	Total	100	100
b. People without secondary education, born in Israel			
1. at least "to some extent"		71	49
2. to a small extent, if any		29	51
	Total	100	100
c. Educated people born abroad			
1. at least "to some extent"		74	29
2. to a small extent, if any		26	71
	Total	100	100
d. People without secondary education, born abroad			
1. at least "to some extent"		79	62
2. to a small extent, if any		21	38
	Total	100	100
χ^2 (education and place of birth vs. the preservation of ethnic culture) =		29.75; $p<0.005$;	100.75 $p<0.005$

Table 8.5 "What are the Principal Groups or Categories with which the People of your Edah will have Social Contacts in 20 Years from Now?" (%)

		Yemenites (N = 139)	Moroccans (N = 152)
(a) As neighbors			
1. People of the edah		13	4
2. Orientals		7	58
3. Ashkenazi		6	11
4. All groups without difference		74	27
	Total	100	100
	$\chi^2 =$	97.64; p<0.005	
(b) As Friends			
1. People of the edah		8	9
2. Orientals		8	50
3. Ashkenazi		7	12
4. All groups without difference		77	29
	Total	100	100
	$\chi^2 =$	77.66; p<0.005	
(c) As brides or grooms for children			
1. People of the edah		11	6
2. Orientals		4	46
3. Ashkenazi		4	14
4. All groups without difference		81	34
	Total	100	100
	$\chi^2 =$	83.44; p<0.005	

primarily expected: the Yemenites are convinced that total *mizug* is on its way, while more Moroccans observe a closening to the other Oriental groups which, as shown below, is dictated more by pessimism *via-à-vis* the probability of *mizug* with "others" than by a strong identification with the concepts of "Orientals."

In sum, while the Yemenites draw a more confident picture with regard to status achievements and social melting with "others," Moroccans are more convinced of the narrowing of cultural differences and political inequalities. Beyond these differences, the present distinctiveness of the edot, which is heavily insisted upon, is basically considered by both samples to be a *transitional stage*. According to their own contention, let us repeat, they voice here images and beliefs widely accepted within their stocks.

THE EDOT VERSUS THE "ORIENTALS."

As a matter of course, ethnic distinctiveness *vis-à-vis* "others" is accompanied by images of distance from other Oriental edot as well. In any event, Table 8.6 shows that according to informants "Orientals-as-a-whole" is but a restricted source of pride in the eyes of the edot.

It is true that the differences found between the two identities are less pronounced among Moroccans (and statistically insignificant). If accepting these views as characteristic not only of mobile cohorts but also of the edot themselves, they may be explained by the fact that the Moroccan edah was from the beginning much less ethnocentric than the Yemenite, a fact which transpired throughout the research. More-

Table 8.6 Ethnic Identity vs. Oriental Identity as Sources of Pride in the Eyes of the Edot and as Reported by Informants (%)

	Yemenite (N = 139)	Moroccan (N = 152)
(a) Ethnic identity (Yemenite or Moroccan) as a source of pride:		
1. very restricted	13	17
2. to some extent	9	42
3. to a large extent	33	31
4. to a very large extent	45	10
Total	100	100
$\chi^2 =$	66.15; $p<0.005$	
(b) Oriental identity as a source of pride:		
1. very restricted	43	23
2. to some extent	26	47
3. to a large extent	20	24
4. to a very large extent	11	6
Total	100	100
$\chi^2 =$	20.45; $p<0.005$	
χ^2 of (a) vs. (b) =	68.51; $p<0.005$	4.75; $p>0.05$

over, additional evidence confirming hypothesis (5), which emerged in Table 8.2, is the existence, in the ethnics' mind—according to informants—of an "illogical" order of importance among the several identities: first comes "Jewishness," the most comprehensive; second, "Israeliness," still comprehensive but more confined than the first; third, the specific edah, the most particular; only in fourth position—and quite distant from the edah—comes "Orientals-as-a-whole," which is less comprehensive than "Israeliness" but more than the edah. This finding corroborates a datum already mentioned, by which no member of an edah automatically becomes an "Oriental only" due to the mere fact of veteranship.

Table 8.7, moreover, shows that for Yemenite informants (more than for Moroccans), offspring identity is generally perceived in the group as ethnic (whether according to the father's or the mother's origin) and mostly related to their own edah; for Moroccans (more than for Yemenites), the identity of offspring of mixed marriages tends to be deleted completely. Among both, only a minority sustains the view that in such cases the "Oriental only" identity is the one endowed. When comparing these findings with Table 8.3, it also appears that mixed marriages among Orientals maintain the particular ethnic identity even more (for the Yemenites) or to no lesser extent (for the Moroccans) than do those between people of these groups and Ashkenazi.

In the same vein, let us add, it is also the samples' conviction—and in this concern again they are convinced of an identity of views between themselves and the norm of their respective edah—that melting is *not* predominant between the edot and other Oriental groups: only a minority considers such processes as intense (27 percent of Yemenites and none of Moroccans) or describes them as quite intense (17 and 10 percent respectively); the majority (56 and 90 percent) sees them as limited, if at all. Hence, compared to the degree of melting with "others," and as expected from hypothesis (6), the edot, according to informants, do not view themselves melting together more than with "others."

However, whatever these perceptions of enduring distinctiveness from each other, it is reported throughout that the edot are undergoing similar processes of change. Table 8.4, for example, reports that traditional customs are weakening, while data mentioned in the for-

Table 8.7 The Ethnic Identity of Offspring of Mixed Marriages as Seen by the Edah (%)

		Yemenites (N = 135)	Moroccans (N = 151)
(a) Mother from the edah (Yemenite or Morrocan) **—father from another Oriental edah** Identity of offspring:			
1. your edah		45	17
2. father's edah		36	3
3. Oriental only		15	22
4. Israeli Jew without label		4	58
	Total	100	100
	$\chi^2 =$	129.07; $p<0.005$	
(b) Father from edah—mother from another Oriental edah Identity of offspring:		(N = 137)	(N = 152)
1. your edah		43	34
2. mother's edah		5	2
3. Oriental only		20	9
4. Israeli Jew without label		32	55
	Total	100	100
	$\chi^2 =$	17.40; $p<0.005$	

mer section insist on socioeconomic or political mutations. Against this background, should we not expect perceptions among the edot of a future Oriental submelting? Table 8.5, in fact, contends that differences exist here between Yemenites and Moroccans and, while the former believe that the future will bring the melting of all Jews, the latter are more prone to forecast a submelting of Orientals. When looking at Table 8.8, however, it is quite evident that this latter eventuality is viewed by informants as basically contradicting the wishes of both groups. The edot, in fact, are depicted as distinguishing themselves from each other mainly with respect to their attitudes vis-à-vis themselves and the Ashkenazi.

Thus, whether or not this "Orientals-as-a-whole" entity will crystallize in future as a step toward the de-ethnicization of Israeli society, it does not constitute, according to the samples, an attractive proposition for either Yemenites or Moroccans. These reports of the inform-

Table 8.8 "What Group/Category is Preferred for Social Closeness by the People of your Edah, in General?" (%)

		Yemenites (N = 139)	Moroccans (N = 152)
(a) as neighbors			
1. people of the edah		52	12
2. Orientals, in general		1	5
3. Ashkenazi		7	47
4. all groups without difference		40	36
	Total	100	100
	$\chi^2 =$	83.36; p<0.005	
(b) as friends			
1. people of the edah		46	34
2. Orientals, in general		1	9
3. Ashkenazi		7	17
4. all groups without difference		46	40
	Total	100	100
	$\chi^2 =$	19.19; p<0.005	
(c) as brides or grooms for children			
1. people of the edah		54	14
2. Orientals, in general		1	6
3. Ashkenazi		10	20
4. all groups without difference		35	60
	Total	100	100
	$\chi^2 =$	51.00; p<0.005	

ants support hypothesis (7) and point to the continuous presence of the edot as real and distinct collectivities vis-à-vis both the "others" and the other edot. Thus, a closer look at their images which are the "personality" behind the identity is now required.

ETHNIC GROUPS: ATTRIBUTES, UNIQUENESS, AND ECLECTICISM

In a novel about the vicissitudes of Iraqi immigration to Israel, one finds a passage quite typical of the kind of problems met by all Oriental groups:

A surprise awaited [Ester who lives in the early 1950s in an immigrant camp near Tel Aviv] when she comes back from work. . . . "Uncle Shlomo! What a surprise!". . . After a while, he explained the purpose of his visit: "Rumors have reached us in the camp of Beersheva. . . . You will come to us with your three brothers. . . and you will be closer to us. . . and won't be abandoned to yourselves. . . . Who would bear such a situation in Iraq? Here everything is upside-down.". . . At night she decided in her heart that if Uncle Shlomo came back to this matter she would tell him clearly: "Uncle Shlomo, if you want take the children; I will go to the army. There will be no reason anymore to postpone my draft."[1]

If the edot, indeed see themselves still as distinct groups, how do they define the present content of this distinctiveness? The eclecticism of models exhibited by Yemenite and Moroccan edot was shown in Chapter 5; let us now consider—as far as they can be learned from informants—those subjective value orientations, concepts of social order, and outlooks toward life in society that both underlie the edot's "objective" participation in the cultural order and substantiate the self-perceived "personalities" designated by their primordial identities.

Though by no means exhausting the subject, the current inquiry focused especially, in this respect, on attitudes widespread among the edot regarding a few major parameters of social life, namely religious and parochial customs, the family, social status, the polity, and the community endeavor. In accordance with the "subjective basic characteristics" pertaining to the encounter in the area of membership and culture, the first hypothesis was that (1) the informants' testimony would support that the eclecticism transpiring in objective features of the edot's cultural endeavor will also be intrinsic to outlooks, since elements recalling the past and appraised as a "legacy" should "coexist" with concepts learned in Israel that are far from being rejected.

Yet if eclecticism may be expected to be a feature common to Yemenites and Moroccans alike, a second hypothesis, based on the historical material of Chapter 3, should insist on the eventuality to be confirmed by informants that (2) beyond their common closeness, relative to "others," to a traditional world-view, the different cultural starting-points of the two edot (mainly regarding religiosity and community cohesion) also account for different respective "collective personalities." On the whole, (3) these "personalites," it should be reported, represent, in the eyes of the edot, the essential difference between each of them and "outs."

When turning to our findings, it first appears that religiosity and tradition are effectively reported as much weaker than in the past among both Yemenites (according to two-thirds of informants) and Moroccans (91 percent). In the eyes of both groups of informants, one may hardly define most youngsters either as religious or (even) traditionalist; and it is mainly the older generation that is still deeply faithful to ancestral traditions (according to 74 percent of Yemenites and 99 percent of Moroccans).

On the other hand, it is also clear that religiosity and adherence to parochial customs are by no means totally vanishing in the edot. Religious knowledge remains a worthwhile educational goal according to 74 percent of Yemenites and 51 percent of Moroccans, while there is still fervent support, including among the young, for certain edah customs such as yearly pilgrimages to the tombs of saints or public festivals (this is the opinion of 84 percent of Yemenites and 70 percent of Moroccans). Moreover, informants think (see Table 8.4) that among Yemenites defection from customs is not overwhelming, even among educated persons born in Israel, while among Moroccans such defection is the case apart from those who lack secondary schooling and who, it should be added, are a majority in the edah (see Chapter 6). Thus, Yemenites in general, it is true—and in accordance with hypothesis (2)—are depicted as more religious and traditionalist than Moroccans, who, as noted earlier, were often much less respectful of parochial values even before they immigrated. Yet in both edot, it is reported that several customary rituals have remained alive and have become symbols of ethnic identity.

As for the concept of family, which in Yemen as in Morocco responded to a like traditionalism, near unanimity exists again among informants (90 percent of Yemenites and 93 percent of Moroccans) about the value, in the edot, of "a well-established family life" as a major goal. Moreover, strong and permanent ties with relatives are described as either "highly commanding" (according to no less than 60 percent of Yemenites and half of the Moroccans) or at least of no negligible importance (another 36 and 45 percent respectively). Inside the nuclear family—a resonance of time-honored norms—relations between parents and children remain imbued with authority (this is strongly emphasized by 46 percent of Yemenites and 50 percent of Moroccans and, to a lesser extent, by 17 percent and 21 percent respectively), while the education of daughters is seen as of far less importance than that of sons. In all these respects, reported differences between Yemenites and Moroccans are minimal. Concomitantly, however, there are many other features reported, such as recognition of the importance of modern education for male offspring, a decline in the number of children desired per family, or the acceptance of women working outside the home, which, according to informants, bring Yemenite and Moroccan families nearer to the models displayed by the "others."

As for outlooks on status, the influence of the dominant ethos is also apparent in informants' reports, and it "coexists" with concepts inherited from the past. Attributes expressing individual achievement, for instance, like talent, "brains," education, and financial resources, are all reported as seen as advantages in society. Yet by no means do the edot underrate factors which are beyond individual control such as "luck" (85 percent of Yemenites and 89 percent of Moroccans considered this at least "quite important" in their edot), or "fate" (77 percent and 59 percent). Again, regarding aspirations especially worthy of commitment, both groups of informants, almost unanimously, insist upon a "well-established economic position" and a "high standard of living" as of great importance in the eyes of their respective stocks; on the other hand, among the major goals, higher education is reported as a less popular one.

In sum, it is the informants' opinion that the edot accept the claims of achievement criteria but do not deny the role of "uncontrollable" ascriptive attributes; they endorse the emphasis on improvement but consider economic gains as of greater value than educational ones. They understand the individualistic rules of social status, but are also less prone than the "others" to adopt them. These "compromising" outlooks, one may conclude, express the difficulty for traditional or quasi-traditional groups—greater for Yemenites than Moroccans since these latter had experienced, for the most part, the colonial version of modernity—in fully internalizing concepts of the current ethos that contrast with their own parochial culture.

A similar eclecticism is depicted with respect to the edot's view of the polity. The main purpose of a democracy is to serve its citizens; hence there is no difference, seemingly, between edot and "others." Yet prominent attributes which the edot consider should also belong to the state are strength and authority as well as control that permeates all domains of social life; at the same time, interest in political matters and information is quite scarce (according to 80 percent of Yemenite informants and 98 percent of Moroccan). Thus the edot's image of the polity, as described by informants, is an aggregate of the modern democratic view, the representative function of the state, and patrimonial orientations, combining a powerful concept of political authority with a very limited personal or collective involvement in politics.

Though in most respects discussed above much resemblance characterizes the eclecticism of these two edot as described by informants, this is less true when turning to the community endeavor proper. For both groups of informants (99 percent of both Yemenites and Moroccans), closeness to people of one's stock is generally thought advantageous by people of the edot. Among the eventual "gains" of this closeness, a like proportion of the two samples (30 percent) mentions better possibilities for people to make friends and enjoy mutual aid when needed. Yet, besides these benefits, which are evenly estimated by each group of informants, Yemenites (53 percent) also insist on the importance among the people of their stock of maintaining parochial customs. For Moroccans special advantages are the provision of self-assurance (34 percent) or economic and political power (28 percent).

These data are consistent with the findings of Table 8.4 which reported stronger feelings of identification among the Yemenites in general with the edah's patrimonium. This was also reported with respect to their clear affirmation of ethnic identity (see Tables 8.3 and 8.7) and pride (Table 8.2). All these, finally, are well summarized in Table 8.8, which shows how Yemenites, in the mind of informants, are much more attracted by each other than are Moroccans. These differences are also expressed in the informants' descriptions of their fellow ethnics' attitudes toward community organizations (Tables 8.9 and 8.10). For the Yemenite informants it is the ethnic synagogue that awakens the greatest interest in the edah; for the Moroccans, it is the social organization that aims to enhance the edah's status in society. While a high degree of readiness to contribute to community frameworks is not reported for either group, these frameworks still arouse much more commitment among Yemenites.

Table 8.9 Readiness to Contribute to Community Organizations among the Yemenite Edah, as Viewed by the Yemenite Informants (%)

Kinds of Frameworks	Degrees of readiness to contribute, widespread in the edah			Total
	high	some	small	
(a) Edah synagogues (N = 135)	56	24	20	100
(b) Charity organizations (N = 138)	26	32	42	100
(c) Organizations for promoting the edah's status (N = 139)	23	34	43	100
(d) Scholarship funds for youth of the edah (N = 128)	30	27	43	100

χ^2 of (a) versus (b) = 27.46; $p < 0.005$
(c) = 33.23; $p < 0.005$
(d) = 22.20; $p < 0.005$

Table 8.10 Readiness to Contribute to Community Organizations among the Moroccan Edah, as Viewed by the Moroccan Informants (%)

Kinds of Frameworks	Degrees of readiness to contribute, widespread in the edah			Total
	high	some	small	
(a) Edah synagogues (N = 152)	3	10	87	100
(b) Charity organizations (N = 145)	-	10	90	100
(c) Organizations for promoting the edah's status (N = 152)	3	33	64	100
(d) Scholarship funds for youth of the edah (N = 141)	-	10	90	100

χ^2 of (c) versus (a) = 22.18; $p < 0.005$
(b) = 28.42; $p < 0.005$
(d) = 28.89; $p < 0.005$

Thus it again appears that Yemenites who, let us remember, have been longer in the country, enjoy more sympathy of "others," are better off than Moroccans, also constitute, according to the informants, a more cohesive stock. This underlines the extent to which the differences between the subjective features of these edot depend less on practical circumstances in Israel itself than on cultural starting-points. The Yemenites' greater cohesion, despite the above-mentioned conditions conducive to greater integration, can be explained only by the longevity of their traditions based upon centuries of a well-institutionalized, collective plight. Jewry in Morocco on the other hand included villagers, *mellah* dwellers, and "Frenchized" bourgeois who, as a whole, were unsure of their horizons and, though concentrating like the Yemenites in compact communities in Israel, suffered greater cultural ambiguities.

Thus in general the testimony of the samples describes at the level of self-images an eclecticism inherent in ethnics' value orientations that is consistent with hypothesis (1). The same findings—as expected by hypothesis (2)—also depict each edah as illustrating, despite the "unifying" effect of a traditional outlook as well as of a like "different" environment, a profile of attitudes and outlooks which remains quite "unique" insofar as it represents a continuation of particular *a priori* features. Moreover, generalizing from the findings to Israel's ethnic groups as a whole, it is suggested that for some groups the ethnic community commands greater loyalty, and henceforth holds more basic sociopsychological value, than for others. Such differences constitute an additional aspect of ethnic diversity of society requiring further investigation in a direction widely neglected by contemporary studies.

In the context of this self-perceived uniqueness of the edah reported by the informants, it is no wonder that the latter were eager to underline precise dissimilarities between their edot and the Ashkenazi as well as (though to a lesser extent) other Orientals, while according to their own feelings, they expressed here again their groups' norm in these respects. Hence, regarding the Ashkenazi's value orientations—among a given range of items two main elements were insisted upon—90 percent of Yemenites and 95 percent of Moroccans viewed Ashkenazi as strongly moved by social ambitions and as highly individualistic—the "heart" of the modern ethos—and their own stocks as being much less so. Only 30 percent of Yemenites and 13 percent of Moroccans classified their group in the same categories regarding the first question and even fewer regarding the second. Moreover, Table 8.11 is another and more general index, which shows how insistently the informants depict their edot as "unidentifiable." Comparatively to "others," it is true, the resemblance between edot is by no means ignored by them; beyond this point, however—and this is the key fact—they also emphasize substantial differences between each other.

Table 8.11 Cultural Dissimilarity between the Edah and the Ashkenazi, Other Orientals, and inside the Edah (%)

	Yemenites (N = 139)			Moroccans (N = 152)		
	vs. Ashkenazim	vs. other Orientals	among themselves	vs. Ashkenazim	vs. other Orientals	among themselves
1. very wide cultural dissimilarity (referring to customs, personal attributes and physical features)	64	39	4	50	34	9
2. wide cultural dissimilarity (referring to two aspects out of three)	22	39	17	33	33	24
3. certain cultural dissimilarity (one aspect only)	12	19	45	14	26	45
4. no dissimilarity	2	3	34	3	7	22
Total	100	100	100	100	100	100
$\chi^2 =$	189.09; $p < 0.005$			98.64; $p < 0.005$		

144

These findings, finally, support hypothesis (3) and well articulate those "contents" of ethnics' self-perceived personalities which, as described by informants, make the edot both eclectic but distinct entities and substantiate their self-affirmation under given labels of primordial identities. At this point, we should turn to another subject of concern here, the practical social meanings endowed the edah concept of distinctiveness.

THE EDAH, A SELF-PERCEIVED MARGINAL ENTITY

The ethnics' primordial identity, is a lens through which people view themselves as standing inside given boundaries, the cement of which is constituted by specific models of behavior and symbols of identification. An objective ethnic sociocultural reality, in turn, must lead, in direct intergroup relations, to some feelings of social aloofness and the diffusion of prejudices—not least to mutual ethnic labelling—which expresses the fact that, in spite of belonging to the same society, one does not live together. Moreover, images of social distance between "ins" and "outs" may spill over and flow through additional social channels, and the more so if, as in Israel, occurrences in the spheres of status and polity reveal the particular objective features of the various ethnic groups.

Hence, our investigation of the mobiles' images of their ethnic groups in these respects hypothesized that (1) according to informants' reports ethnic cleavages are resented among the edot as most salient in society. Regarding "others," more specifically, (2) feelings of cultural and social aloofness, prejudices, and ethnic labelling imbuing social interactions should be reported as widespread among ethnics. Furthermore, and as a reflection of "objective" occurrences, (3) informants should also emphasize the existence of perceptions of wide differences between "ins" and "others" with respect to status and power.

As for the edot's images vis-à-vis other Oriental groups, however, it was expected that (4) considering the edot's greater objective cultural, social, and political closeness, the informants would report weaker perceptions of distinctiveness; yet, as each edah remains a discrete entity, (5) its self-images should still be depicted as showing an awareness of relative differences in every way envisaged above.

In sum, and in the context of the "objective basic characteristics" analyzed in Part II, the general expectation of this part of the research was that in the informants' descriptions the edot's condition in society evokes self-images of *distinct and marginal cultural, social, and political entities.*

Findings, let us emphasize immediately, are in full agreement with hypothesis (1) while our respondents who are widely unanimous within each sample on many items, present, as a rule, their own feelings as identical with their edot's norm.

Thus among *all* social cleavages dividing Israeli society, that opposing Ashkenazi to Oriental groups is seen as one of the most acute (the Yemenites) or the most acute (the Moroccans) (Table 8.12). This cleavage, at least as far as the "others" are concerned, is detailed by our informants in reference to all major points of social interactions. Among Yemenite informants, two-thirds (65 percent) do not admit that the Ashkenazi are really prejudiced against their edah, while the large majority of Moroccans feel so (76 percent). This corroborates what was said above concerning difference in prestige among these two edot. However, when informants discuss the Ashkenazi's attitude toward their groups, very few Yemenites (6 percent) or Moroccans (11 percent) consider it directed toward "Israelis without any label." Thirty-three percent and 29 percent define it respectively as toward "Oriental Israelis," and no less than 61 percent and 60 percent as toward "Israelis of a definite edah." Hence, despite, the variance of views on the intensity of prejudice, according to the informant of both samples, ethnic labels are deeply inherent in intergroup relations.

Concomitantly, only a small minority of informants (about 7 percent of Yemenites and 9 percent of Moroccans) consider that Ashkenazi are the main focus of social contact with their stocks in areas like the neighborhood, friendship, or friends of children. Differences, however, appear between the samples under the heading of "all groups without distinction"; for Yemenites the percentage varies here from 32 (friendship) to 35 (neighborhood) to 50 (friends of children), while the respective figures for Moroccans are 2, 1 and 10. Thus, many Yemenite informants report that their more veteran and more popular edah has much wider contacts with "others" than as reported for the Moroccan group by the nearly unanimity of Moroccan respondents. Yet, as expected by hypothesis (2), the picture emerging even with regard to

Table 8.12 Saliency of Various Cleavages in Israeli Society (%)

Cleavages		Yemenites	Moroccans
a. Religious people versus secular		(N = 132)	(N = 148)
1. very significant		57	34
2. significant		27	50
3. unimportant		16	16
	Total	100	100
b. Right versus Left		(N = 135)	(N = 151)
1. very significant		38	28
2. significant		22	46
3. unimportant		40	26
	Total	100	100
c. Rich versus poor		(N = 136)	(N = 147)
1. very significant		57	22
2. significant		20	63
3. unimportant		23	15
	Total	100	100
d. Ashkenazi versus Oriental groups		(N = 139)	(N = 152)
1. very significant		70	88
2. significant		16	7
3. unimportant		14	5
	Total	100	100
e. All ethnic groups, one versus the other		(N = 139)	(N = 152)
1. very significant		23	79
2. significant		31	20
3. unimportant		46	1
	Total	100	100
χ^2 of (d) vs. (a) =		6.00; $p<0.05$	92; $p<0.005$
(b) =		30.76; $p<0.005$	110.75; $p<0.005$
(c) =		4.89; $p = 0.10$	132; $p<0.005$
(e) =		61.18; $p<0.005$	13.07; $p<0.005$

the former—as depicted by a wide majority of informants, besides one item—is still one of substantial social distance between the edot and non-Orientals. This dimension is superimposed on stratificational and political levels.

Thus, 80 percent of Yemenite informants and 90 percent of Moroccans, consider that there are few Ashkenazi in the lower and lower-middle class, but substantial numbers of them in the highest social strata. Only 30 percent of Yemenites, contrasted with 89 percent of Moroccans, think a large group of their own stocks belongs to the lowest stratum of society, while respectively 44 and 73 percent think so with regard to the lower-middle class; yet about 75 percent of the former agree again with 92 percent of the latter that people of their edot are very few in the highest strata. Thus *both* Yemenite and Moroccan informants do feel that social inequality exists between their respective groups and the Ashkenazi, although the Moroccan image is more polarized. On one item, it must be stressed that even more than a consensus character-izes both samples; almost all Yemenites (97 percent) and Moroccans (91 percent) complain that their representation on the political scene is much inferior to that of Ashkenazi. Again, it should be repeated, that in all these aspects informants reported an identity of views between their own perceptions and those existing among the edot in general. If we accept this stand of the respondents, it means that by no means are the edot unaware of the stratificational and political situations de-scribed by statistics in former chapters.

When looking at *inter-edot* relations, however, it is still impossible to speak of totally different descriptions. Table 8.12 shows, indeed, that the division of Israeli society into various ethnic groups is reported by many informants as at least a "significant social cleavage." This con-viction transpires from other data as well. Thus Table 8.11 reports that the cultural dissimilarities seen among themselves by edot contrast with images of wide similarity *inside* the respective edot.

To be sure, these distances between groups are reflected in images of social interaction. Seventy-two percent of Yemenite informants report that other edot are not prejudiced against their stock, but 65 percent of Moroccans share the opposite view. Further on, a wide majority in both groups (71 percent of Yemenites and 83 percent of Moroccans) think that attitudes of people from other edot toward them are imbued with ethnic labels and but a minority describes it either as toward "Israeli Orientals" (respectively 20 percent and 12 percent) or toward "Israelis without a particular label" (9 percent and 5 percent). If accepting here too, that informants voice the norms of their respective edot, when compared with the data concerning Edot-

Ashkenazi interaction mentioned above, *ethnic labelling among edot is perceived as even sharper*.

Differences between Yemenite and Moroccan informants, however, appear in their reports of the intensity of inter-edot relationships. According to the Yemenite sample, the edah itself is the main factor of social interaction for the people of the group, followed by "all groups without difference" (for instance, half of the Yemenite informants report that the edah is the main factor of neighbors' proximity and 35 percent, "all groups"; respectively 54 percent and 32 percent concerning friendship). For the Moroccan sample, "Orientals-as-a-whole" is the main factor and the edah only second (72 percent of the Moroccan informants report "Orientals" as the main factor of neighbors' proximity and 25 percent the edah; respectively 55 and 43 percent concerning friendship). The paradox here is that as just seen, it is the Moroccan informants' who report the existence of sharper prejudice against their group among the other edot. Thus, though they report narrower social distances between their edah and other edot than do Yemenites, by no means do they acknowledge their edah's disappearing among "Orientals."

In sum, despite the similarity of problems reported—that is, the marginality of edot in the setting—the various groups, according to informants, remain quite acutely aware of their social distinctiveness from each other. Yemenite and Moroccan informants, moreover, are outspoken about status and the political peculiarities of their respective stocks. The stratificational descriptions of the Yemenite and Moroccan edot by informants show that while only 30 percent of the Yemenite respondents think that many of their stock belong to the lowest social strata, 90 percent of Moroccan respondents do so; 44 and 73 percent, respectively see many more of their groups in the lower-middle class; and 53 and 2 percent share the view that a number are middle class. In a general manner, when asked to estimate the socioeconomic achievements of their edot compared to other Oriental groups, Yemenite informants incline to overstate the plight of their stock, while the opposite is true of Moroccan informants.

These perceptions are confirmed by objective findings (see Chapter 6), but contrasting positions appear as regards political participation. Half the Yemenite respondents but merely 11 percent of Moroccan respondents feel the location of their edah in the polity is inferior to

that of other Orientals: 37 and 24 percent respectively see no difference, while 13 percent of Yemenite respondents and 65 percent of
Moroccan respondents are convinced that their respective groups are
stronger in this matter (also confirmed by observation in Chapter 7).

If, again, we accept the divergent trends transpiring in the samples'
opinions as indicative of their edot's attitudes in general, it may be said
that while both edot perceive their lot quite similarly compared with
Ashkenazi, each stresses different self-images. Anyway, the data confirm hypotheses (4) and (5) and support the statement that according
to informants, edot see themselves chiefly as culturally marginal groups,
inferior in status and power and, finally, distinct—nay even quite
isolated—communities.

THE "IN-ITSELF" CONFLICT GROUP

Yet, as suggested by the "basic subjective characteristics," the way
ethnics interpret their actual sociocultural "particularisms" and react to
it should bring out a fundamental contradiction. As groups defining
their "personalities" by reference to a "worthwhile legacy," they
should effectively "recognize themselves" in many behavioral features or models which distinguish them from "outs." On the other
hand, this "faithfulness" to a special culture is not limitless, since
Yemenites and Moroccans, as well as all other groups they are representative of, adhere to the *mizug* perspective and the overall unifying
of the Nation. This is all the more so since edot people are also quite
eager to embrace many aspects of the modern ethos despite the pain
involved in giving up certain parochial value orientations or customs.
This problem, to be sure, is primarily *theirs* and this is why the edah
phenomenon, though basically cultural, does not appear on the public
scene as a major issue. There, ethnicity pertains mainly to material and
practical exigencies and expresses the ethnics' sharp sensitivity to their
condition of inferiority *vis-à-vis* "others," which bluntly contrasts with
the *mizug* perspective and the aspirations attached to it. One's plight,
from this viewpoint, cannot but awaken feelings of alienation as it
represents a fate imposed by "others," contradicting even the latter's
own declared ideals. However, and by the same token—that is, the
ethnics' adherence to the *mizug* perspective—the development of
edot into conflict groups cannot be unrestrained. The very nature of

their expectations—their disappearance as special entities at whatever respect—is bound to an unwillingness to endorse a militant "for-itself"-group outlook which would but institutionalize their particular location in the setting.

It is against the background of these considerations that the research in this concern, was oriented by four major hypotheses. The edot, it was assumed, (1) would appear in the images informants share about them, as clearly expressing positive appreciation of both their cultural personalities and parochial models even if convinced of their irremediable weakening; however, in view of the social and political characteristics which are theirs, and of the nature of their expectations, (2) the ethnics' understanding of their collective plight should be depicted by informants as clearly conflictual. In response to what they perceive as "unfairness," even "injustice," they (3) should be described as demonstrating an alienated minority behavior protecting itself from the "establishment." But as conflict groups bound by beliefs in their future "disappearance" into the "whole," it is expected that (4) informants confirm the lack of eagerness of both Yemenites and Moroccans, in general, to willingly embrace overt patterns of political confrontation.

The significance of these hypotheses resides in their describing the Israeli case of ethnicity as exemplifying the paradoxical situation where entities form compact communities (as shown by Chapter 5), potentially powerful (see Chapter 7), but which do not become "for-themselves" conflict groups despite the antagonisms they perceive in relations with "others."

In brief, and as expected by hypothesis (1), these behavioral models and parochial customs like festivals, religious rituals, speech formulae, styles of cooking, and so on, which make up their cultural particularisms, are interpreted by the people of the edot—according to our informants—as a fairly faithful reflection of the group's "personality." The gradual vanishing of many of these features in Israel is not ignored and a large majority (from 70 to 90 percent, according to items) report at least "some regret" on the part of ethnics in general, at their irreversible weakening. Moreover, on the desirability—in the edot's eyes—of conserving the edot's cultural essentials as a national boon, most informants again, were vigorously affirmative.

On the other hand, the case is different with informants' reporting the ethnics' attitudes toward other components of their sociocultural particularisms. It has been noted that according to respondents, the basic aspiration of edot is to melt notwithstanding, and in tandem with their wish to remain faithful to "legacies." However, informants have also pointed out the discrepancy between these aspirations and images of social, economic, and political realities. In fact it is enough to look at Table 8.12 to validate hypothesis (2): ethnic cleavages are seen—assuredly on behalf of the edot as a whole—as especially salient in Israeli society. This perception measures the extent to which ethnics are described by informants as sharing conflictual images of their collective plight.

In turning now to descriptions of feelings of alienation that were expected by hypothesis (3), findings, it must be said, go much further than was forecast by the researchers. The severest expression of this alienation was reported by the informants in the groups' lack of commitment to normative requirements of the "establishment." To some extent these reports even recall the ethnics' attitudes, prior to their immigration, when they made up quasi-alien enclaves hardly identifying themselves with any civic duty imposed from "outside," an attitude strikingly illustrated in the following speech of a rich Aleppo merchant:

He who steals from a thief is exempt from punishment. . . . If a simple goy [non-Jew] at the market is a petty thief, he who climbs up the steps of bureaucracy is a real criminal; otherwise he could not make it and reach the highest spheres. . . . Governing means that citizens accumulate gold and silver day and night by the sweat of their brow; eventually, the official comes and takes it from them as if this money belonged to him. This is the fate of simple citizens and the more so for Jews whose fat, blood and gold are considered goods without owner. Thus, he who is able to cheat the authorities and tax-collectors does a saintly deed and is blessed in this world as well as the next.[2]

This degree of estrangement, it is true, is not reported in our research. Nevertheless, the disappointments encountered by the edot in Israel as well as the very maintenance of communities may explain that many are unready to cooperate with the establishment at the expense of ethnic solidarity. For example, about 70 percent of both Yemenite and Moroccan informants think that a thief who has acted outside the community, though blamed by it, would not be ostracized nor handed over to the police by his fellow ethnics. Similarly, it is reported that illegal transactions at the expense of the government (such as receiving social security benefits by false reports) are not considered a felony, and for all Yemenite and a 90 percent of Moroccan respondents even desertion from the army would not break the taboo on notifying the authorities. These findings show a level of alienation unperceived by any former work, and its description, which is hardly exhausted by our own data, remains a challenge for researchers.

These findings, if remembering Chapter 4, echo the fears of many an Ashkenazi of the dangers of "levantinization" of society, referring to the level of civility in Israeli society. Considered in the more general context of ethnic communities of North African and Middle Eastern origins, they also constitute an important element in the discussion of democratic prospects in Israel. In order to safeguard her democratic regime in the face of a protracted state of belligerency and difficult economic circumstances, Israel is particularly in need of firm institutionalization of civil norms and a wide consensus of disciplined public behavior.

The overall discussion of this issue, however, requires the detailed examination of many additional factors, such as power relations between social sectors, the structures of the political system, and the history of the country's challenges that are not in the scope of a specific study of ethnicity. Another contribution of this study to such a discussion is its finding that, according to informants, ethnic slogans in any form, originating outside the existing political establishment have little or no appeal for the ethnic community.

Hence, and as predicted by hypothesis (4), despite its strength, the antiestablishment mood expressed in deviancy from given norms of civility has no correlation, in the informants' reports, with support for politicians who try, from time to time, to set up ethnic parties that independently voice the claims of the "underprivileged Oriental." Yemenite informants (73 percent) for instance, report no readiness at all among their stock to sustain a Yemenite political organization, and among the more bitter Moroccans this figure is even higher (90 percent). As seen in Table 8.12 the reason for this is not explained by informants by lack of conflictual perceptions of ethnic cleavages, which supports our own interpretation. In Chapter 4, indeed, it was contended that the denial of overt ethnic politics relates mainly to the edot's self-defining as "temporary groups" and their general belief in future melting; this accounts at the same time for the depth of their disillusionment and their unwillingness to contribute to the institution-alization of pluralism. It is in this context that many among the edot do share the position of Ketsef, a member of Parliament of Persian origin, when he states:

> I am opposed to ethnic lists. . . .I think that the more elections are democratic. . . the larger the representation of all strata in the population. . . . There is no need in Israel for any ethnic party.[3]

CONCLUSIONS

The informants, let us remember, are random samples, representative of the cohorts of mobile Yemenites and Moroccans—not just individ-uals selected arbitrarily. On the basis of the information they yield about their edot, this chapter corroborates the "subjective basic char-acteristics" suggested in Chapter 4, along with their inconsistencies and paradoxes:

(1) The concept of *edah* represents a certain type of ethnic group charac-terized by a primordial identity interpreting a given attribute, the origin, as a meaningful criterion of distinctiveness between "ins" and "outs"; this distinctiveness is formulated in terms of an ascriptive subdivision of a "nation" though it does not exclude—and in fact aspires to—its self-deletion.

(2) Though given to new influences accounting for the present eclecticism of their value orientations, the edot still share many attitudes reflecting a continuity of their historical and cultural personalities, which are viewed by them as legacies worthy of commitment; it is in this sense that edot remain "unique" not only *vis-à-vis* "others" but also *vis-à-vis* each other.

(3) Distinctiveness from "outs" is endowed with practical social meanings in all dimensions of the social endeavor, from culture and social life to status and politics; on the whole, *vis-à-vis* "others," the edot see themselves as marginal entities reduced to a general condition of inferiority, while *vis-à-vis* other edot each group emphasizes a particular profile of its objective sociocultural particularism.

(4) As for the interpretation of their plight, the edot, to be sure, "recognize themselves" in these features which present their endeavor as a contin-uation of the past, while, at the same time, their social, economic, and

political condition arouses among them feelings of alienation which do *not* come out in velleities to crystallize into "for-themselves" groups.

These findings, it must be repeated, are a first attempt at generalizations with regard to the subjective side of Israeli ethnicity on the basis of the comparative study of edot; it is hoped that future studies will test their significance and make available fresh data on this model of ethnic encounter.

A major purpose, however, of this study was to analyze more particularly the impact of social mobility of individual ethnics. It is to this issue that we now turn.

NOTES

1. S. Balas, *Hamaabarah* [The camp] (Tel Aviv: Am Oved, 1964), pp. 159-61.

2. A. Shamosh, "Comment s'Enrichir," *Noam* 2 (1977): 88-89.

3. I. Ketsef, "Ryaun Hahodesh" [Monthly interview], *Bamaaraha* 219 (March 1979): 14-15.

The Impact of Social Mobility

9

INTRODUCTION

The Jewish Israeli case of ethnicity (as seen in all the foregoing) shows a strong correlation between inferior class positions and ethnic groups; this is crucial in the way ethnicity appears on the public stage. At the same time, however, many ethnics do achieve social mobility. Thus, more than in many other instances of ethnic encounter, a major question here is the impact of mobility on the encounter as a whole.

Some sociologists, confronted by such cases, define the ethnic entity as a "tangential group," meaning that from the stratificational viewpoint[1] the angle of social barriers changes from a horizontal to a tangential position. In other words, in addition to a numerous lower-class stratum, the ethnic group gradually comprises no few members holding middle- and higher-class positions. On the other hand, and as emphasized by Gordon,[2] a structural assimilation of ethnics among "outs," (i.e. a more and more undifferentiated participation in social positions), together with acculturation, (i.e. their gradual acceptance of the dominant culture), must entail a deletion of group boundaries. When applied to a minority of successful and more acculturated persons from a stock otherwise showing evidence of lower positions and cultural aloofness from the rest of the setting, Gordon's statement in fact allows added alternates and moves the theory of tangentiality to a new possibility: to the extent that only a given part of the group accedes to social mobility and tends to assimilate with "outs," or at least to form a new entity, the ethnic group does *not* necessarily disappear or become a tangential entity; more likely, by the removal of its active elements and their closeness to "outs," it is finally reduced to what we have called in Chapter 3 a "truncated ethnoclass."

To illustrate the several possibilities, it is useful to recall Horowitz's "processes of ethnic fusion and fission."[3] "A" represents the ethnic group; "A_1" the stock in general; "A_2" the mobiles; and "B" the "outs." One then obtains, according to the case:

1. Mobiles remain bound to their stock, which becomes a tangential group:
   $$A + B \rightarrow (A_1 + A_2) + B$$

2. Mobiles distinguish themselves from their stock but do not yet assimilate:
   $$A + B \rightarrow A_1 + A_2 + B$$
3. Mobiles assimilate to "outs" but the rest of the group preserves its existence:
   $$A + B \rightarrow A_1 + (A_2 + B) \rightarrow A_1 + B$$

At all events, the appearance of a subgroup, differing from the rest of the ethnic stock by its degree of cultural distance from the dominant culture and its status features, formulates anew the ethnics' sociocultural particularism in the setting, and is thus a determinant element of their overall objective engagement in social spheres.

The question which now arises is: What type of situation may be expected in what circumstances? Many factors of a conjunctural order might well be relevant here; the size of the group and of the cohorts of mobiles, the ethnic diversity of the setting, external political threats, or economic developments in the country are all elements which by influencing, in one way or other, the ethnic's plight generally, also determine the shaping of paths of mobility and of their issues. Due to their versatile character, however, these factors can hardly be conceptualized systematically; beyond them are two further elements which, according to our theoretical approach, should receive special attention. The first is the attitude of "outs" toward ethnics who manage to "make it" and move socially closer to them. In a competitive setting, achievements of ethnics, if substantial, cannot but endanger the status of given categories of "outs" and awaken among them a self-protective spirit expressed in tendencies of *rejection* at least at the level of social acceptance. The overtness and severity of such a rejection, however, depend on its legitimacy in the eyes of the dominant culture—in fact, the culture of the "outs" or at least some category of "outs"—and its general perspective on the encounter as a whole. Whether it insists on a "melting pot" future or on the contrary, on some "separate developent," should influence the extent to which it is permissive of these "outs'" discriminatory practices and self-closure toward people entitled by their achievements to status and recognition. This relative "openness" or "closure" of "outs" to mobile ethnics—as determined by the dominant culture—is a crucial factor, of course, as for the very objective possibilities available to them to integrate new strata and detach themselves from their ethnic community.

On the other hand, one may also assume that such mobile elements are also influenced by the expectations toward them on the side of their stock of origin, as they still represent, in some way at least, its cultural "personality." At this viewpoint, what is to be especially emphasized is that any ethnic group, because of its very self-defining as such, tends to require from its members, including the mobile ones, commitment to itself. Yet, according to its own basic view of the ethnic encounter—whether or not it aspires to full integration—it is also more or less confined when discouraging *assimilatory tendencies vis-à-vis* "outs" among those mobiles who enjoy more opportunities of "escaping" from the group, insofar as "allowed" by the dominant culture.

In sum, against the twofold background of an ethnoclass or ethnoclasses "monopolizing" social inferiority and of cohorts of ethnics achieving mobility individually, the interaction between the dominant culture's and the group's respective perspectives on the encounter widely accounts for the social fate of mobile ethnics. By dichotomizing each factor, and keeping conjunctural circumstances outside theoretical considerations, we can develop different profiles (Figure 9.1), which refer to processes of fusion or fission of the ethnic stock as affected by social mobility.

The first case is when the dominant culture generally encourages melting of ethnics among "outs," while the ethnics themselves remain shy of this perspective. Here, mobiles are by no means unambiguously anxious to seize every chance offered to detach themselves. More than a few, of course, may succumb to temptation, but through these mobile individuals who remain bound to the group, the group as a whole becomes a "tangential" entity now comprising heterogenous social positions and different degrees of acculturation. This "tangentialization" should be even more conspicuous if the negative orienta-

Figure 9.1 Social Mobility and the Structures of Ethnics Groups Heavily Concentrated in Lower Class

Attitudes of "outs" toward mobile ethnics

	Social openness — dominant culture encourages melting	Social rejection — dominant culture justifies some separateness
ATTITUDES Reticence toward total assimilation	**- 1 -** Ethnic group : tangential entity Mobiles : some assimilate and others remain identified with the group $A + B \longrightarrow (A_1 + \text{many } A_2) + B$	**- 2 -** Ethnic group : tangential entity Mobiles : many remain a part of the group $A + B \longrightarrow (A_1 + A_2) + B$
OF		
ETHNICS Endorsement of melting perspective	**- 4 -** Ethnic group : truncated ethnoclass Mobiles : assimilate among "Outs" $A + B \longrightarrow A_1 + B$	**- 3 -** Ethnic group : between ethnoclass and tangential group Mobiles : either part of the group or inbetween entity $A + B \longrightarrow A_1 + A_2 + B$ or $(A_1 + A_2) + B$

tion of ethnics toward complete assimilation joins a tendency, legitimized in the dominant culture, of social rejection by "outs."

When, however, the ethnics' aspiration to total melting contradicts this rejection, the mobiles who are "allowed" by their stock the wish to be accepted confront a refusal by "outs", mobile elements may either maintain themselves as a new in-between group of marginal men or go back to their community of origin. In the latter case, they contribute, though involuntarily, to the "tangentialization" of the group. The final case is that of mutual endorsement of a melting perspective. The greater this endorsement by both the group and the dominant culture, the greater the authorization of assimilation away from their stock and the weaker the obstacles to social acceptance by the "outs." Here, since much of the group remains lower class and more remote from the dominant culture, loss of contact between mobiles and the bulk of their stock signifies the latter's becoming a "truncated ethnoclass." This "disappearance" of higher-status, more acculturated elements, moreover, deprives the group of a natural reservoir of leadership and prolongs the juxtaposition of ethnicity and class.

In a general manner, whether or not mobile elements remain an integral part of their ethnic group, constitutes an objective reality. However, underlying this reality there is the subjective fact. As emphasized by Glaser and Moynihan,

Individual choice, not law or rigid custom, determines the degree to which any person participates, if at all, in the life of an ethnic group, and assimilation and acculturation proceed at a rate determined in large measure by individuals.[4]

Hence the impact of social mobility of individuals on the development of an ethnic group otherwise widely participating in lower-class positions is to be primarily sought in the *contents of their own ethnic awareness of kind* and through them, in the extent to which *mobiles differentiate themselves from their communities of origin as well as from "outs."* Thus, the four questions raised by the concept of awareness of kind, when referring to such a subgroup within a larger entity, ought be termed as follows: (1) How far do mobiles perceive themselves as close to what they understand as the cultural personality of their stock? (2) How much do they endorse concepts of primordial identity and group boundaries widespread among their community of origin? (3) What are the social and practical meanings they confer on ethnic distinctiveness regarding themselves comparatively to those they associate with their group as a whole? (4) To what extent do they interpret their plight in society as bound to their group? and, a parallel question: How do they define their relation with "outs?"

Insofar as mobile ethnics see themselves (1) remote from ethnic culture, (2) define their ethnic identity in more flexible terms than their group in general, (3) are less concerned than their group by meanings of ethnicity, and (4) are detached from the collective plight of their stock, they respond more readily to the assimilatory model, the objective consequence being their leaving the ethnic group a "truncated" ethnoclass. On the contrary, the more mobiles share opposite features, the more they contribute to and reflect the "tangentialization" of their group.

If focusing now on the cases of mobile ethnics under study and remembering Chapter 4, *it is the assimilationist type of situation* (see Case 4, Figure 9.1) *which is the most likely here*, where melting is expected by ethnics and the dominant culture alike. For an edah, joining the "others" is a fulfillment of the ideal of *mizug*, which must have an impact on the mobiles' response to opportunities available for assimilation. These opportunities are the more numerous as no social barrier can legitimately be set up once mobile ethnics achieve a status entitling them to acceptance by the nonethnic middle and upper classes. The truth of this contention could be validated by our research, as our samples of Yemenites and Moroccans were random samples representative of mobile elements among their edot.

The general hypotheses of this part of the project were derived from both the different aspects of ethnic awareness of kind as defined with respect to the issue of social mobility, and the particular Israeli context. Hence, the first three hypotheses, which deal with respondents' attitude to their group, take into consideration the fact that most mobile ethnics in Israel are the first generation mobile offspring of their stock. Accordingly:

1. Mobile ethnics emphasize affinity with many aspects of what they see as the *ethnic cultural personality*, but in numerous other respects—due to the endeavor itself of mobility consonant with rules that pertain to the dominant culture—they perceive themselves as closer to this dominant culture. As a corollary by expressing the divorce of given cultural atti-

tudes from other aspects of social life, mobiles should be conscious of being a centrifugal element in their edot.

2. Mobile ethnics identify with the concepts of *primordial identity* as they seem generally endorsed by their stock. On the other hand, the effect of mobility is that they consider themselves as interpreting these concepts in more flexible terms, leaving greater leeway for "escape" from ethnicity.

3. They consciously minimize the *practical meanings* of ethnic distinctiveness for themselves in comparison to what they perceive as the norm for their stocks.

If confirmed, these hypotheses signify that mobile ethnics do *not* see themselves an effective part of their groups. These hypotheses also represent a "minimalist" answer to the first question implied by the fourth component of mobiles' ethnic awareness of kind, namely, to what extent do they interpret their individual destiny as bound to their groups in general.

As for the second question implied by this component, that is, the nature of their relation to "outs," one must here too, differentiate between "Orientals-as-a-whole" and "others." In view of the social characteristics attached to the Oriental category, a whole of distinct low-class ethnic groups, it is expected that:

4. Mobile ethnics see themselves detached from "Orientals-as-a-whole" at least as much as they see their edot in general, detached from this concept as regards self-perceived identity, cultural personality, and practical social endeavors.

On the other hand, since it is the "others," that is, the nonethnic but predominantly Ashkenazi middle and upper class, who are identified with the dominant culture,

5. It is with this category that mobile ethnics feel the greatest affinity on all counts specified by hypothesis (4).

The hypotheses now under study are comparative in two distinct ways. While the respondents were asked earlier to provide data on their edot in general, they were questioned at this stage on their attitudes toward many of the same issues. This made it possible to compare self-images of mobiles and what they reported about their edot. On the other hand, as two samples of different groups were involved, differences between them could also be analyzed.

Regarding the first point, our data from this angle indicate now, not the comparative strength of given attitudes among groups and mobiles, but *the extent to which the latter see themselves different from the images they share of their edot.* This question becomes the issue of major interest when investigating the subjective impact of social mobility.

As for the second point, it derives its interests from our formulation of the hypotheses. Implicit in these hypotheses was the expectation of *an overall tendency of convergence among the two groups of mobiles, notwithstanding*—as assumed by the fourth hypothesis—*a common remoteness from the "Orientals-as-a-whole" category.*

CULTURAL FEATURES OF MOBILES

If we follow the mobiles' value orientations in areas already analyzed with regard to their groups, one easily concludes that they see themselves, as exhibiting, like their stocks in general, an amalgam of traditional and modern features, though the latter are more emphasized in their own self-images than in those they report of their edot.

With respect to *religion, traditions, and parochial customs,* many Yemenite respondents, it is true, consider themselves more religious than their stock in general (no Yemenite defined himself as "secular" but no less than 26 percent referred to their stock as such). The Moroccans, on the contrary, view themselves as much less religious than their edah (23 percent declared they were "secular" and only 1 percent placed the Moroccan community in this category). Both groups however, affirm themselves less enthusiastic than their stocks about parochial customs and symbols such as pilgrimages to tombs of saints (while 84 percent of Yemenites and 68 percent of Moroccans think these customs are favored by their stocks, only 13 and 58 percent respectively do so personally), or accord the rabbi a role of community leader (77 and 100 percent respectively do not consult him on nonreligious matters). Moreover, while all Yemenites and half the Moroccans feel that religious education is important in their edot, only two-thirds of the former and about one-third of the latter share the same attitude personally. Thus, as a whole, Yemenite respondents are more tradition-oriented than Moroccans, but both groups see themselves less so than their own stocks. Even if, as is the case of mobile Yemenites, religion may gain in importance, it is seen as less bound to parochialism.

As for the *concept of family*, the same trend is evident: though many Yemenites and Moroccans declare that they maintain strong ties with relatives (respectively 45 and 21 percent), they feel less "familial" than their edot (60 percent of Yemenites and half of Moroccans reported "strong ties with relatives" as a major value among their groups). Moreover, although several questions related to authority in parent-child relationships have not shown any significant self-differentiation, attitudes toward the value of formal academic education—and mainly the schooling of girls—do contrast with those reported of the edot (see Table 9.1). The main difference that emerges here between Yemenite and Moroccan respondents concerns the importance of a "well-settled family" as a goal. Yemenites, seemingly because of their stronger religious outlook, insist on this even more than in their images of their stock (83 percent see it this way though only 64 percent think it true for people of their edah); Moroccans, by contrast, are less family-oriented than they perceive their group to be (14 percent only view it of major importance for themselves but 70 percent think it applies to their edah at large).

In sum one may say that families of both groups are depicted as more modern than in the reports about the respective stocks, since ties with relatives are seen as looser, the education of children as more appreciated, and girls as enjoying a more equal status with their brothers. In all these aspects there is a convergence between mobile Yemenites and Moroccans.

Regarding *criteria of social status*, the mobiles' attitudes were studied from two angles: factors of individual success in social life and one's motives of action in society. From the first angle, no substantial differences appear between distributions of personal attitudes and of images of the edot concerning the importance of achieved attributes (talent, "brains," education, or money). The mobiles emphasize only slightly more some attitudes inherent in the modern ethos which, in fact, they also see as widespread among the edot. More self-differentiation emerges (especially among Yemenites) regarding "uncontrollable" factors: "luck," for instance, is "important" in the edah's eyes according to 80 percent of the Yemenite sample but is rated as such by only

Table 9.1 Attitudes toward the Education of Boys and Girls (%)

		Yemenites		Moroccans	
		In the eyes of the respondents	As perceived by the respondents regarding the edah	In the eyes of the respondents	As perceived by the resondents regarding the edah
(a) the attitude towards academic education of boys:		(N = 137)		(N = 150)	
1. very important		77	58	36	14
2. important		15	22	26	38
3. some importance		8	20	38	48
	Total	100	100	100	100
	$\chi^2 =$	12.64; p < 0.005		33.56; p < 0.005	
(b) the attitude towards academic education of girls:		(N = 135)		(N = 148)	
1. very important		75	.4	26	14
2. important		17	7	29	28
3. some importance		8	89	45	58
	Total	100	100	100	100
	$\chi^2 =$	182.75; p < 0.005		17.25; p < 0.005	

63 percent of the subjects. The respective figures for Moroccans are 84 and 72 percent. "Fate" receives among Yemenites 77 percent on the first count but only 42 percent on the second, while the respective data for Moroccans are 58 and 44 percent.

As for motivations to action, the mobiles tend to differentiate themselves mainly with regard to two issues: the desirability of modern education for children and of a well-established economic position. On the first issue they are more positive than the images of their stocks (44 percent of Yemenite respondents think modern education for children is a very strong motive of action in their edah, but 72 percent consider it so for themselves; the respective figures for Moroccans are 40 and 50 percent). On the second issue, the mobiles emphasize a preoccupation for financial success that is less exclusive (60 percent of the Yemenite sample and 97 percent of the Moroccan think it is a primordial aim within their edot, but only 48 and 55 percent, respectively, describe themselves this way). Thus mobiles converge again toward each other and, as may be surmised, see themselves as more concerned by social promotion based on educational achievement than on economic success as such.

Regarding *the polity*, one obtains again a similar picture. In several respects, mobiles are closer to the images they perceive in their edot: government should "serve the citizens" but also be strong and deeply involved in all social matters of importance. On the other hand, awareness of and interest in political issues on the part of respondents remain weak. Yet this syndrome is altered in the subjects' personal views by a firmer emphasis on the representative function of the polity: 96 percent of Yemenites and 60 percent of Moroccans consider this attribute essential, but only 54 and 35 percent respectively think it is endorsed as such by their edot.

To conclude the cultural standpoints analyzed in the above, let us add that differences as such between mobiles and their stock are deliberately emphasized by the subjects on many questions. Confirming their general estimate that legacies are less sustained by people of a higher educational level, namely themselves (see Table 8.4 in Chapter 8), a majority of 60 percent among both samples is convinced that at least some substantial cultural difference exists between them and their edot. These data, however, already concern the mobiles' attitudes toward the ethnic community.

ATTITUDES TOWARD THE ETHNIC COMMUNITY

This dimension, the fifth cultural parameter of social endeavor and already considered with regard to the edot's attitudes in Chapter 8, takes on a most crucial significance in the context of this part of our research. More specifically, the centrifugal role of mobiles *vis-à-vis* their edot also anticipated by our first hypothesis was viewed here under four main heads: (1) feelings of special ethnic obligations, (2) preferences for social proximity, (3) attitudes toward abandonment of the community, (4) and images of everyday intercourse between mobiles and their edot.

From all these standpoints, findings are here too, consonant with the hypothesis. Only 25 percent of the Yemenite subjects and 34 percent of the Moroccans do feel, for instance, a special obligation toward their edot, compared respectively with 75 and 66 percent who reject any idea of a particular "duty" in this regard. This is confirmed by the preferences of subjects concerning all types of social closeness, such as neighborhood, friendship, or friends of their children: in each case "all groups without distinction" is by far the most popular category. This feeling is stressed far more than "one's own edah," and again, mobiles contrast here with what they report of their groups (see Table 9.2).

Table 9.2 Preferences for Social Interaction (%)

	Yemenites		Moroccans	
	In the eyes of the respondents	The respondents' perceptions of the edah's preferences	In the eyes of the respondents	The respondents' perceptions of the edah's preferences
(a) as neighbors				
1. Ashkenazi	15	7	25	47
2. One's own edah	22	52	9	12
3. Orientals in general	–	1	8	5
4. All groups without distinction	63	40	58	36
Total	100	100	100	100
χ^2 =	27.94; p < 0.005		18.9; p < 0.005	
(b) as friends				
1. Ashkenazi	9	7	9	17
2. One's own edah	15	46	23	34
3. Orientals in general	–	1	11	9
4. All groups without distinction	76	46	57	40
Total	100	100	100	100
χ^2 =	33.31; p < 0.005		31.81; p < 0.005	
(c) as friends for one's children				
1. Ashkenazi	15	13	9	23
2. One's own edah	3	24	3	4
3. Orientals in general	1	4	4	8
4. All groups without distinction	81	59	84	65
Total	100	100	100	100
χ^2 =	31.25; p < 0.005		14.58; p < 0.005	

Table 9.2 presents three items, out of a whole range, that are consistently representative of respondents' social preferences. Interestingly enough, the main difference between Yemenites and Moroccans here is their respective views of Ashkenazi compared to those they reported about their edot: while mobile Yemenites do not prefer Ashkenazi much more than does their edah in their eyes, Moroccans favor them far less. This phenomenon, seemingly, can be explained by the mobile Moroccans' velleity to show their greater sensitivity to the Ashkenazi's prejudices toward their stock. On the other hand, they are by no means much less prone than Yemenites to insist on their own preference—comparatively to the edah—of "all groups without distinction." Moroccans, it is true, depict the people of their edah as much less attracted by each other than do the Yemenite respondents; hence, their greater own neglect of their stock, is less salient comparatively to their fellow ethnics' attitudes, as they see them, than in the Yemenite sample. Yet, it remains that a similar trend appears in all three respects in Table 9.2. Furthermore, both Yemenites and Moroccans (the latter far more so) point out that people of their edot leave them once they can economically do so: only 27 percent of Yemenites and 5 percent of Moroccans consider that such people stay in the community; 20 and 9 percent respectively that they move to places relatively close to it; 53 and 86 percent emphasize their moving completely away.

These attitudes, to be sure, are not gainsaid in any way by the images of practical behavior of respondents and of the nature of their actual social links with the edot: only 35 percent of Yemenites and 28 percent of Moroccan testify that their main friends belong to their respective edot. Another instance: 60 percent of Yemenites and 52 percent of Moroccans report that their children's best friends are either Ashkenazi or "children from all groups without distinction," while just 34 and 8 percent respectively acknowledge that such friends belong to their edah. These findings are not at the level of the aspirations given above, but they confirm the mobiles' image of loosening links with their stocks. Let us add here that as far as North Africans are concerned, Doris Bensimon-Donath provides supporting evidence. She found[5] that among youth, nonmobile elements—the blue-collar workers—have fewer friends among Europeans than do students, and two-thirds have friends only among people of their own edah or of other Oriental origin. For high school and university students, this figure drops to about one-third.

In the same vein, Table 9.3 shows that regarding mobiles, strong ties with people of one's edah are viewed only in connection with relatives, and (though to a much lesser extent) friends, among Yemenites. In wider respects, ethnicity is seen as of almost no social meaning.

Table 9.3 Ties with People of the Edah at Various Levels of Social Life (%)

		Yemenites (N = 136)	Moroccans (N = 149)
(a) relations with relatives from the edah			
1. strong and continuous		63	29
2. quite continuous		10	37
3. weak		27	34
	Total	100	100
(b) friendship relations with people of the edah			
1. strong and continuous		45	13
2. quite continuous		19	44
3. weak		36	43
	Total	100	100
(c) importance of people of the edah in one's social life, in general			
1. strong and continuous		13	17
2. quite continuous		25	30
3. weak		62	53
	Total	100	100
(d) importance of people of the edah in one's occupational life			
1. strong and continuous		17	12
2. quite continuous		9	20
3. weak		74	68
	Total	100	100

χ^2 of (a) vs. (b) = 6.23;p<0.05 11.75;p<0.005
(c) = 72.10;p<0.005 11.78;p<0.005
(d) = 66.13;p<0.005 34.04;p<0.005

Not surprisingly, both groups of mobiles feel but to a limited extent involved in community activities and organizations: 63 of Yemenites and 81 percent of Moroccans stated that they do not belong to an ethnic synagogue; 82 and 90 percent respectively that they have no ties with local charity groups; and 85 percent of both samples report that they never—or almost never—participate in meetings held by national organizations of their edot.

These data, however, should not mislead us on the mobiles' feelings regarding the lot of their edot in society: a large majority do resent unfairness in this matter and look forward to substantial change in the ethnics' general situation. On the other hand, it is quite evident that the flag of ethnic conflict will not be raised by their own actions: 75 percent of Yemenite respondents and 86 percent of Moroccan do not endorse ethnic political organizations (62 percent of the former and 71 percent of the latter even show a hostile view of such attempts), while 85 percent of Yemenites and 91 percent of Moroccans oppose the setting up of ethnic parties (with 73 and 71 percent being sharply negative). More positive feelings among respondents are evident toward community groups that help strengthen the edot's status in society (only 12 percent of Yemenites and 28 percent of Moroccans are convinced that they make no contribution), though mobiles themselves show little readiness to join these either.

In conclusion to the preceding sections, which focused on the mobiles' expressing and interpreting ethnic "personalities," it may be said that our relevant hypothesis was confirmed. The issues under study concerned value and cultural orientations toward five major parameters of the social endeavor, namely religion and traditions, family, criteria of status and motives of action, the polity, and the community.

Regarding the first four parameters, and in accordance with our hypothesis, it appears that a similar cultural eclecticism transpires from the mobiles' own orientations as when reporting about their edot. Yet, those cultural features contributed by the dominant culture are more insisted upon in the respondents' self-images. Moreover, the mobiles are fully conscious of a cultural gap between themselves and their edot and, on the whole, of their gradual detachment from parochial legacies. When considering the fifth parameter, we see how clear is the mobiles' consciousness of being, *vis-à-vis* their edot, a centrifugal element for which ethnicity is less and less associated with involvement in, or commitment to, the community.

In all these respects, Yemenite and Moroccan mobiles express a convergence toward each other: not only do they view themselves as representing a change, but this change, it has been shown, takes the same direction for both, that is, a greater closeness to the dominant culture and a stepping out from their edot. It is in this context that the question rises as to their very definition of ethnic identity and boundaries.

ETHNIC IDENTITY AND BOUNDARIES

Ethnic identity, it must be said, is graded (see Table 8.2) by respondents quite similarly to the pictures they draw, in this regard, of their edot. Moreover, as shown by Table 9.4, substantial differences with respect to the attachment to ethnic identity (as well as to Jewishness, Israeliness or the Oriental label) appear only among the Moroccans, who describe their stock as more "proud of" ethnic identity than they are themselves (this is also the case for "Israeliness" and the "Oriental label" but goes the other way around with respect to "Jewishness"). When looking at Table 9.5, however, it appears that respondents of *both* groups tend to define belongingness to the edah in terms more open to possibilities of "escaping" than—in their eyes—is characteristic of their stock in general. For all kinds of offspring of mixed marriages, respondents stress the category "Israeli Jew without label" more than they do as informants, while, in a related way, they also insist on their own underrating the perpetuation of the particular ethnic identity (with the exception of Moroccans for item b).

Thus, in a general manner and as expected by hypothesis (2), though mobiles still identify themselves with ethnic labels in quite the same way as they perceive it among people of their stocks, this identity, in their own eyes, is more "erasable." In other words, group boundaries are viewed by them as more flexible and open. Again, regarding this issue too, a convergence appears between the two groups of mobiles.

When considering this "reassessment" of ethnic identities against the background of the findings reported earlier, which show the mobiles on their "way out" from the edot, it emerges that they also share, quite clearly, an awareness of distinctiveness from the latter. At this viewpoint, let us remember the various aspects of self-perceived ethnic distinctiveness from "outs" discussed in Chapter 8, namely images of cultural and social aloofness and of status and power distances. When turning these same questions to the mobiles' views of their relation with their own stocks, not every item, of course, is relevant and makes sense. The problem of political power, for in-

Table 9.4 The Various Identities as Sources of Pride among Mobile Ethnics (%)

	Yemenites		Moroccans	
	as perceived by the respondents regarding themselves	as perceived regarding the edah in general	as perceived by the respondents regarding themselves	as perceived regarding the edah in general
(a) As Jews				
1. small source of pride	12	11	14	57
2. important source of pride	11	10	60	36
3. very important source of pride	77	79	26	7
Total	100	100	100	100
χ^2 =	0.20; p>0.10		66.24; p<0.005	
(b) As Israelis				
1. small source of pride	13	14	18	21
2. important source of pride	23	32	63	47
3. very important source of pride	64	54	19	32
Total	100	100	100	100
χ^2 =	3.41; p>0.10		9.29; p<0.01	
(c) As "Orientals"				
1. small source of pride	71	69	98	70
2. important source of pride	20	20	2	24
3. very important source of pride	9	11	–	6
Total	100	100	100	100
χ^2 =	0.36; p>0.10		45.17; p<0.005	
(d) As "Yemenites" or "Moroccans"				
1. small source of pride	32	22	73	59
2. important source of pride	33	33	25	31
3. very important source of pride	35	45	2	10
Total	100	100	100	100
χ^2 =	5.02; p>0.05		12.26; p<0.005	

stance, is meaningless when we address individuals; another issue which here is obviously deprived of any significance is that of ethnic prejudices. As for the remaining items, our earlier discussion of two of

Table 9.5 The Ethnic Identity of Offspring of Mixed Marriages in the Edah and in the Eyes of Respondents (%)

	Yemenites		Moroccans	
	In the eyes of respondents	description of the edah	In the eyes of respondents	description of the edah
(a) The father is Ashkenazi, the mother from the edah	(N = 139)		(N = 152)	
Identity of offspring:				
1. edah	14	22	14	13
2. Ashkenazi	14	11	12	17
3. Oriental	4	31	1	6
4. Israeli Jew without label	68	36	73	64
Total	100	100	100	100
χ^2 =	45.26; p < 0.005		24.54; p < 0.005	
(b) The mother is Ashkenazi, the father from the edah	(N = 139)		(N = 152)	
Identity of offspring:				
1. edah	27	37	31	29
2. Ashkenazi	4	10	2	10
3. Oriental	4	3	2	1
4. Israeli Jew without label	65	50	65	60
Total	100	100	100	100
χ^2 =	8.32; p < 0.05		10.42; p < 0.01	
(c) The father is from other Oriental group, the mother from the edah	(N = 135)		(N = 151)	
Identity of offspring:				
1. edah	13	45	10	17
2. the father's edah	12	36	–	3
3. Oriental	22	15	28	22
4. Israeli Jew without label	53	4	62	58
Total	100	100	100	100
χ^2 =	101.88; p < 0.005		8.24; p < 0.05	
(d) The mother is from other Oriental group, the father from the edah	(N = 137)		(N = 152)	
Identity of offspring:				
1. edah	32	43	14	34
2. the mother's edah	3	5	1	2
3. Oriental	13	20	23	9
4. Israeli Jew without label	52	32	62	55
Total	100	100	100	100
χ^2 =	11.14; p < 0.025		24.96; p < 0.005	

them is also relevant in the present context. Thus it was shown earlier that value orientations expressed by the mobiles represent a cultural self-differentiation from the edot. Similarly, later discussion was quite indicative as concerns the aloofness mobiles perceive, from the same viewpoint, regarding direct social intercourse.

Finally, as far as status distances are concerned, let us add that it is in this respect that the widest gap appears between the mobiles' self-definitions and those they associate with their edot: no Yemenite or Moroccan respondent considers himself a member of the lower class; only a small minority (respectively 8 and 9 percent) define themselves as "lower-middle class"; more than half (56 and 62 percent) put themselves in the middle class; and about one-third (36 and 29 percent) on an even higher level. These self-definitions, on the whole, bluntly contrast with their perceptions of the general lot of their groups (see Chapter 8). In fact, most respondents—and again convergently— were quite eager to underline their socioeconomic closeness to the "others."

These findings confirm hypothesis (3) by showing how firmly mobiles minimize the practical meanings of ethnic distinctiveness as regards themselves. Hence, these findings cannot but provoke the question heading the following section.

THE MOBILES, WHERE TO?

Looking now at the mobiles' perceptions of distinctiveness from other components of the setting, let us immediately stress that despite the numerous lines of convergence demonstrated above, Yemenite and Moroccan samples alike do not feel more attracted by the "Orientals-as-a-whole" category than do their edot in general, according to them. Table 9.4 shows that a wide majority (71 percent of Yemenites and 98 percent of Moroccans) do not consider being an Oriental an important source of pride. Moreover, while for Yemenites no significant difference appears here between their own images and those they share about their edah, for the Moroccans reluctance as regards this label is even significantly stronger in personal attitudes than in images of the group. Table 9.5 moreover, testifies that both groups do not attach much importance to this category when defining the ethnic identity of offspring of mixed marriages. When the non-edah spouse is from another Oriental group, it must be said, one may see from (c) and (d) in Table 9.5 that from 13 to 28 percent of the samples define offspring as "Oriental." Moreover, in one case for Yemenites (though not significantly) and in both cases for Moroccans (significantly), these percentages are higher than when they report their edot's images. The Moroccan data contradict hypothesis (4); however, it remains that in both (c) and (d), from 79 to 87 percent of the subjects have chosen different labels, which as a whole confirmed our expectations.

To be sure, the existence of a distance between mobiles and "Orientals-as-a-whole" is specified by respondents with regard to every one of its various aspects. From the status viewpoint, "Edot Mizrah" is depicted as referring mainly to people of lower-class positions, while (as just mentioned) they define themselves in quite different terms. Culturally, they do not confuse their respective edot with other ethnic groups and a fortiori themselves with "Orientals-as-a-whole." Regarding social intercourse, it is true, an image exists according to which this entity does play a role in respondents' social life, mainly among Moroccans (for 5 percent of Yemenites and 38 percent of the latter, for instance, best friends are reported as recruited among people of Oriental edot in general, and for 3 and 40 percent respectively this is also the case of one's children); but from the angle of expectations (Table 9.2), "Edot Mizrah" is by far the most neglected category in one's preferred social contacts. Moreover, it appears quite convincingly—and congruent with the fourth hypothesis—that mobiles who loosen ties with their stock do not move closer to a new ethnic label, nor are they especially attracted by people of "neighboring" edot.

As a matter of course, the fact that "Orientals-as-a-whole" is not a referent for mobiles only underlines their strong assimilatory attitude toward "others." As a rule, distinctiveness in this latter respect is most often underrated, and among other findings, Table 9.5 shows their stronger tendency to define offspring of mixed marriages as "Israeli Jews without label"—even when both parents are from different Oriental edot.

Though in Table 9.5, differences between respondents' personal feelings and their images of the edot are not always substantial, they go the same way regarding all patterns envisaged. Moreover, and as already discussed, mobiles see themselves from the status viewpoint as belonging to strata predominantly Ashkenazi; culturally, they consciously express orientations on many issues closer to the dominant stock than those they perceive in their edah in general; regarding social intercourse, "Ashkenazi" and "all groups without distinction" are reported by them as their main factors of proximity in most social contacts. Let us add here that only a minority (14 percent of Yemenites and 19 percent of Moroccans) complains about some personal experience of prejudice on the part of Ashkenazi.

In this context, it is no wonder that a low degree of readiness to support ethnic politics and conflict was found among mobiles of both edot, as their chief aspiration is but to deepen and increase their social interaction with "all groups without distinction" (see Table 9.2). Thus, when speaking about mobile ethnics and their evolving in society, it becomes—in accordance with our fifth hypothesis—quite inappropriate to use the term "others" at all. Despite numerous cultural features that still recall their origins and faithfulness to the ethnic label, these mobiles primarily aspire to, and do, in fact, intermingle with the nonethnic Israeli middle class. In conclusion, let us quote Deshen's description of a particular group of mobile ethnics which corroborates the foregoing:

The *yeshivot*, mostly founded by European scholars, foster the European variants of Jewish scholarship and religiosity.... In fact there is comparatively little demand among Oriental youth for advanced Talmudic education. However, a fair number of these attend the more recently established *yeshivot*.... *These students have become absorbed in the Yiddish language and even switch their particular prayer-ritual to the European style. Hence they emerge, in fact, from their studies more or less acculturated to European tradition.*[6]

CONCLUSIONS

To be sure, some difference separates the Yemenite and Moroccan samples regarding issues analyzed above. The major trend shows that Yemenites appear as closer to given value orientations widespread among their edot. This difference may be accounted for by the more solid *a priori* crystallization of the Yemenite stock. Moreover, Yemenites, at the same time, share stronger images of mingling with "others." This, seemingly, is due to their longer residence in Israel.

Yet, on the whole, the twofold comparison between the images of the edot and the samples' own attitudes, and between the samples themselves, clearly indicates a general and convergent trend of assimilation with "others" among both Yemenite and Moroccan mobiles that "skips over" the "Orientals-as-a-whole" label. In this context differences between samples simply represent different rhythms of the same process of de-ethnicization, which excludes the prospects of a new ethnic entity.

These findings, as discussed in the introduction of this chapter, can be related to the combined impact of the melting perspective shared by the dominant culture and ethnic groups. The first hinders the setting up of any overt obstacles to social acceptance by "others" of mobile ethnics, and the second is hardly able to discourage the latter from exploiting opportunities to integrate into new groups. In other words, in the same measure as mobile ethnics of different edot do not create a new common ethnic entity, neither do they crystallize ethnically loyal middle-class groups according to specific origins. In fact, let us repeat, mobile ethnics in Israel tend to assimilate among "others," while, despite their mobile cohorts, most ethnics perpetuate their groups in marginal communities "monopolizing" social inferiority. For these communities, the "disappearance" of active elements means, objectively, their maintenance as "truncated ethnoclasses."

It is at this point that one touches upon the significance of the data reported in the two latter chapters. By introducing the subjective side of ethnicity, this research completes—and in many respects accounts for—the objective characteristics described in Part II and, finally, permits us to consider the contribution of the ethnic encounter as a whole to the shaping of a new society *comprising* the ethnics.

NOTES

1. See G. E. Hendershot, "Ethnic Stratification," in *Racial Tensions and National Identity*, ed. E. Q. Campbell (Nashville: Vanderbilt University Press, 1972), pp. 57-61.

2. M. M. Gordon, "Toward a General Theory of Racial and Ethnic Group Relations," in *Ethnicity*, ed. N. Glazer and D. Moynihan (Cambridge, Mass.: Harvard University Press, 1975), pp. 84-110.

3. D. L. Horowitz, "Ethnic Identity," in *Ethnicity*, ed. N. Glazer and D. Moynihan (Cambridge Mass.: Harvard University Press, 1975), pp. 111-14.

4. N. Glazer and D. Moynihan, *Beyond the Melting Pot* (Cambridge Mass.: MIT Press, 1974), pp. XXIV.

5. D. Bensimon-Donath, *L'Integration des Juifs Nord-Africains en France* (Paris, La Haye: Mouton, 1977), p. 191.

6. Quoted from an early draft of S. Deshen, "Israeli Judaism: Introduction to the Major Patterns," *International Journal of Middle East Studies*, 9 February 1978, pp. 141-69.

PART IV

ETHNICITY AND SOCIETY

The Shaping of Society by Ethnicity

10

UNREALISTIC EXPECTATIONS

In a general way, our analysis of both the objective and subjective sides of the encounter was consistent with the "basic characteristics' " broad outlining of the case. To recall the main points, Table 10.1 sums up briefly the rules of the ethnic encounter as defined by, and pertaining to, the Israeli version of dominant culture.

Table 10.1 Rules of the Ethnic Encounter in the Jewish Israeli Case

Spheres of Social participation	"Rules" of ethnicity as defined by the setting
Membership and culture	- open concept of membership for Jews of any origin in the presence of a melting perspective and a secular national culture
Stratification	- "generosity" expressed in a wide scope of rights relatedly to acceptance into membership
	- requirements to accept the modern ethos
Polity	- endowment of democratic privileges of citizenship
	- integration of new groups under "guidance" of a dominant stock

In brief, the "rules" express a general expectation that groups of newcomers will gradually be integrated by acceding to full membership and due to the "generosity" of the setting in resources and services. Adjustments to the economic sphere and modern socialization, under the "guidance" of buffering institutions, will favor the groups' assimilation into an ethnically undifferentiated (and more or less egalitarian) periphery of the dominant stock.

From some viewpoints, it is true, the absorptive setting's expectations originated in an accurate assumption that the various edot were also willing to "melt" into it without reservation. However, our analysis of the historical, social, and cultural background of these groups in their countries of origin—at least for those two under study (see Table 10.2) —shows that there was by no means total compatibility from the start.

Thus, while the dominant culture expected to implement *mizug* through its acceptance by the newcomers for whom it implied more efforts of adjustment than for itself, the immigrants expected mainly to concretize their *a priori* belonging to the Jewish Nation as well as to definitively solve their problem of collective inferiority. While the former factor was more determinant among Yemenites and the latter among Moroccans, in their resettlement both groups primarily expressed a faithfulness to themselves. These incompatibilities between the expectations of each side of the ethnic encounter explain the unrealistic character of both.

To be sure, the different sizes of the edot, their specific features and the periods of immigration account for the numerous disparities between them in Israel. Yet, and as reflected in Table 10.3, similar problems were to confront them in their new environment. In a general manner, the findings effectively coroborate both the objective and subjective "basic characteristics" and, in this sense, validate the interpretative framework wherein they were formulated.

The two sides of ethnicity form in themselves key contributions to the shapes, structures, and conflicts presently known by Israeli society. If we ask "What is the Jewish Israeli society today composed of as regards ethnicity?" and use the center-periphery model,[1] one may now describe this setting as characterized by three principal discontinuous circles located at different distances from the center, and hence involved at different levels with social spheres, which exhibit diverse sociocultural shades and processes of *mizug*.

Table 10.2 Background Features of the Groups under Study

Aspects of Background	Jews in Yemen and Morocco	Jews in Yemen	Jews in Morocco
The environment and the statute of Jews	Muslim traditional regime defining Jews as dhimmis	Arab country at the heart of Islam dominated by Shi'ism; Jews sharply segregated	Berber kingdoms dominated by Sunnism and Maraboutism; since 1912, French colonialism de-institutionalizes the Jews' statute
Socioeconomic characteristics and the community setting	General poverty; major occupational strata: artisans and peddlers; community organized around synagogue and religious leadership	Wide homogeneity of the Jewish condition; small communities dispersed all over the country	At the French epoch; high degree of urbanization; new middle-class strata concomitantly with expansion of mellah misery
Cultural features and orientations	Importance of religious elementary education for the great number; of Kabbalah studies for the learned man; strong familism and, generally, outlook toward life expressing a traditional mind; on the other hand urban or urban-like social endeavour	Importance of ritualistic and precise patterns of behavior; high degree of cohesion of community isolated from non-Arabic population	Expanding French education and new structures of social opportunities result in a crisis of the traditional culture among big-city dwellers; cultural differentiation between various types of communities and strata; weakening of community organization

183

Table 10.3 Yemenites and Moroccans in Israel

I. The objective side	Common characteristics of Yemenites and Moroccans (crypto-pluralistic model)	Particular characteristics of Yemenites	Particular characteristics of Moroccans
a. Culture	"dispersed" ecological concentrations wherein strength of traditional models and symbols are concomitant with newly acquired patterns. As a result: salience of sociocultural pluralism	most communities in central area of the country; special salience of parochialism	most communities in further periphery; culture imbued with Mediterranean features and reference to French
b. Status	ethnoclassization of main bulk of groups despite cohorts of mobiles. As a result: pronounced social pluralism	poverty mainly with regard to income	poverty mainly with regard to wealth
c. Polity	"liberation" from buffering institutions evokes a working class frequently oriented to the right but feebly incorporated in political elites de facto political pluralism	unsustained attempts to set up party	intense participation in politics of individuals; sporadic outbursts of protest.

184

Table 10.3 Yemenites and Moroccans in Israel (continued)

II. The subjective side	Common characteristics of Yemenites and Moroccans (crypto-pluralistic model)	Particular characteristics of Yemenites	Particular characteristics of Moroccans
a. *Primordial identity*	origin becomes primordial identity, defined as *temporarily* meaningul, in framework of more comprehensive labels	more pride of edah identity and more *mizug* perceived	less pride of edah identity and *less mizug* perceived
b. *Collective personality*	amalgamation of traditional and modern value-orientations and concepts, including a view of community as a source of advantages	more tradition-oriented and sociocultural attraction of community to members	less tradition-oriented and more instrumental attraction of community to members
c. *Practical meanings of distinctiveness*	*vis-à-vis* "others": sharp cultural, social status, political distances perceived; *vis-à-vis* other Orientals: each edah has own images distinguishing it from other edot	more cultural distance *and* less social distance from "others"	less cultural distance *but* more social distance from "others"; less social distance from other edot

Table 10.3 Yemenites and Moroccans in Israel (continued)

II. The Subjective side (cont.)	Common characteristics of Yemenites and Moroccans (crypto-pluralistic model)	Particular characteristics of Yemenites	Particular characteristics of Moroccans
d. *Interpretations of plight*	expectations of *mizug* in future but conflictual interpretation of present reality: self recognition in cultural particularism but alienation regarding other components of particularism though *refusal of ethnic militantism;* "*in-itself conflict group*" sharing a "minority mentality"	perceptions of relative status achievements as well as more closeness to "others" than other edot: *general mizug* expected in future	emphasis of advantages in realm of culture and politics relative to other edot; Oriental submelting first expected—pessimistically

III. Impact of mobility

	Common Characteristics of Yemenites and Moroccans
a. *the mobiles and the edah*	still define themselves according to edah identity, but less than their stocks; more "flexible" concept of edah membership; cultural, social, and status *remoteness from the edah* though sharing some of its cultural traits
b. *the mobiles and "Edot Mizrah"*	in all respects: mobiles of the two groups, while converging toward each other, remain remote from this concept;
c. *the mobile and the others*	movement toward "others" in all areas of social endeavor; clear *assimilatory tendencies*

The circle of the dominant stock, located at the very center, is partly determined by ascriptive criteria (veteranship and descent from veteran families) and partly by achievements of national significance. This stock is widely characterized by specific origins—Russian, Polish, Rumanian, or Central European—as far as these are related to one's contribution to the building of the setting and early immigration (of oneself and/or one's family). Over time, it is true, persons of other origins have been coopted, but Orientals especially constitute here but a small fraction. The cultural shade of this stock is modern, largely secular, and often still inspired by ideological views of the era of the Yishuv.

The second circle is made up of various components of the middle class on the immediate edge of the dominant stock. This group founds its position on material resources, educational achievements, and occupational status; it has developed mainly since the industrial expansion of the mid-1950s. Most of its members are Euro-American or of like descent, but it also includes numerous mobile Orientals of various origins (mainly Iraqi, Egyptian, Persian, and Lebanese, who arrived with material assets and had already received a modern education abroad). The cultural character of this middle class is mostly as Westernized and secular as that of the dominant stock; yet, more than the latter, it is also highly cosmopolitan in outlook. Because of its recent formation and varied composition it still shows some cultural heterogeneity, but the "melting of edot" is at its peak here and emerges from Western perspectives and styles of life.

The third circle is the periphery of the setting as a whole and comprises the bottom of all social hierarchies. Euro-Americans are few here; most of its members belong to these Oriental edot that were the subject of this study, illustrated by the cases of Yemenites and Moroccans. It is in this circle that *mizug* is at its lowest and Diasporan symbols and cultures the most popular.

As a whole, the reality of Israeli life today as shaped by ethnicity is characterized by a twofold principle: the more remote the circle from the center, the stronger the traditional outlook and the weaker the "melting of edot." This principle makes ethnicity a most salient aspect of Israel's daily routine in populous neighborhoods.

The street is overflown with Moroccan, Iraqi and Rumanian faces. In the air are odors from Iraqi and Hungarian soup. . . . This is New Safed painting its ruins with its doubts. Young couples, old people, lonely persons and the batallions of welfare cases.[2]

This face of Israel, to be sure, is but feebly apparent in "higher spheres" and ethnics themselves play a major role in this situation. As deplored by an ethnic activist who thus confirms our findings, "Something is lacking [in the Sephardic and Oriental edot]. There is no unity nor common orientation and this large public is left. . . without any *leading leadership.*"[3]

An intimate knowledge of Israeli society, it is true, does not always endow these three circles with the same distinctiveness as summarized above. One may find, for instance, among both the dominant stock and the middle class, families of diverse Oriental origin that, mainly if religious, still adhere to symbols and norms reflecting a continuity related to the past, despite their anchorage among "others." Further, many ethnics, though still close to their community, are already marked by "de-ethnicization," chiefly if they share prospects of social mobility. At the same time, on the other end of the ethnoclass spectrum there are those whose conditions of life are especially hard and among whom remoteness from any normative patterns may also be the rule. These remarks, however, though attenuating our description of discontinuities in the Israeli human panorama, do not gainsay as such the latter's reality.

RECENT DEVELOPMENTS

Any projection of the *future* of interethnic relations, however, must also include nowadays consideration of several factors only succinctly mentioned up to now. In recent years the functions of the military, the integrated school, and mixed marriages have become an integral part of the overall picture, and the question that arises, and cannot be avoided at this point, concerns the extent to which they may be seen as leading to a new ethnic reality.

If turning first to the impact of the military, what is to be emphasized is that more and more children of the immigrants of the late forties and fifties reach service age in the seventies and early eighties and ethnics have come to constitute a large proportion of the army. As already noted, the military represents one of the major pillars of Israeli society. Due to the Jewish-Arab conflict, a permanent state of belligerence since the British Mandate, "the Israel Defense Force (IDF) is unique among national armies in the degree to which it is an integral part of the society rather than peripheral to it."[4]

Nearly all male Israeli Jews serve in the army and almost the only ones exempted from military duties are the physically handicapped and those who have a too low level of education[5] (about 4 percent receive exemption each year). Jewish women are also drafted, although exemptions for them are much more numerous and include married women as well as religious or traditional ones.[6] (In total about half of the female candidates for military service are exempted.) The military duty required today is three years for men and two years for women. As a rule, induction takes place at age eighteen and postponement for the purpose of higher education is rare.

It is in this context that the army's role in shaping interethnic relations takes on particular interest. In this institution both males and females of all origins are brought together, in a situation of relative isolation from civilian vicissitudes, for some of the most crucial years of their lives. This experience occurs before the start of individual careers, and it repeats itself every year in the form of reserve duties.[7] It is periodically intensified by the outbreak of wars or emergency states. As Greenberg describes it, "Zahal [IDF] is an exciting arena for unusual human relations. . . . Ashkenazi, Sephardi, new immigrants and old-timers, . . . serve together in life and death situations which wipe out all differences in background."[8]

In addition, since the military service involves participation in collective challenges, it is rewarded by social prestige,[9] and the completion of military service is accompanied by quite a few practical privileges (particularly important for people of lower class extraction). It is frequently a nonofficial prerequisite for jobs on the private market, while government housing, social security, and scholarships for higher education are all granted with preference to former soldiers.

The IDF, more than many other national armies, also constitutes a relatively open channel of social mobility for gifted persons. As emphasized by Horowitz and Kimmerling, "Israel has no military academy whose graduates are drafted as officers; there is no requirement of a high-school education for promotion to an officer's rank. . . . Every draftee must follow the same path which begins at the recruit's base and continues through various courses in order to reach officership."[10]

Moreover, the army itself constitutes a vast school for vocational and technical training. For the "educationally weak," who are often of

North African or Middle Eastern origin, the skills acquired in the army may be essential in their postmilitary careers.[11]

Finally, general education is provided the soldier throughout military service in programs intended to bridge cultural differences and to impart a common framework of values and symbols.[12] More particularly, general education is primarily concerned with the study of Hebrew and with basic elementary education, offered in special three-month courses for those who have had less than eight years of education. A four-month optional course is offered for soldiers who have completed eight to nine years of schooling. Moreover, a program for information comprises a wide range of cultural and educational activities that are an integral part of the weekly schedule of every unit. Most of these activities are organized by "education officers" who serve throughout the army, and in all ranks.

Thus, considering the structural nature and the cultural and educational activities of the IDF, military service seems to constitute a major agent of social integration in Israel. Closer examination of the ethnic encounter in the military framework, however, reveals that the IDF reflects Israel's dominant culture, and knows the same intrinsic dilemmas of simultaneous influence of different foci of cultural development as we see in general Israeli society.

Overwhelming importance is placed on *Zionist ideology*. Hence, Jewish history, the Land of Israel, and Israel's contemporary challenges constitute major focal points of the cultural and educational programs. These issues are generally presented from a nonreligious point of view; soldiers of traditional background are encouraged to identify with a national secular state.[13] As for the solidaristic principle of *mizug*, it finds expression in a declared aspiration to ensure ethnic heterogeneity in military units. This ideal assumes a symmetry of all groups in their mutual evolution toward a socially and culturally unified whole.

However, as in Israeli society at large, this latter premise is overshadowed in practice by the *meritocratic ethos*. Educational programs in the army also focus on specific knowledge, and assign importance to intellectual achievements. Promotion to officership as well as selection for elite units is directed to those possessing appropriate ability and skills; psychotechnical tests constitute an equivalent for formal scholarly diplomas.

This selectivity tends to preserve the status quo of ethnic division. Horowitz and Kimmerling[14] note a wide overrepresentation of youngsters from peripheral strata of Israeli society in nonessential and auxiliary units. Parallel to this, the higher-status units have relatively few ethnics. The IDF, then, has de facto developed an internal status differentiation generally superseding society's ethnic divisions. The ethnic encounter inside the military framework is geared towards the acculturation of those soldiers who are more remote from the modern ethos than others, by encouraging identification with those who are closer. Inequality of the "underprivileged" is taken for granted.

The internalization of inferiority, however, arouses tensions and leads to alienation. According to Lipset, "The worse consequence of ethnic, racial or class stratification is that people who are defined as inferior by the powerful accept the definition of their own inferiority."[15] This problem is intensified in the present context by the expectation of solidarity and mutual concessions central to the ideal of mizug.

This explains the findings of an educational experiment carried out in the IDF during the 1960s, related by Shild. Until 1962, the IDF conducted the special courses for soldiers with minimal education during their last three months of service. In 1963 and 1964, the course was given during the soldier's first months in the army, with the hope that it would improve further performance in the army. The experiment did not succeed: "Not only did the participants not learn much, if anything, but severe disciplinary problems arose. Although the curriculum was identical to the one offered at the end of the service, and although the teachers had the same qualifications, a massive resistance to learning was encountered."[16] In light of the above, it seems likely that starting military service by participating in a special course for "underprivileged" was perceived as a kind of institutionalization—implying stigmatization and arising frustration—of inferior status within the military "integrated" framework. On the other hand, at the end of the service such courses could be accepted as a facility offered by the army to further one's career in the outside world.

This basic conflict, however, between the solidaristic orientation associated to the mizug perspective and the differentiation of socioethnic status resulting from the meritocratic ethos is attenuated by the impact of the egalitarian principles based in the social and democratic ideologies predominant in Israel. As an heir of the prestate underground armed forces, which were molded mainly by members of the socialist sector of the population, the IDF has a particularly strong egalitarian orientation. This is reflected primarily in the model of officer-soldier relationships. The Israeli officer maintains direct contact with his men and he participates directly in any task of his unit—including active combat.[17] As emphasized by Shild, "From time to time heated controversies have broken out [in the military hierarchy] concerning the importance or lack of importance, of hierarchical differences and symbols of formal discipline and authority. But whatever the shifts in doctrine and practice in this respect, the pervasive undertone has always been one of egalitarian ideology."[18] This egalitarian ideology —with the consequent "generosity" in educational facilities and opportunities for mobility available to the "weak"—lowers the "cost" of inferiority in terms of the quality of relationships with superiors.

On the other hand, superiority which unavoidably remains as part of the hierarchy, is accompanied by "patronizing" attitudes that reflect the Israeli ethnic scene as a whole. As shown by Greenberg, "officers to a large extent are parent figures to their young charges despite the fact that they tend to be but a few years their senior."[19] Underlying this type of inferior-superior relationship is the

correlation between the degree of orientation to the center. . .and the tendency in Israeli society to serve in selected voluntary units [and, let us add, at higher officer ranks]. In these elite units [and in these ranks] the number of members of kibbutzim and moshavim and of highschool graduates who are sons of oldtimers and in particular of members of the pioneering elite groups is far greater than the relative representation of these segments in the population.[20]

Hence, beyond the expressions of socioethnic differences outlined above, the IDF also reflects in its elite, the same principle of "dominant stock" that exists in Israeli society in general. This stock consists mainly of persons who, because of the position and traditions of their particular sectors of origin, are especially motivated to contribute actively to the country's security. This stock mitigates the alienating impact upon those who do not belong to it by the "guiding" role it assumes towards the regular soldiers, particularly the "underprivileged."

In this general picture, it is therefore no wonder that only a minority of ethnics joins units or ranks where Europeans are predominant, let alone envisage a military career and join the senior hierarchy. This fact was bluntly pointed out by a former chief of staff who openly declared, "...when I look around me in the Army, I see rather a small number of officers from Oriental communities....there are 30% Orientals in junior commissioned ranks...[and] this number gets much smaller from the rank of captain and up."[21] Concomitantly, and by the same token, cultural differences among groups inside the military framework are far from being erased. Even here, culturally determined social distances do not disappear. The following description of two young Kurds in the IDF is by no means exceptional:

Both Jacob and Moshe were good soldiers. Yet they were also deeply rooted in their edah....They never split and in the camp they were known as the 'couple.'...In the evenings they sat wrapped in a cloud of smoke and in short and monotonous sentences talked about things close to their heart, telling each other about their families.[22]

Those who do "make it," it is true, face few obstacles to social acceptance among their European comrades and even—if they reach seniority—by the dominant stock. (It is the author's own observation that officers of North African or Middle Eastern descent are quite frequently even more authoritarian than Europeans in their dealings with privates of the same origin.) This implies also increased social mobility outside the army and prospects of total assimilation among nonethnics. For the majority of ethnic individuals, however, those who do not belong to this category, the army does not entail the deletion of ethnic bonds. Army service, it is true, because of the status it endows as such, contributes to greater self-confidence, and this self-confidence is still strengthened by the ideological values and the general and vocational knowledge acquired[23] that undoubtedly forward acculturation to the dominant culture. Yet, while the Ashkenazi ex-soldier will start a middle-class career, the majority of ethnic ex-soldiers will re-enter ethnic communities where they will mainly contribute to a stronger general sense of stability.

Among other circumstances, it is this context of greater stability and self-confidence that best explains the recent multiplication of open expressions of ethnic culture. In recent years, actually, Oriental edot seem to be experiencing "a swell of pride"[24] and exhibit a new enthusiasm for their own literature, poetry, and music. Two examples among many: "The Moroccan King," a play about Moroccan Jews staged in 1979 at the National Habimah Theater, and the "Last-Choice" group, a North African song group that was very popular in Israel in 1980. Hence, paradoxically enough, the military, which represents one of the most powerful means of sociocultural integration of ethnic groups, and in fact, contributes much to the eclecticization of values and outlooks, constitutes at the same time an indirect factor "vitalizing" ethnic cultures.

As a matter of course, quite similar effects may be attributed to the educational integration implemented during the 1970s in a large part of the Israeli school system, principally at the junior high school level. This intermediate level of education was instituted in 1971. Comprising the two upper grades of the formerly eight-year elementary school and the lower grade of the formerly four-year high school, the new junior high school was intended as an integrative framework, to be "supplied" with pupils from different ethnic and socioeconomic neighborhoods. These frameworks have now been established in almost the entire Israeli educational system; integration, however, exists in only about 50 percent of them.

As in the IDF, it is the *mizug* perspective that is at the root of the goal of integration; it is assumed that integrated schools forward ethnic integration in society. However, again parallel to the IDF, school curricula and educational philosophy have remained essentially meritocratic, while at the same time special facilities are also provided "generously" for the "underprivileged" (guidance, counselling, individual tutoring, or special classes). The general atmosphere of the Israeli school, moreover, attempts to promote a sense of equality among pupils (through, for example, extracurricular activities), as well as between pupils and teaching staff. (In many schools, pupils address teachers by their first names.)

The ethnic encounter created by the integrated school is a subject passionately debated in Israel today. There is, however, general agreement with respect to certain specific results. All researchers have found no substantial reduction of the gap in the scholarly achievements of the various groups,[25] and they emphasize the continuity of broad ethnic division in the form of scholarly differentiation. Many studies,[26] it is true, indicate that non-European pupils are quite prone to accept the meritotcratic criteria for academic status, and that, as a consequence, they most often see "good pupils" as preferential choices for social interaction in the classroom. This success at acculturation should be seen, however, in the context of the fact that these "good pupils" are generally of European descent; these findings actually represent an internalization of inferiority. It is difficult to evaluate the extent to which this factor is responsible for tensions and conflictual feelings. It is most probable, however, that it is related to the numerous outbursts of violence on the part of non-European pupils in several integrated schools that took place in the late 1970s. This violence is most often expressed in vandalism against school property and sometimes even in insulting behavior against teachers and physical terrorization of European children.

On the other hand, it should be emphasized that successful pupils of non-European origin are easily accepted by their fellow pupils of European origin.[27] While most of the less successful ethnics will continue in vocational programs—where ethnics are a large majority— and a few will even drop out, these "achievers" will most often follow the academic track in senior high school where Ashkenazi are predominant. They will probably also succeed in the army and continue to higher studies, and are likely to find their way out of the ethnoclass. In the same vein, moreover, observers of the Israeli school system emphasize that high-level schools in peripheral towns not only contribute to a better educational level of the community as a whole, but also— and this is less appreciated by the same observers—to a strong orientation among the gifted toward the center, and to the eventual emigration of the well-educated to middle-class neighborhoods in central cities.

Thus both the army and the school, rather than promoting a qualitative change of the ethnic encounter, actually amplify the dynamism of its basic characteristics. They forward acculturation—promoting eclecticization of ethnic cultures—and they also provide means for the more active persons to join the nonethnic middle class, but they do not delete the very existence of the ethnoclass.

We now turn to the most crucial index of social integration, the rate of interethnic marriages. It has not yet been investigated as to what extent sexually mixed and ethnically heterogenous institutions such as high school and the army contribute to this rate. However, the statistics themselves provide a useful indication of the current developments.

Table 10.4 testifies to the steady increase of marriages between members of different ethnic groups. In 1955, such marriages com-

Table 10.4 Persons Marrying, by Bride's and Groom's Continent of Origin (Jews)

Years	Endogamy Index [a]	Groom from Europe-America		Groom from Asia-Africa		Absolute numbers-Total
		Bride from Europe-America	Bride from Asia-Africa	Bride from Europe-America	Bride from Asia-Africa	
		PERCENTAGES				
All persons marrying						
1955	0.81	48.4	7.5	4.3	39.8	13,530
1960	0.78	43.1	9.5	5.0	42.4	14,467
1965	0.70	40.5	7.4	7.9	44.2	18,097
1970	0.66	42.8	8.3	9.3	39.6	23,983
1972	0.64	39.3	9.6	8.8	42.3	26,433
1974	0.64	37.2	10.4	8.7	43.7	28,568
1975	0.64	37.5	10.2	8.7	43.6	28,583
1976	0.64	35.3	10.4	8.7	45.6	25,805
1977	0.63	34.1	11.1	8.8	46.0	25,361
Single persons						
1968	0.69	41.8	7.5	9.3	41.4	17,851
1970	0.66	41.3	8.3	9.7	40.7	21,085
1972	0.63	37.4	9.7	9.0	43.9	25,265
1974	0.63	35.0	10.5	8.8	45.7	26,277
1976	0.63	33.1	10.5	8.8	47.6	22,742
1977	0.62	31.8	11.2	8.9	48.1	22,174

SOURCE: Israeli Central Bureau of Statistics, *Statistical Abstract of Israel: 1979*, No. 30, Jerusalem, 1980, p. 83.

[a]Index was calculated on the base of continent of origin.

prised 11.8 percent of all marriages in Israel, in 1977, 19.9 percent. Further analysis of the data, considering specific groups of origin and social status provide additional details. Kraus[28] studied nationwide data concerning twenty-four groups of origin in 1971-1974; her findings indicate the major importance of social status in interethnic marriages. Peres,[29] who concentrated on intercategory marriages (Europeans with North Africans and Middle Easterners), made the same conclusion. Both studies showed that the greater the ethnic's social mobility (in terms of occupational achievements leading to middle-class status), the greater the probability that he or she will marry a European spouse.

However, recent statistics show that to marry an European spouse is generally easier for females originating from the edot than for males of the same origins (this is expressed in the figures for most years shown in Table 10.4). This is particularly significant considering that girls of Oriental origin are generally less educated and less socially mobile than their male fellow ethnics. Moreover, a large proportion—about 60 percent—of non-Ashkenazi girls are exempt from military service for religious reasons and thus do not participate in the the vast marrying mart that this institution represents.

It can therefore be concluded that status plays a less important role for females than for males in the issue of intermarriage. This phenomenon is best understood in the context of the twofold assumption that the individual's principal status asset is occupation, and that this asset is primarily determined in society by the male member of the family. Hence, Ashkenazi males, most of whom have higher- or middle-class occupations, do not lose much status by marrying lower-status non-Ashkenazi females. An Ashkenazi female, on the other hand, is likely to marry a non-Ashkenazi male only if he has already "made it" socially.

It is in this context that intercategory marriages may be seen as an additional indicator of the general model of ethnic encounter exemplified in Israel: the predominantly Ashkenazi nonethnic middleclass is quite open to accept non-Ashkenazi people who, either by their achievements or by marital union, are entitled to middle-class status; on the other hand, this openness does not extend to an elimination of ethnosocial differentiation as a whole.

Furthermore, marriages between members of different Oriental edot have an essentially different effect; they are also more numerous.

In these cases, as discussed in an earlier chapter in reference to Yemenites and Moroccans, there is no process of "de-ethnicization." Rather, most frequently, we witness a "passing" from one group to the other; offsprings generally identifying with the group with which the family has located.

To summarize, the relative frequency of intercategory and interethnic marriages does not signify a future much different from the present. These marriages do underline the fluidity of ethnic divisions, but it appears that the currents of this fluidity are directed by the basic characteristics of the encounter: these marriages actually strengthen the nonethnic character of the predominantly Ashkenazi middle class, while they do not cause any radical change in the condition of the lower-class ethnic communities. The influence of "mixed marriages" on the ethnic encounter, then, is parallel to the impact of other integrative frameworks such as the army and the junior high school.

Considering again these latter institutions, a major phenomenon which has been revealed, let us repeat, is the glaring contrast between the amount of effort invested in them on behalf of sociocultural integration and their actual relative impact on ethnic reality. Hence, a final question that cannot be ignored concerns the very rationale of these efforts. No precise solution has been given for this problem and many of Israel's social scientists actually justify integrative policies by minimizing the importance of their results, emphasizing instead the ideological tenets they represent.[30] Inserting this issue within the general analysis of this study, however, allows an additional interpretation to be suggested that relates the scope of integrative policies to the fundamental contradictions inherent in the Israeli crypto-pluralistic syndrome. Ethnic pluralism, that is, differentiated and enduring participation of ethnic groups in given areas of social activity, exists indeed in all major spheres of the Israeli setting, though Zionist ideology does not—in normative terms—allow any recognition of this as a permanent aspect of the social order (and in particular as an autonomous focus of political power). In this context, the heavy investments in the name of integration if not aimed at effectively implementing *mizug*, may be understood at least, as intended to maintain, reaffirm, and reinforce, in society at large, the ideological taboo of ethnic pluralism (and eventually to "truncate" the active and successful from the edah). This interpretation becomes more plausible if one considers

again the edot's share in the population and the overwhelming potential power which is theirs in democracy.

THE FUTURE OF THE CRYPTO-PLURALISTIC SYNDROME

In the context of the foregoing remarks, several problematic aspects of
political connotation that were discussed throughout these pages are
to be recalled in the light of additional comments, and in view of the
consequences they bear for the future of ethnic relations in Israel. First
it should be repeated that the reluctance of ethnics to express blunt
political dissent is not to be taken for granted. The very transformation
of edot into ethnoclasses represents for the people involved an alienating reality, in the background of which, let us add, is also the general
state of belligerency that has both an attenuating and an aggravating
impact. On the one hand, the external threat enhances national
solidarity and impedes unrestrained political expressions of conflict;
on the other hand, after participating in a war for a cause common to
all Israelis, returning to the slums sharpens the feelings of deprivation.
It is no coincidence that the Haifa riots broke out in the aftermath of the
Sinai Operation, and the Jerusalem Black Panthers events erupted at
the end of the War of Attrition on the Suez Canal.

Moreover, seeing the increased self-assurance of the ethnic born in
the country evoked in the former section, it cannot be excluded that
ethnic tickets could be viewed by him as merely politically profitable
and that he would be less sensitive than his father to normative
restrictions on independent ethnic politics. It is on such an attitude that
ethnic lists led by leaders of low-class extraction hang their hopes to
enter the Parliament.

Up to now these attempts were unsuccessful. However, in the 1981
elections three seats (and 2.3 percent of the votes) were won by
another type of ethnic ticket, namely the Movement for Israel's Tradition (Tami). To understand this phenomenon one has to refer to the
very dynamics of political recruitment inherent to the crypto-pluralistic
syndrome. According to this syndrome, individual cooptation by
nonethnic parties is the main pattern of political career available to
ethnics. Such a pattern, however, leads quite inevitably to the
strengthening of ethnic lobbies within these parties, since cooptated
figures who worry about their effective power in the political apparatus

are inclined to crystallize an internal ethnic constituency. Such a development, moreover, frequently witnesses coalitions of the various Oriental groups belonging to a same party.

From this situation, the way is short to the model exemplified by Tami. This party was created by two Moroccan MPs (one of whom was the Minister of Religious Affairs in the actual government and of the National Religious Party and by a Tunisian former Labor MP (a Minister of Agriculture in the pre-1977 government). Unsatisfied with their location on their parties' lists, they created a new organization as many have done before them, on the basis of several advantages which were at their disposal. These experienced politicians had sup- porters of diverse Oriental origins within their respective parties ready to join them. They also had many links to foci of power outside partisan structures inside Israel (the moshavim federation, municipal councils, and the rabbinical hierarchy) as well as outside the country (the World Federation of the Sephardim). Moreover, they were identi- fied as a part of the national political elite and, as such were less vulnerable than other ethnic tickets to public criticism. Last but not least, they openly affirmed their rejection of radical protest and their aspiration to participate in government. The close competition be- tween the rightist Likud and the left-of-the-center Labor seemed, anyway, to ensure an overproportionate parliamentary bargaining power to small centrist formations.

The results of the elections, however, shows that support for Tami came principally from this minority among the Oriental edot, from the Moroccans in particular, who were former supporters of the NRP. Hence, the ethnic character of the Tami vote intermingled with the factor of religious-political allegiance. At this point, it is important to notice that the creation of Tami took place one month before the elections while the minister of Religious Affairs remained in charge on behalf of the NRP. This party, henceforth, was prevented from "reconquering" this basis of power which had always belonged to it. Evident here is that Tami rarely infringed on the ethnic clientele of either the Likud or the Labor Party, and both these parties in fact, increased their support among the edot. At the same time, the NRP lost half of its supporters and in sum, Tami succeeded in drawing 50 percent of its deserters. Thus, seeing the type of its leaders and their intentions, as well as the relativity of its numerical success in the

context of the NRP's crisis, it is quite hazardous to consider Tami—
under its present form at least—as a breakdown of the crypto-pluralistic
syndrome.

Generally speaking, the 1981 elections took place in particular
circumstances as far as ethnic issues are concerned. They followed,
indeed, the very first term of a right-wing coalition in Israel. This
coalition (as noted formerly in Chapter 3) was raised to power in 1977,
among other factors, by the massive support of edot. This government, however, has not brought about any substantial change in the
social configuration of ethnic problems while in a strict economic
sense, ethnic gaps have rather slightly widened during the 1977-1981
period. Hence, the repeated greater support of ethnics for the Likud
(see Appendix 3), than for the Labor Party, their ignorance of leftist
forces and of three ethnic lists more radical than Tami, and, finally, the
weak sympathy for the latter, all provide confirmation to our interpretation of ethnics' political behavior (see Chapter 3) based on the
notions of crypto-pluralism and in-itself conflict group.

This behavior, however, and as also already stated, cannot be seen
as irrational, since the edot's becoming a floating element on the
political map, beyond their affinity to the Right, is bound to increase
their latent bargaining power. As a confirmation, it is the role edot
played in the Right's 1977 victory, concurrently with the stronger
standing achieved by ethnic politicans within their parties over the
years, which explains that in 1981 not less than five parties (including
the two largest, the Labor Alignment and the Likud) set up ethnics in
the second or third place of their lists of candidates to Parliament.
Moreover, MPs of Oriental origins increased their number by 45
percent and from 17 percent of all MPs (18 percent of the Jews), they
became 26 percent (29 percent of the Jews), Tami's own representation represented but one-tenth of MPs of Oriental origins.

The very emergence of Tami, notwithstanding its small following, is
a sign that reminds us, it is true, that the crypto-pluralistic syndrome is
given to many factors of instability. However, it is also to be emphasized that all ethnic tickets, (and Tami more than any other) remain
bound to the framework of the premisses of crypto-pluralism. Their
programs reaffirm the exigeny of a better integration of the edot in
Israeli society; by no means do they express a velleity of independence from the center. On the contrary they fight for the center's

endorsment of greater responsibility for the condition of ethnic groups, that is to say, they themselves reject a pluralistic society and try to draw the legitimacy of their endeavor from the ideology of *mizug* itself. In this is revealed the fundamental contradiction of these attempts of independent politics, which accounts for the limits on their potential development.

However, it must be taken into consideration that a much more serious threat to crypto-pluralism may spring from another source. A major element of the crypto-pluralistic syndrome, let us recall, is the assimilation of successful ethnics among "others," and the number of these mobiles, as debated in the former section, is at the measure of the growing investments of the center in the edot. It should now be underlined that their assimilation, which brings support to the ideal of *mizug*, cannot be assumed as a state of affairs that must persist. Should grave disparity occur between the cohorts of potential upwardly mobile ethnics on the one hand, and available opportunities for social mobility on the other, one cannot exclude the possibility that ethnic tensions could be aggravated by self-protective reactions of "others," notwithstanding the dominant *mizug* ideology. Such reactions could in turn induce mobiles, or candidates to mobility, to adopt a new attitude toward their groups of origin. Deteriorated relations between ethnics and "others," in the context of a relinking of mobiles to their edot could constitute a most drastic change in the general Israeli model of ethnic encounter and a powerful factor of crystallization of ethnic protest.

NOTES

1. See E. Shils, "Centre and Periphery," in essays presented to Michael Polanyi, *The Logic of Personal Knowledge* (London: Routledge and Kegan Paul, 1961), pp. 117-30.

2. Y. Saaroni, *Nisim Betsfat* [Miracles in Safed] (Tel Aviv: Am Oved, 1961), p. 10.

3. Y. Sofer, "Hasera Manhigut Movilah" [There is no leading leadership], *Bamaaraha* 216 (December 1978): 8.

4. H. J. Greenberg, *Israeli Social Problems in Perspective* (Tel Aviv: Dekel Academic Press, 1979), p. 100.

5. See M. Bar-On, *Education Processes in the Israel Defense Force* (Tel Aviv: Israel Press, 1966), pp. 22-23.

6. M. Roumani, *From Immigrant to Citizen* (The Hague: Foundation for the study of Plural Societies, 1979), p. 38.

7. D. Horowitz and B. Kimmerling, "Some Social Implications of Military Service and the Reserve System in Israel," *Israeli Society 1967-1973*, ed. R. Kehana and S. Kopstein (Jerusalem: Academon, 1974), p. 120.

8. Greenberg, *Israeli Social Problems*, pp. 100-101.

9. Horowitz and Kimmerling, "Some Social Implications of Military Service," p. 123.

10. Ibid., p. 126.

11. See Roumani, *From Immigrant to Citizen*, pp. 62-63.

12. Z. Schiff and E. Haber, "Leksikon Lebithon Israel" [Israel, army and defense, a dictionary] (Tel Aviv: Zmora, Bitan, Modan Publishers, 1976), pp. 212-13.

13. See Roumani, *From Immigrant to Citizen*, p. 95.

14. Horowitz and Kimmerling, "Some Social Implications of Military Service," p. 123.

15. S. M. Lipset, "The Israeli Dilemma," in *Israel: Social Structure and Change*, ed. M. Curtis and M. Chertoff (New Brunswick, N.J.: Transaction Books, 1973), pp. 349, 430-31.

16. O. Shild, "On the Meaning of Military Service in Israel," in *Israel: Social Structure and Change*.

17. Roumani, *From Immigrant to Citizen*, p. 43.

18. Shild, "On the Meaning of Military Service," p. 424.

19. Greenberg, *Israeli Social Problems*, pp. 102-3.

20. Horowitz and Kimmerling, "Some Social Implications of Military Service," p. 123.

21. M. Gur, "Riayun" [Interview], *Yediot Aharonot*, 25 May 1978.

22. J. Erlich, *Haarariim* [The highlanders] (Tel Aviv: Am Oved, 1961), p. 10.

23. See Roumani, *From Immigrant to Citizen*, p. 125.

24. J. Friedman, "Israel's Oriental Jews are First-Class Citizens Now," *New York Times*, 9 November 1980.

25. Editors, "Hakdamah" [Preface], *Megamot* 23, nos. 3-4 (December 1977): 3.

26. See, for instance, M. Chen, A. Lewy, and D. Kfir, "Efsharuiot Hamifgash Habein-edati Behativot Habeinaim, Mimusho Vetotsaotav" [The possibilities of interethnic contact in the junior high schools: implementation and results], *Megamot* 23, nos. 3-4 (December 1977): 101-23; J. Levin and M. Chen, "Behirot Sotsiometriot Bekitot Meuravot Mibehinah Edatit" [Sociometric choices in ethnically heterogeneous classes], *Megamot* 23, nos. 3-4 (December 1977): 189-208.

27. R. Shapira and M. Hadad, "Shlitah Bemashavim Vehithabrut Hevratit" [Commanding resources and social integration], *Megamot* 23, nos. 3-4 (December 1977): 161-173.

28. V. Kraus, "Social Segregation as a Function of Social Class and Ethnic Status," (Jerusalem: Hebrew University, Department of Sociology and Social Anthropology, 1978) (mimeographed).

29. Y. Peres, *Yahasei Edot Beisrael* [Ethnic relations in Israel] (Tel Aviv: Sifriat Hapoalim, 1977), p. 159.

30. Editors, "Hakdamah" [Preface] *Megamot* 23, nos. 3-4, pp. 9-14.

The Jewish-Arab Case

11

INTRODUCTION

Another case of ethnic encounter in Israel is that between the Jews and Arabs. Since this is an important aspect of Israeli society, a brief comparative outline of this case is relevant to the study at this point, especially in the light of the cultural and socioeconomic closeness of Arabs to the Oriental edot and the interaction between them in actual reality.

The following pages will apply—to the extent possible with available data—the same theoretical approach *vis-à-vis* this case of ethnic group as *vis-à-vis* the edot. In this case, however, the various foci of cultural development pertaining to the dominant culture participate differently in the shaping of ethnic occurrences in the diverse spheres of the encounter while, in some respects, from these foci different orientations and rules also derive. On the other hand, beyond the similarities, the Arabs confronting these rules also differ significantly from the edot in crucial *a priori* features. Hence, the model revealed is essentially different and this accounts for the kind of interactions that exist between the Jewish-Arab and the inter-Jewish cases.

CULTURE AND MEMBERSHIP

In 1948, the State of Israel was separated from the rest of the Palestinian territories, and many of its Arab inhabitants fled. Those who remained then numbered 156,000 out of a total Palestinian population of 1,320,000.[1] Today, Arabs constitute 15 percent of the Israeli population. Among them, the Druze make up 8 percent, Muslim Bedouins, 10 percent; the non-Bedouin Sunite Moslems, 67 percent; and the Christians who are subdivided into five major congregations, 15 percent.[2]

This population confronts, in the sphere of culture and membership, rules deriving from three major foci of cultural development pertaining to the dominant culture that to a certain extent contradict each other. As a democracy, Israeli society considers those Arabs, who have lived in the country since before the creation of the state, an integral part of it and *formally* endows them *full membership*. However, their position is affected by the protracted belligerency between Israel and Arab countries, which is one of the principal circumstances characterizing the setting's recent historical endeavor. As a cultural consequence, concern for national security receives the highest priority among all other social and national challenges, a concern deeply embedded in the entire Jewish community. With respect to the Arab inhabitants, who in the past belonged to the hostile environment, this orientation is translated in a velleity to sustain control over the group regarding any matter relevant to this concern. This principle, when translated, for instance, into the exemption of Arabs (with the exception of Druze) from compulsory military service—a major symbol of belongingness to "Israeliness"—and the enrollment of volunteers in special minority units reduces the significance of full membership. From this angle, the Arab condition in Israel is best described by the label of *de facto partial membership*.

At the same time, the Zionist ideology that calls for the building of a Jewish nation-state draws its secular symbols from a given religious-national tradition. From this viewpoint, all Jews, including those who *vis-à-vis* the edot constitute a nonethnic stock, represent, *vis-à-vis* the Arabs, a separate ethnic entity. This entity aspires to maintain both its *distinctiveness* from the Arabs and its *predominance* over the historical and cultural personality of society. In this pluralistic perspective, Arabs make up what Rose[3] calls a *national minority* entailing a *wide cultural autonomy* together with a *subordinate status*.

As for the Arabs themselves, the following deals mainly with the Sunite Moslem non-Bedouin communities and the Christian groups. Comprising the greater part of Israel's Arab population, these groups may actually be considered one ethnic stock. While the Bedouins and Druze have, on the whole, remained in the margins of events because of their separatist traditions, for the Sunite non-Bedouins and the Christians, the *Arabic language and culture* had already crystallized a sense of Arab *Palestinian nationalism* in the frame of the British Mandate (1921-1948). These groups are included in Nakhleh's statement that "there existed [before 1948] a group of people in a determinate territory who perceived themselves to be, and were referred to as Arabs of Palestine."[4] For those who, since 1948, have become "Israeli Arabs," as concluded by Stock, "Arab solidarity has tended [ever since] to transcend religious difference in confrontation with the larger Jewish community."[5]

This confrontation, it should be emphasized, is only partial and up to a certain point, a *convergence* exists between the Arabs' *a priori* features and the dominant culture's approach toward the ethnic encounter. Thus, the group's *a priori* self-definition and perception in terms allying nation and culture, which emphasize the belonging to a larger whole excluding the Jew are, in fact, taken for granted and recognized by the pluralistic approach of the dominant culture.

So it is that today some 85 to 90 percent live in villages (about 150 in number) and towns (15) that are populated by Arabs alone. That this concentration is not just imposed from "above" is shown by the fact that about 10 percent of Arabs live in Jewish-Arab cities.[6] This geographical division between Jews and Arabs is, of course, concomitant with the low rate of intergroup marriages—one hundred Arab men marry Jewish women *every year* on average and many fewer Jewish men marry Arab women.[7]

As a national minority, moreover, the Arab community—much more than the edot—possess many autonomous institutions. Religious courts have legal authority on matters of personal status, an Arabic-speaking school system enrolls the wide majority of all pupils from kindergartens to teacher colleges, and there are Arab newspapers, television and radio broadcasting.

The convergence between the Arabs' *a priori* features and the dominant culture, however, is widely *negative* as, within the framework of a label of identity—"Israeliness"—pertaining to a common geopolitical reality, both refer to particular collectives that exclude each other. Hence, for the Jew as well as for the Arab, "Israeliness" is only a predicate to their different—Jewish and Arab—primordial identities.

Here is revealed the basic divergence. For the Jew, "Israeliness" means, in accordance with the Zionist perspective and as already discussed in Chapter 2, the *fulfilment* of the idea of Nation intrinsic to Judaism. For the Arab, on the contrary, "Israeliness" represents the *divorce* between citizenship and national-cultural identity. In this context the endowment of substantial meanings to their "Israeliness" is all the more problematic, as their position as a controlled minority inside a Jewish nation-state sharply contrasts with the multiple examples of Arab sovereignty all around them. Moreover, the state of belligerency between Israel and Arab countries as well as the conflict over the Palestinian Cause—a Cause that according to its spokesman, includes them—result in a dramatic dilemma of loyalty. As stated by an Israeli Arab personality,[8] "My people are at war with my country."

This dilemma, understandably, has become more and more acute as the Israeli-Arab conflict has developed. In 1948, the Israeli Arabs were weak and bewildered, and eager to find practical accommodation with the regime. The Six-Day War and the conquest by Israel of Judea, Samaria, and the Gaza Strip provided renewed contact between Israel's Arabs and the majority of the Palestinians, and, through them, with the Arab world as a whole. In the following years, the Palestinian issue achieved an overwhelming resonance on the international scene, further amplified by the Yom Kippur War (1973) and the Camp David Agreements (1978).

The drastic impact of such events on the Israeli Arabs' approach towards "Israeliness" is shown, for instance, by a twofold survey that investigated attitudes toward the state in 1966, one year before the Six-Day War, and was duplicated in aftermath of the war, in 1967.[9] In 1966, 81 percent of the Arab respondents endorsed the existing pluralistic model of Jewish-Arab relationships and 6 percent even an assimilationist approach, while 13 percent advocated the Arabs' separation from the Israeli state; one year later, only 53 percent favored pluralism, while the rest of the sample supported separation or even Israel's replacement by a Palestinian state. The 1967 survey showed, moreover, that only one-third of the sample accepted unreservedly the right of Israel to exist while, on the other hand, 57 percent stated that they feel more "at home" in an Arab country than in Israel. It should be emphasized that these attitudes parallel the development of Jewish public opinion. A 1976 survey[10] shows that a wide majority of

Jews (83 percent) think that "it would be better if there were less Arabs in the country." In the same vein, many said that "Arabs are exempted from duties but enjoy privileges and numerous economic and educational facilities they do not deserve as a hostile minority."

The foregoing reveals the fundamental difference between the Jewish-Arab and the inter-Jewish ethnic cleavages in the sphere of culture and membership. For the Arabs, as aforesaid, the major problem revolves around the meanings to be endowed to the comprehensive allegiance referring to the setting as a whole. In the background, there are both a primordial identity and, associated to it, a self-perceived distinct culture, which were already "given" by the group's a priori features and were originally alien and hostile to that comprehensive allegiance. In contrast, the Oriental edot's major problem concerns the meanings to be endowed to their primordial identity and cultural "uniqueness" within the frame of an "Israeli Jewishness." The unalienable belonging to this latter label is taken for granted beyond the differences of formulations between them and "others," and notwithstanding their own ethnic conflicts. It is this fundamental difference which accounts for the minimal impact, in this sphere of the ethnic encounter, afforded the similarities between Oriental edot and Arabs. Though in several respects—from styles of family life to religious attitudes—these edot may have greater cultural resemblance to Arabs than to other groups of Jews, and though both the Arabs and the edot remain distinct communities inside the setting—even if confronted by different rules, this distinctiveness knows very different degrees of institutionalization—these facts do not indicate any connection between the two types of ethnic encounters. This reality accounts for several aspects of the encounter in the realm of stratification.

CLASS STRUCTURE AND SOCIAL MOBILITY

The Arabs' status as a national minority, and the impact of the security situation bear segregative consequences in the area of stratification as well. Higher ranks of the civil administration, the clients of which are principally Jews, are generally closed to Arabs. This is even more so regarding areas related to national security, such as the military hierarchy, the Ministry of Defense, or the diplomatic service.

Beyond these limits, however, the socialist ethos and its inherent egalitarian orientation assure all citizens a wide range of rights and social services. This applies to Arabs as well, and they also participate by right in all-Israeli professional associations and unions. The development of schools under the National Education Law (1953), the expansion of governmental health centers as well as of the trade union's Sick Fund, and development projects implemented in Arab villages since 1961[11] are all factors that together with the Israeli norms in matters of salary and income, account for Lustick's observation:

It is definitely the case that the Israeli Arabs enjoy a much higher standard of living than they did in 1948 and that this living standard surpasses by a wide margin that of most of the inhabitants of the Arab states bordering Israel.[12]

Furthermore, in those spheres where no ascriptive criteria impede their steps—agriculture, commerce, civil industry—Arabs participate indiscriminately on the basis of meritocratic requirements. However, in this latter respect it is to be emphasized that the Arabs in 1948 constituted another example of a traditional stock. Hence, like the Oriental edot, their absorption in Israeli economy was also to signify deep cultural changes concomitantly with a general trend to concentrate at the lower steps of the social ladder.

The Arab community today is quite different from the 1948 reality, indeed. Although work outside of the village began in the days of the Mandate,[13] Zureik[14] shows that while before 1948 about 57 percent of the Arab manpower eked their living from farming their own land, this figure in 1972 was only 20 percent. The social and cultural consequences of this change are overwhelming. As described by Stock,

[when based on household agricultural economy], the family unit is . . . patriarchal; women play a distinctly subordinate role and the sons owe absolute obedience to their father. . . . In Israel, in recent years, however, this patriarchal relationship has been undermined. As the sons have gone off to work in the town . . . family ties have been weakened. Income is no longer automatically surrendered to the father. . . . Increased opportunities for secondary education have given rise to a class of young intellectuals . . . educational and vocational training have been emancipating the young Arab woman.[15]

Yet, Arabs, as a rule, are still more remote than Jews from the modern ethos. What Stock calls the "constraining influence of tradition" still expresses itself, for instance, in the fact that many parents prevent their daughters attending school after the age of twelve despite legal stipulations. Poorly equipped to meet the requirements of better-paying positions, many Arabs attain only lower-status jobs, and as a group widely constitute an *underclass* of unskilled manpower. Thus, a survey shows that in 1972[16] only 10 percent of the Arab manpower was employed in professional, executive, and clerical jobs, as opposed to 37 percent of Jewish manpower; on the other hand, with respect to industrial blue-collar jobs, the respective figures were 51 percent and 36 percent.

The term "underclass" is use in order to emphasize that this development is even more salient with respect to Arabs than to Jews of North African or Middle Eastern origin. This fact is due not only to the restrictions applying to the former—and which were mentioned in the above —but also, and principally, to differences of starting-points: the majority of Israeli Arabs, including those who now work outside agriculture, are offspring of peasants, while most Oriental Jews (as shown in Chapter 3 regarding Yemenites and Moroccans), though also from traditional settings, are sons of craftsmen, peddlers, or tradesmen. Relatedly, these Jews—again in contrast to the Arab peasant in Palestine—belonged to the segment of their respective societies showing the lowest rates of illiteracy. These differences of background widely account for the date of Table 11.1, computed from findings provided by a 1971 survey.[17]

In the context of drastic sociocultural change inside the group, Jews, it is true, are often seen by Arabs as people they should—and effectively do— learn from, with respect to technology, education, or family models.[18] On the other hand, social inferiority in the frame of Israeli society is one more factor that accounts for feelings of deprivation and resentment. In the context of the pluralistic model wherein Jews firmly maintain their predominance, Arabs are quick to decry discrimination against the group as such. As examples they point to the governmental aid accorded for housing mainly to young Jewish couples (although this assistance is granted to all ex-soldiers and it is as such that it excludes most, but not all, Arabs); the lower educational standard of Arabic-speaking schools— where, however, it is Arabs who teach; or the restricted government resources invested in the Arab village economy—while this

Table 11.1 Comparison of Family Income and Per Person Income (1971)

Israeli families according to origin of family head	Average income per family as % of average income of Israeli family	Per person income[a] as % of average income of an Israeli-born Jew of European or American father
Non-Jews[b]	66%	26%
Jews, Asia-Africa	83%	44%
Jews, Israeli-born, father from Asia-Africa	86%	54%
Jew, Israeli-born, father born in Israel	105%	72%
Jew, Europe-America	112%	90%
Jew, Israeli-born, father from Europe-America	126%	100%

[a]calculated on the basis of gross per family income and family size
[b]this category includes, besides Arabs, non-Arab non-Jews
(who amount to less than 1%)

economy, it has been shown, is only of secondary importance today, anyway.

But whatever the weight of these contentions, a less debatable issue is the existence of discrimination against Arabs on the part of individual Jews. This is expressed in areas such as the rental of lodgings or employment. Though formally illegal, this discrimination finds an indirect and informal justification in the state of belligerency that may account for diffidence. It is further latently supported by the emphasis of the dominant culture's pluralistic perspective on maintenance of distinctiveness between groups.

Interestingly enough, Oriental Jews are among the most discriminatory. As a rule, this group expresses stronger anti-Arab attitudes than those of European extraction.[19] Researchers trace this phenomenon to the memory of discrimination against Jews in Moslem countries as well as the Orientals' desire to "draw the line" between them and the Arabs *because* of their cultural resemblance. One may add here, on the basis of Myrdal's poor-white theory,[20] that as ethnoclasses, it is also in the Oriental edot's interest to be more militant against Arabs because they are the first threatened in terms of social status by the latter's eventual achievements. Such a defensive "rejectionist" attitude, it is true, finds no equivalent among Jews *vis-à-vis* each other; with respect to this case, however, *mizug* and not pluralism is emphasized, and discriminatory practices are much more unambiguously opposed by the dominant culture.

However, it is with respect to the issue of social mobility that the most essential difference is revealed between the edot and the Arab minority in the sphere of stratification. As in the case of the edot, the number of Arab mobile individuals is continually increasing and while for instance, in 1965 there were only 511 Arab students in Israeli universities, in 1975 their number was already 1,281, that is, an increase of 150 percent.[21] Many of the mobile Arabs are employed in public service and schools in the Arab settlement itself. In 1972, it was found that 83 percent of the Arab graduates of the University of Haifa held such positions.[22] In the same vein, among all Arabs who graduated from Israeli universities during 1961-1971 and turned to white-collar occupations, about 47 percent became elementary or secondary teachers in Arabic-speaking schools.[23] Yet the further increase of educated people over and above the needs of the Arab community requires occupational absorption outside the Arab sector. Inevitably, and despite the difficulties, Arabs find their way to hospitals as physicians or nurses, to courts as lawyers, to the mass media (and not only in Arabic) as journalists or to the research institutes as scientists.

However, recalling both the former section of this chapter and the general discussion of Chapter 9 about the impact of social mobility on ethnic groups otherwise widely concentrated in lower strata, it is significant that the Israeli Arabs' case of social mobility occurs in a situation where neither the dominant culture nor the ethnic group aspire to mutual assimilation. Thus, the dominant culture does not encourage mobile individuals to detach themselves from their original stock, and neither does the latter see their social success as a justification for loosening their ethnic commitment. The pressure from both sides of the ethnic encounter for mobile Arabs—whether employed inside or outside the Arab settlement—to remain socially an integral part of their ethnic group, contributes to the Arab community becoming a "tangential" entity, that is, a group more and more heterogeneous in terms of occupational status. This model—see Case 2 in Figure 9.1—contrasts with that of the "truncated ethnoclass" exemplified by the edot.

The differences of practical impacts between these two models are crucial. To recall, socially mobile individuals from among the edot see their social mobility as a solution to their ethnic problem, and they factually quit their group. For the mobile Arabs, social mobility represents quite opposite consequences. Above all, their social mobility involves the well-known problem of status inconsistency:[24] in terms of social class, mobile Arabs belong to the Israeli middle or upper strata; on the other hand, they *remain* a part of an ascriptive lower-status group.

This inconsistency, to be sure, is reflected in subjective aspects: the survey of Haifa Arab graduates,[25] for instance, shows that respectively 35 percent and 59 percent of them consider themselves as belonging either to the middle or higher class of Israeli society; at the same time, as shown by Peres's investigation,[26] educated youth constitute the Arab population's most radical group *vis-à-vis* the Israeli state. Moreover, and again in contrast to mobile elements in the edot, these individuals, because they remain inside their ethnic group, do not escape the cultural confrontation with the bulk of their stock that arises from their greater acculturation to modern values as a result of their very endeavor of social mobility. The sharpness of this problem is shown by another finding of the Haifa survey:[27] not less than 74 percent of the respondents see their own world of concepts as basically different from their parents'. Furthermore, these new elements also face the challenge represented by the traditional Arab elites countering their aspirations to affirm their status at least inside their own group.

In sum, while the most salient aspect in the sphere of stratification of the edah model lies in the ethnic communities remaining at the bottom of the social ladder, with respect to the Arabs, it is the issue of the new middle class that is particularly problematic. These differences imply meaningful consequences in the area of the polity.

ARAB ETHNIC POLITICS

Most significant with respect to the polity is again the dominant culture's definition of the Arabs as a national minority. This definition legitimizes—in contrast to the inter-Jewish crypto-pluralistic syndrome—autonomous ethnic politics. Hence, in the context of a democratic regime, Arab parties participate in both local and national elections. Moreover, the center has also developed buffering institutions *vis-à-vis* Arabs, as *vis-à-vis* the edot. In this case, however, they are not intended to promote social integration, but rather to crystallize a permanent framework of Jewish-Arab coexistence, and to serve as mechanisms of control.

Thus, during the first year of the inception of the Israeli state, a special Ministry for Minorities was instituted, and every government office had its own special Arab Department. In 1949, this arrangement was replaced by the position of advisor to the prime minister for Arab matters; it has been maintained ever since. Aside the regular channels of the various ministries, the advisor heads a complex web of formal and informal channels with the diverse Arab communities.[28] A special military administration was set up to prevent hostile activities. Comprising a few dozen employees[29] who dealt personally with Arab notables, this administration was abolished in the mid-1960s and its functions were handed over to regular security services.

As for the Arabs, the weakness of the group in the aftermath of the 1948 War, its traditionalism, and the preeminence of political blocs led by notables, have resulted in a readiness to cooperate with the center within this client-patron pattern of relationship. The Arab parties have always exhibited a permanent allegiance to what was until 1977 the principal force in the Jewish establishment, the Labor Party while direct links of the Arab elite with the governmental officials constitute a useful resource—far from the limelight—for overcoming occasional difficulties in Jewish-Arab relations.[30]

However, because of their restricted numerical importance and minority status, the Arabs' power on the national scene is marginal. An unwritten consensus among the Zionist parties neutralizes their bargaining power in Parliament and as Lustick puts it, they enjoy "no effective access [of participation] to those institutions and organizations that dominate the life of the State."[31]

Hence, and, in this respect like for the edot, inferiority in the polity accumulates with that in the spheres of social stratification and membership. All these sharpen conflictual feelings against the domination of the Jew which are nourished—instead of being attenuated, as for the edot—by the development on the international scene of both the Israeli-Arab conflict and the Palestinian Cause. Furthermore, the emergence inside the group of new elites of inconsistent status, who are also hostile to the traditional—and pragmatic—leadership, reinforce a tendency to radicalization. Hence, in Peres's survey[32] of 1967, it was found that only 38 percent of a random sample of Israeli Arabs firmly opposed war of Arab countries against Israel. Similarly, verses of Israeli Arab poets calling for ultimate resistance against the "robbing" of land by the Jew[33] have become very popular among their stock.

Much more data about the Arabs' general interpretation of their plight in Israeli society are unavailable; however, one can point to political behaviors that are consistent with such sentiments. As early as 1960, a movement called "El-Ard" (The Land) proclaimed its aspiration "to restore the Palestinian People's autonomy, to guarantee its complete and legitimate rights. . . [in accordance] with the high ideals of the Arab Nation."[34] This movement, which actually called for the separation of Arab-populated areas from the State of Israel, was banned by the Israeli Supreme Court.

However, another form of anti-Israel politics was to be more successful. Support of Rakah, the virulently anti-Zionist New Communist List is widespread among the Arabs. During the 1970s, this party had about 2,000 Arab members and 500 Jews.[35] While it generally obtains less than 1 percent of the Jewish vote, its support among the Arab population varies between 35 percent and 40 percent. Yet, as a Communist faction tied to the U.S.S.R., Rakah does not evolve as an independent Arab force; hence it represents an Arab protest vote rather than a focus of ideological identification.

As such this party is unable to impede the appearance of more ethnic-oriented organizations such as the "Movement of the Sons of the Village" (Tnuat Bne Hakfar) which in the early 1980s constitutes the main force in Arab student organizations, and is expanding its activity to villages and towns. Though its pamphlets mainly denounce the discrimination of Arabs by the "establishment" and endorse the Palestinian Cause only for Palestinians of non-Israeli territories, its aggressive slogans and its open sympathy for Palestinian guerrilla movements reveal its basic anti-Israeli attitude.

Militant Arabism of whatever form shows that Israeli Arabs constitute, contrarily to the edot, a "for-itself" grouping. However, this militantism only deepens the division between Jews and Arabs. As such, it isolates this ethnic issue even more from that which divides

Jews among themselves—as well as, let us add, from any other political cleavage in the Israeli polity.

It is this context, factually, which alongside the Arabs' "gains" in Israel in terms of standard of living, educational facilities, civil rights, and citizenship in a democratic country, explains that protest constitutes but one political expression of a conflictual awareness of kind. The other expression, which persists despite the radicalization of many Arabs, still recognizes the ethnic condition inherent in the label "Israeli Arabs," and the imperative of positive arrangements with, and within Israeli society. Ever since 1949, all general elections have shown a strong support of Arab votes—between 50 and 65 percent—either for Arab parties allied to the Israeli establishment or for Zionist parties themselves, wherein they have representatives; this support is generally even greater at the local level, which is more directly and practically important for the ethnic community.

All these contrast with the crypto-pluralistic syndrome that applies to the edot. The illegitimacy in this case of open ethnic politics explains the marginality of ethnic independent militantism which actually takes place mainly inside nonethnic frameworks. At the same time issues related to ethnic problems are deeply embedded in the center's policies, which are articulated in the name of a strong integrative ideology. Hence, one cannot find any expression of conjunction between Arabs and Jewish ethnic groups in the realm of polity either.

THE IMPACT OF ETHNICITY

In terms of the Jewish-Arab ethnic encounter, Israel is a "deeply divided"[36] society, its divisions drawn along the lines of common belonging to a given geopolitical entity. This division is openly recognized in a pluralistic model that widely institutionalizes the distinction between and hierarchy among groups.

Major problematic aspects of this model reside in the terms and arrangements of its formulation and implementation. It is thus, for instance, that the principle of control imposed by belligerency represents, in a democratic regime, a permanent focus of tension between the Jewish establishment and the Arabs. Moreover, an acute problem for the group is its limited and isolated power and, as a consequence, the position of its cultural, social, economic problems in the center's list of priorities. Furthermore, the social development of the Arab community and the apparition of new elites gradually make the client-patron patterns that relate the group to the center more and more obsolete.

Beyond such points of friction, there is the basic "negative convergence" of both the Jews' and the Arabs' perspectives on their ethnic encounter, namely, the unambiguous, mutually exclusive boundaries. It is this "negative convergence" that explains the absence of any common point of reference between the Jewish-Arab and the inter-Jewish ethnic cleavages, the two major cleavages in Israeli society. Many Jews belonging to the Oriental edot, it is true, are closer to Arabs than to other Jews in many cultural and social respects, but what is entailed by the foregoing is that each case but "amplifies" the particular dynamism of the other. Thus the Oriental edot, by virtue of the logic of the pluralistic model of the Jewish-Arab encounter consider themselves an integral part of the dominant group. The Arabs, similarly, by virtue of the logic of the crypto-pluralistic inter-Jewish cleavage, do not seek allies among the edot and remain concentrated on their own ethnic problems. Hence, the two ethnic encounters occurring in Israeli society are of no accumulative impact on its stability; on the contrary, the divergence of their respective pressures may even be viewed as contributing to this stability.

The influence of belligerency between Israel and Arab countries, however, is a crucial factor in this picture. This situation, one may hope, will vanish sometime in the future when peace would ease Jewish-Arab relations in Israel herself. The abolition, for instance, of special control mechanisms would open new areas of participation to Arabs. In addition, this population could play an important role in Israel's relationship with the rest of the Middle East.

Yet, in the long run, the solidification of Jewish-Arab partnership cannot be grounded only in instrumental considerations deriving from the mere coexistence inside a given geopolitical reality; it is also a function of development of common cultural contents and symbols drawn from shared endeavors. What is required for such a development, from Arabs as well as from Jews, is that "Israeliness" would stand as an identity on its own and not only as a predicate—differently interpreted by each side—of another primordial identity of "Arabness" or "Jewishness."

For the Israeli Arab, however, the crystallization of such a concept of "Israeliness" bearing substantial intrinsic meanings would be likely to arouse acute subjective difficulties when unlimited free contacts with the Arab world—and mainly, with a Palestinian entity—will be possible.

In the same vein, an era of peace would also impart new roles to the Oriental edot inside the Jewish stock because of their better knowledge of Arab culture. But, at the same time, and by the same token, a Middle East open to free movement and relations would also constitute a challenge to the Jews' social and cultural cohesion. This problem would re-emphasize the importance of *mizug*. Mizug, to recall, revolves around the twofold principle of deepening cultural values inherent to all versions of Judaism, and encouraging the contribution of every group of immigrants to an all-Israeli Jewish patrimonium.

In *theory*, "Israeliness" on the one hand, and "Israeli Jewishness" or "Israeli Arabness" on the other, do not exclude each other, since each label applies to another circle of intergroup relations. In *practice*, however, these labels represent, in their respective circles of interaction, implications that are basically divergent. These *simultaneous* divergences will probably be a major nexus of conflictual dynamism of Israeli society if and when it finally becomes an undisputed reality.

NOTES

1. R. Bastuni, "The Arab Israelis," in *Israel: Social Structure and Change*, ed. M. Curtis and M. Chertoff (New Brunswick N.J.: Transaction Books 1973), p. 411.

2. I. Lustick, *Arabs in the Jewish State* (Austin and London: University of Texas Press, 1980), p. 83.

3. A. Rose, "Minorities," *The International Encyclopedia of Social Sciences*, vol.10, ed. D. L. Sills (USA: Crowell, Collier and Macmillan Inc., 1968), pp. 365-71.

4. K. Nakhleh, "Cultural Determinants of Collective Identity: The Case of the Arabs in Israel," in *Problems of Collective Identity and Legitimization in Israeli Society*, ed. R. Kehana and S. Kopstein (Jerusalem: Academon 1980), p. 362.

5. E. Stock, *From Conflict to Understanding, Relations between Jews and Arabs in Israel since 1948* (New York: Institute of Human Relations Press, 1968), p. 20.

6. Lustick, *Arabs in the Jewish State*, p. 84.

7. Stock, *From Conflict to Understanding*, p. 94.

8. Quoted from newspaper, in A. Benyamin and R. Peleg, *Haskalah Gvohah Vehaaravim Beisrael* [Higher education and Arabs in Israel] (Tel Aviv: Am Oved, 1977), p. 21.

9. Y. Peres, *Yahasei Edot Beisrael* [Ethnic relations in Israel] (Tel Aviv: Sifriat Hapoalim, 1977), p. 186.

10. S. Smooha, "Mediniut Kayemet Vealternativit Klapei Haaravim Beisrael" [Existing and Alternative Policy Towards the Arabs in Israel], *Megamot* 26, no. 1 (September 1980): 14.

11. Stock, *From Conflict to Understanding*, pp. 24-25; 47; 59; 65.

12. Lustick, *Arabs in the Jewish State*, pp. 182-183.

13. S. Carmi and H. Rosenfeld, "The Origins of the Process of Proletarianization and Urbanization of Arab Peasants in Palestine," in *Migration, Ethnicity and Community, Studies of Israeli Society*, vol. 1, ed. K. Kraucz (New Brunswick and London: Transaction Books, 1980), pp. 183-98.

14. E. T. Zureik, *The Palestinians in Israel, A Study in Internal Colonialism* (London: Boston, and Henley: Routledge and Kegan Paul, 1979), p. 123.

15. Stock, *From Conflict to Understanding*, pp. 23-24.

16. Zureik, *The Palestinians in Israel*, p. 123.

17. O. Remba, "Income Inequality in Israel: Ethnic Aspects," in *Israel: Social Structure and Change*, ed. M. Curtis and M. Chertoff (New Brunswick N.J.: Transaction Books, 1973) p. 207.

18. Peres, *Yahasei Edot Beisrael* [Ethnic relations in Israel], pp. 178-79.

19. L. Adar and H. Adler, *Hahinuh Learahim Bebeit Sefer Leyaldei Olim* [Education for values in schools for immigrant children] (Jerusalem: The School of Education, the Hebrew University, 1965), pp. 101-3; 137-38.

20. G. Myrdal, *An American Dilemma*, vol. 2 (New York, Toronto, London: McGraw Hill Company, 1962), pp. 592-99.

21. Council for Higher Education, *Statistics of Higher Education* (Jerusalem) 1979, p. 15.

22. A. Benyamin and R. Peleg, *Haskalah Gvohah Vehaaravim* [Higher education and Arabs], p. 80.

23. E. Rekhess, *A Survey of Israeli-Arab Graduates from Institutions of Higher Learning in Israel (1961-1971)* (Tel Aviv: Shiloah Institute, Tel Aviv University, 1974), p. 9.

24. G. Lenski, "Status Crystallization: A Non-Vertical Dimension of Social Status," *American Sociological Review*, 19 August 1954, pp. 405-13.

25. Benyamin and Peleg, *Haskalah Gvohah Vehaavarim* [Higher education and Arabs], p. 96.

26. Peres, *Yahasei Edot Beisrael* [Ethnic relations in Israel], p. 180.

27. Benyamin and Peleg, *Haskalah Gvohah Vehaaravim* [Higher education and Arabs], p. 27.

28. Bastuni, "The Arab Israelis," p. 412.

29. Stock, *From Conflict to Understanding*, p. 43.

30. Lustick, *Arabs in the Jewish State*, pp. 208-14.

31. Ibid., p. 116.

32. Peres, *Yahasei Edot Beisrael* [Ethnic Relations in Israel], p. 187.

33. Samih al-Kassem, "A Speech from the Market of Unemployment," quoted in Lustick, *Arabs in the Jewish State*, p. 11.

34. Zureik, *The Palestinians in Israel*, p. 174.

35. Lustick, *Arabs in the Jewish State*, p. 242.

36. E. Nordlinger, *Conflict Regulation in Divided Societies* (Cambridge, Mass.: Harvard University Press, 1972), pp. 6-13.

The General Meanings of the Analysis

12

The previous chapter has shown the essential differences between the inter-Jewish model of ethnic encounter grounded in a Fusion of Exiles concept and the Arab-Jewish case where pluralism is taken for granted. Another case that emphasizes the variety within the universe of ethnicity, and which is worth raising in this concluding chapter, is the one wherein (1) the dominant culture aspires to the implementation of a melting model but conditions the full acceptance of the ethnic group into membership upon its thorough acculturation, and where, on the other hand, (2) the group shares more favorable predispositions to meet the requirements of modern socioeconomic markets but is also committed to maintaining itself as a distinct cultural community.

Thus, for instance, the problems of some American white ethnic groups are altogether different from those analyzed above. Originally alien to the labels of identity pertaining to the dominant culture and though by their ability to "adjust," groups such as Italian or Irish Americans fully legitimize their presence in society, their basic velleity to preserve themselves in at least some cultural respects, accounts for their aspiration to institutionalize cultural pluralism "beyond the melting pot." By the same token, and in the context of the opposed perspective of the dominant culture, one may explain not only the diffusion of ethnic prejudices within the absorptive setting at the first steps of these groups' settling, but also the segregative impact these prejudices may imply in intergroup relations. Hence, unlike the Israeli edot, the interest of such groups refers primarily to liberalism, which is associated with a greater tolerance of cultural particularisms and a "lowering of the price demanded" for social integration. Thus these groups are quite mobile and manage to join the middle class, thereby minimizing their salience on the stratificational map. Yet, at the same time, cultural pluralism gains in popularity despite a shrinkage of objective sociocultural differences. In Israel, as far as the edot are concerned, such pluralism remains quite evident in daily life as cultural disparities widely overlap class positions; however, the "temporary" character of the situation is taken for granted by all. Thus, if at the level of an individual ethnic, the main problems in America are: How and how far should he remain an ethnic?, in Israel, the questions are: Why has assimilation not fully occurred yet, and who is to blame? It is this kind of shortfall which is the essence of the Jewish-Israeli model of ethnicity. In other words:

The idea of pluralism was voiced as a human condition in the reality of American society, as one leading to recognition of ethnic and religious differences among groups of people who settled there. Then, it came to replace the assumption of a melting pot. . . . This was a concession to minorities by the majority. . . . Here (in Israel) ethnic differences are not spoken of. At most, variations are mentioned depending on the society of origin.[1]

These comparative remarks bring us back to the discussion of contemporary theoretical approaches. To recall, some of these approaches chiefly stress integrative processes while others point out conflictual aspects, each one referring variously to cultural, stratificational, and political problems. Moreover, while some give special attention to characteristics of ethnics, others focus principally on the setting's structure.

In fact, it appears that not every feature singled out by these approaches is equally relevant to the case of the edot. Parsons' "ethnic de-socialization," for instance, has only a relative impact upon edot, which maintain themselves culturally. As for stratification, the case of the edot confirms Lenski's emphasis on the issue of culture-determined predispositions while Van den Berghe's theory about the impact of socioeconomic competition also explains the ethnics' becoming ethnoclasses. In these circumstances, cross-cutting lines of solidarity— as emphasized by Shils—barely affect their cohesion (which greatly depends in fact on their a priori own cultural features). Yet, in contrast to another assumption of Van den Berghe as well as to Myrdal's approach, ethnics remain ethnoclasses, not because of the impeding of mobility by "others," but rather because of the latter's readiness to assimilate mobile elements. The case of the edot, in this respect, challenges sociopsychological theories by showing that the social impact of prejudices is widely subordinate to "rules of membership." Mobility, therefore, does not entail, as for the edot, any "tangentialization" of the groups as implied by Hendershot, while, on the other hand, and in contradiction to Bell's hypothesis, the edot, which see themselves as "temporary" groupings do not become autonomous political forces despite their numerical importance and Israel's democratic regime. Thus, on the whole, though some of these concepts, views, and topics have contributed to our study, they are of but limited help.

Our own theoretical approach is much indebted to comparative sociological models that investigate modern societies by focusing on their specific character and, beyond those developments more or less common to all, point to features of their self-perceived cultural and historical personality. In brief, we contend that the shape of ethnicity in modern societies is related not only to models of economic and stratification systems, but also to the contents of their particular culture.

These contents may differ from one society to another, be diversely evident in each or even be common to many. They are not necessarily accepted and internalized by all—not even a majority—in the setting, but they are the ones represented and diffused by the center. Their impact is directly perceived in cultural orientations and rules orienting the practical working of various spheres and their related institutional arrangements. Those foci, orientations, and rules that most influence the ethnic encounter, insofar as it depends on the setting, are those which refer to the defining of membership in society, rights of participation in the several spheres, requirements conditioning participation, and criteria eventually justifying the "monopolization" of preeminence by certain subgroups. It is in this set of factors that, we suggest, resides the answer to one of two "large" questions which concluded the introductory chapter, namely: What elements pertaining to the social order would clarify the dissimilarities between societies otherwise quite similar and in which a same ethnic group may meet a different fate? But whatever the setting's characteristics, an ethnic encounter is a process of interaction where the group itself does play its part.

The general statement which began our discussion in this respect was the defining of an ethnic group as a group of people who originally shared certain primordial attributes, value orientations and behavioral models and who, when met with a given dominant culture, develop a subjective awareness of kind and some objective sociocultural particularism. According to this definition, it is in *a priori* features that one should find the answer to the second "large" question, namely: What factors may explain why separate ethnic groups evolve differently in a same setting?

The main point here is that our definition of an ethnic group makes it a *result* of the encounter with a dominant culture, and what emerges as an ethnic group cannot, in itself, explain the occurrence of ethnicity. It follows that the encounter should be viewed as a process of *ethnicization* of the group. In this process, to be sure, some original features of the group are lost and new ones acquired, some people leave and others are—by marriage, conversion or other means—incorporated. These people were not necessarily an ethnic group outside the context of the encounter. For instance, the Italians were not an ethnic group until they reached America, and groups such as some Protestant immigrants to America were ethnics in their former situations but are not in the United States. Moreover, as in the Israeli case, those who were ethnics in the past may now illustrate a totally different type of ethnic group.

These considerations are hardly new, but the conclusion they entail has not yet been elaborated in theories of ethnicity. This conclusion demands that we view ethnicity as a transformational occurrence and requires an analysis of it that focuses on those nexi of problems inherent in the encounter. Such an analysis cannot avoid the complexity of its object, caused by the diversity of its interrelated sequences: on the one hand, the encounter takes place in distinct—though interacting—spheres where, in the confrontation of relevant rules with features of the group, the latter's engagement is molded; on the other hand, each sphere engenders additional elements of the group's overall sociocultural particularism and awareness of kind—which influence each other as well. It is this whole set of factors, which, obviously, also vary with conjunctural circumstances, that finally accounts not only for ethnicity but also for the transformation of society itself, resulting from the encounter. Because of its current ethnic diversity, indeed, new cleavages of *sociocultural discontinuity* characterize it and are potential foci of conflict, even, eventually, of the reformulation of its historical and cultural personality. Because of the complexity of the study of ethnicity, as well as the wide varieties of possible dominant cultures and features of groups, any general paradigm that is proposed is likely to become rapidly a sterile taxonomy. Yet specific case studies, by pointing out the very possibility of given realities in the universe of ethnicity, do, as such, bear theoretical significance while, at the same time, contribute to our understanding of aspects eventually pertaining to other cases as well.

The Jewish Israeli model, anyway, highlights several issues of general interest in this field. First, we see that an essential aspect of the type of concept exemplified by "ethnic group" resides in the fact that it does not necessarily suggest a symmetric opponent: some category of "outs" may consist of a nonethnic stock. This discussion is close to an additional topic not usually stressed, namely the distinction between a sociocultural category and an ethnic group. Sociocultural categories that indicate broad wholes differing in certain objective respects cannot as such be defined unrelatedly to each other. Moreover, and again in contrast to an ethnic group, they do not presuppose the presence of any conscious commitment among their members and have but a restricted significance as regards the dynamic aspect of social reality. The Jewish Israeli case illustrates a situation where two cultural categories exist, but ethnicity refers to groups relating to just one of them.

These distinctions are confused in Israel itself with respect to the edot, where inappropriate labels are often used even by social scientists. The main reason for this is the wide overlapping of sociocultural categories with socioeconomic cleavages, which endows the former with a particular saliency, leaving the edot—at the bottom of social hierarchies—quite undistinguished, from the outside, from each other. Yet, if in Israel ethnic groups assume the form of ethnoclasses, this is hardly explained, let us repeat, by their exclusion from opportunities of social mobility. Israel, from this viewpoint, is an instance where a quasi-absence of open discrimination and segregation encourages not only ethnic mobility as such but also—and in this respect, supported by the ethnics' own orientations—the assimilation of mobile elements into new strata. Thus, in a general manner, this model demonstrates the paradoxical possibility for an ethnic group of remaining an ethnoclass *despite* the existence of social mobility and, in part *because* of the openness of "others" to ethnics. This phenomenon further explains the lack of an accurate perception of ethnic reality in higher social spheres where ethnic cleavages are weak and of marginal significance and appear mainly as linked to problems of stratification concerning "Orientals-as-a-whole."

In this context, however, it may be argued that two basic contradictions characterize our description of the Israeli model. If mobile ethnics assimilate into "others," is it still possible to contend (as we do) that it is the ethnic encounter at the level of membership and culture which explains the maintenance of the edah as a sociocultural community? Is it not more plausible simply to refer the enduring existence of ethnic groups to questions of stratification *per se*—that is, the lack of mobility of most ethnics? Moreover, if the eagerness of mobiles to assimilate is accounted for, at least partially, by the *mizug* perspective also inherent in the edot's own outlook, how can we justify our other contention— that edot which are socioeconomic "neighbors" do not assimilate among themselves and stand removed from this "Orientals-as-a-whole" concept?

These contradictions, in fact, are only apparent. To begin with the last question, the lack of mutual assimilation between Oriental edot: it follows from the very definition of the encounter at the level of membership and culture that traditional or quasi-traditional groups of Jewish immigrants do meet difficulties in "escaping" from their own circle of reference both in their definition of comprehensive concepts of identity and in their interpretation of cultural differences from the "others." Thus, if it is by these factors that we can explain the lasting endurance of the edah in the face of the nonethnic stock, then even more valid is this explanation when considering the edah *vis-à-vis* other edot sharing also a particular sense of awareness of kind. Thus, from this standpoint, Israel is an instance where submelting processes appear as fraught with even more difficulties than more comprehensive melting.

Accordingly, the main issue remains the significance of the "escape" of mobile elements from their ethnic community. There are several answers which have been mentioned throughout these pages. The first factor, of course, is the very "openness" of "others" to mobile elements and the availability of their cultural symbols and styles for anyone having the material and educational resources of the nonethnic middle class. Where no "conversion" is required, the temptation to get rid of ethnic obligations is equalled by its social reward, which is the social recognition of one's status achievements in the eyes of both "others" and of the group itself. This latter factor brings us to the edah's own ambivalence toward its maintenance. Let us recall here that the encounter with a dominant culture displaying in different terms the same religious and national allegiance represents a partial delegitimization of the group's parochialism. This entails for tradition-minded people not merely problems of adjustment to a new environment but also forming a new image of themselves. Thus, beyond the emergence of the group as an edah, its lack of self-confidence as well as its own belief in its future disappearance account for the fluidity of its boundaries and its weak power of attraction for those who find an alternative to the "ethnic way." More than anything else, the issue of mobile ethnics shows how far "ethnicization" of traditional or quasi-traditional groups of origin under the form of edot is imbued with elements of crisis.

It is against this background that one best understands an additional paradox of theoretical interest, namely that the ethnic group constitutes a real unit that expresses conflictual claims but does not evolve into a "for-itself" group. Hence it endorses the national consensus for which ethnic pluralism is both a taboo and a permanent preoccupation.

Precisely because of this trait, our model could be interpreted from an altogether different perspective. Following Parkin,[2] it may be remarked, in a conflict-theory vein, that an Israeli dominant class maintains itself by controlling entry to valued positions through reliance upon criteria of achievement, while the "hidden" assumption is that only a predictable few can meet these. Thus "mizug galuyot" ("one people") and other tokens of the national consensus simply blur the reality of class antagonisms to the advantage of the better-off. They hinder the growth of a political class-consciousness among ethnics who belong massively to the working class and on the other hand, undermine their readiness to engage in ethnic politics.

Yet, whatever the attractiveness of such a rational interpretation, how can it plausibly explain conspicuous aspects of the case such as the direct and immediate endowment of membership on newcomers or the extent of "generosity" far beyond that which is common in other instances of immigration? Moreover, by no means has the notion of edah and all its related concepts been forged by the dominant culture alone in the framework of Israeli reality; their premises are the outcome of the encounter of given legacies with a culture which is also tributary of particular cultural endeavors.

Thus the one fact, at least, unequivocally confirmed by our study is the strength of myths in society; this strength, seemingly, is the most common denominator of ethnicity in general.

NOTES

1. N. Rotenschtreich, "Sikum" [Conclusions], in *Mizug Galuyot*, ed. O. Cohen, (Jerusalem: The Magnes Press, 1969), p. 189.

2. F. Parkin, "Strategies of Social Closure in Class Formation," in *The Social Analysis of Class Structure*, ed. F. Parkin (London: Tavistock Publications, 1974), pp. 1-19.

Appendix A

The Numerical Importance of Groups of Origin in Israel's Jewish Population

A. Groups According to Country of Origin[a]	Percentage in the Total Jewish Population	Groups according to country of origin	Percentage in the total Jewish Population
Morocco	14.1	Turkey	3.3
Poland	13.4	Greece & Bulgaria	2.6
Rumania	10.5	Libya	2.5
Iraq	8.9	Egypt & Sudan	2.3
Israel[b]	8.5	America & Oceania	2.1
U.S.S.R.	6.2	Hungary	1.8
Yemen & South Yemen	5.7	Czechoslovakia	1.7
Algeria & Tunisia	3.8	Syria & Lebanon	1.3
Iran	3.6	India & Pakistan	1.0
Germany & Austria	3.5	Other groups of origin	3.2
		Total:	100.0

B. According to Continent of Birth	Percentage in the Total Jewish Population
Asia, not including Israel	24.4
Africa	22.9
Europe, America, Oceania	44.2
Israel[b]	8.5
Total:	100.0

SOURCE: This table is based on the 1972-Population Census reported in the Israeli Central Bureau of Statistics, *Statistical Abstracts, 1975,* Jerusalem, 1975: 52-3.

[a]The country of birth refers to oneself if not Israel, or to the father's in the other case.

[b]This category includes all third-generation Israelis.

Appendix B

Status Hierarchies and Origin

		Born in Asia-Africa	Israeli-born Father from As.-Af.	Born in Israel, Father also	Born in Europe-America	Israeli-born, father from Eur.-Amer.
1. Occupational distribution (1978)[a]	Total	100.0	100.0	100.0	100.0	100.0
Industrial and service workers		60.1	51.3	32.6	37.3	22.0
Agriculturalists		5.4	4.1	7.4	4.5	6.9
Salesmen and small businessmen		8.4	6.1	5.9	10.2	5.3
Clerks		13.6	25.0	25.9	19.0	20.9
Managers, professionals, technicians, businessmen		10.2	11.4	21.1	19.3	31.1
Scientists and Academics		2.2	2.2	7.2	10.4	13.8
2. inequality ratios of gross average annual money per urban employee family[a]						
in 1970		0.73	0.78	0.92	1.00	1.18
in 1978		0.80	0.73	1.03	1.00	1.13

3. Years of schooling completed, for population age 14 and over[a]

	Born in Asia-Africa		Israeli-born Father from As.-Af.		Born in Israel, Father also		Born in Europe-America		Israeli-born, father from Eur.-Amer.	
Annual data for	1961	1978	1961	1978	1961	1978	1961	1978	1961	1978
Total	100.0	100.0	100.0	100.0	100.0	100.0	100.0	100.0	100.0	100.0
0-4	41.6	25.7	8.6	1.7	7.5	1.9	10.8	8.6	1.5	0.9
5-8	36.2	30.9	52.3	21.0	34.2	13.1	37.9	26.3	14.5	5.3
9-12	19.1	35.0	34.6	68.1	45.1	61.9	38.5	39.2	64.5	54.4
13+	3.1	8.4	4.5	9.2	13.2	23.1	12.8	25.9	19.5	39.4

4. Political representation[b]	Total for each period	All Jews of Asian and African Origin		All Jews of European and American Origin	
		Late 1950s	Late 1960s	Late 1950s	Late 1960s
Highest rank of political elite	100.0	4.0	14.0	96.0	86.0
Second highest rank	100.0	11.0	17.0	89.0	83.0
Other ranks	100.0	20.0	37.0	80.0	63.0

SOURCE: [a]Israeli Central Bureau of Statistics (ICBS), *Society in Israel, 1980*, Jerusalem: 1980, pp. 69, 96, 160-61.
[b]S. Smooha, *Israel: Pluralism and Conflict*, (London, Henley: Routledge & Kegan Paul, 1978), p. 340.

Appendix C

Selected Results of the 1977 and 1981 General Elections in Israel (%)

Settlements according to categories	Likud[a]		Ma'arah[b]		Religious[c] Parties		Dash[d]	Tami[e]	Miscel.[f]	
	1977	1981	1977	1981	1977	1981	1977	1981	1977	1981
Yemenite settlements										
Rosh Ha'ayin (a town)	27	57	7	8	32	29	—	3	34	3
Mishan (a village)	28	40	28	35	42	19	—	—	2	4
Towns predominantly Moroccan										
Beit She'an	45	55	22	17	21	18	1	6	11	4
Sderot	34	35	22	20	20	10	2	28	22	7
Ofakim	37	40	23	22	26	13	2	15	12	10
Kiryat Shmonah	42	54	23	26	12	7	6	6	17	7
Ashkenazi villages										
Kfar Hasidim	23	25	21	9	32	32	9	—	15	34
Nahalal	11	7	41	77	—	1	37	—	1	15
Upper-class neighborhood										
Savyon	33	19	10	41	3	5	45	—	9	35
Middle-class urban area (predominantly Ashkenazi)										
Givataim & Ramat Gan	37	39	23	45	8	7	17	—	15	9

SOURCE: For 1977, Israeli Central Burea of Statistics (ICBS), *Totsaot Habehirot La-Knesset Hatshiit, Sidrat Pirsumim Meiuhadim mis.* 553 [The Results of the Elections for the 9th Knesset, Special Series number 553], Jerusalem, 1978, pp. 25-36.

NOTES: [a] = Right-wing Alignment;

[b] = Left-of-center Labor Alignment with leftist ally;

[c] = includes National Religious Party and two conservative factions;

[d] = centrist party that dislocated before 1981;

[e] = Movement for Israel's Tradition;

[f] = extreme right Thiah (Renaissance), liberal factions, Arab parties, the Communist Party and other small lists.

Glossary

HEBREW TERMS

Ashkenazi (pl.: Ashkenazim): the term nowadays refers to Jews descendent from Central and Eastern European Jewish Communities.

Edah (pl.: edot): the term designates, in general use, groups of Jewish immigrants according to their origin.

Edot Mizrach: the term designates, in general use, all groups of Jewish immigrants originating from North African and Middle-Eastern countries.

Galut or Golah: literally "Exile," refers to the Jewish Dispersion throughout the world outside the Land of Israel.

Hillulah (pl.: hillulot): literally "feast" or "wedding feast"—a Tunisian Jewish memorial rite commemorating the death of a famous rabbi or scholar.

Histradrut: General Federation of Trade Unions.

Kabbalah: literally "Acceptance;" the mystic teachings of Judaism.

Kibbutz (pl.: Kibbutzim): collective settlement based on agriculture and industry.

Knesset: Israeli Parliament

Mizug galuyot (in brief, mizug): refers to the ideal of the fusion of all groups of Jewish immigrants into a unified national and sociocultural entity.

Moshav (pl.: Moshavim): cooperative agricultural settlement.

Oleh (pl.: olim): Jewish immigrant to Israel.

Sephardi: the term refers to Jews descendent from Jewish communities in Spain.

Yeshivah (pl.: Yeshivot): a traditional Jewish institution of religious learning.

Yishuv: the pre-1948 Jewish community in Palestine.

Zahal: Israel Defense Forces (abb.IDF).

Zohar: literally "Splendor;" the fundamental work of Jewish mysticism which takes the form of commentary to the Pentateuch.

ARABIC TERMS

Dhimmis: term used by Moslem authorities referring to Jews and Christians and defining them as subordinate but protected communities.
Jizyah: special tax paid by the Jewish communities to the Moslem authorities.
Mellah: segregated Jewish neighborhoods in Moroccan cities.

Bibliography

Adams, Charles. "The Islamic Religious Tradition." In *Judaism, Christianity and Islam*, edited by Janet O'Dea, Thomas O'Dea and Charles Adams. New York: Harper & Row, 1972, pp. 159-214.

Almond, Gabriel A., and Verba, Sidney. *The Civic Culture*. Princeton: Princeton University Press, 1963.

Banton, Michael. *Race Relations*. New York: Basic Books, 1967.

Bar-On Mordekhai. *Education Processes in the Israel Defense Forces*. Tel Aviv: Israel Press, 1966.

Bar-Yosef, Rivkah. "Hamarokaiim, Reka Habayah" [The Moroccans, the context of the problem]. *Molad* 17, no. 131 (June 1959): 247-51 (Hebrew).

―――. "Absorption versus Modernization. In *Israeli Society 1967-1973*, edited by Reuven Kehana and Simhah Kopstein. Jerusalem: Academon, 1974, pp. 8-43.

―――, and Ramot, Tamar. "Immigrants in Jerusalem: Residential Status." In *Israeli Society 1967-1973*, edited by Reuven Kehana and Simhah Kopstein. Jerusalem: Academon, 1974, pp. 55-96.

Bastuni, Rustum. "The Arab Israelis." In *Israel: Social Structure and Change*, edited by Michael Curtis and Mordecai Chertoff. New Brunswick, N.J.: Transaction Books, 1973, pp. 409-18.

Bell, Daniel. "Ethnicity and Social Change." In *Ethnicity*, edited by Nathan Glazer and Daniel Moynihan. Cambridge, Mass.: Harvard University Press, 1975, pp. 141-74.

Ben-Ezer, Ehud. *Hamahzevah* [The quarry]. Tel-Aviv: Am Oved, 1963 (Hebrew).

Benyamin, Abraham, and Peleg, Rachel. *Haskalah Gevohah Vehaaravim Beisrael* [Higher education and Arabs in Israel]. Tel Aviv: Am Oved (Hebrew).

Ben-David, Josef. "Diyun" [Discussion]. In *Mizug Galuyot*, edited by Ofrah Cohen. Jerusalem: The Magnes Press, 1969, pp. 89-91 (Hebrew).

Bensimon-Donath, Doris. *L'Integration des Juifs Nord-Africains en France.* Paris, La Haye: Mouton, 1977.

Berler, Alexander. *Arim Hadashot Beisrael* [New towns in Israel]. Jerusalem: Israel Universities Press, 1970 (Hebrew).

Bourla, Yehudah. *Ishto Hasnuah* [His hated wife]. Tel-Aviv: Am Oved, 1959 (Hebrew).

Carmi, Shulamit, and Rosenfeld, Henry. "The Origins of the Process of Proletarianization and Urbanization of Arab Peasants in Palestine." In *Migration, Ethnicity and Community, Studies of Israeli Society,* vol. 1, edited by Ernest Kraucz. New Brunswick and London: Transaction Books, 1980, pp. 183-98.

Chen, Michael; Lewy, Aryeh; and Kfir, Drorah. "Efsharuyot Hamigfash Habeinedati Behativot Habeinaim, Mimusho Vetotsaotav" [The possibilities of interethnic contact in the junior high schools: implementation and results] *Megamot* 23, nos. 3-4 (December 1977), pp. 101-23 (Hebrew).

Chouraqui, André. *La Condition Juridique de l'Israelite Marocain.* Paris: Presse du Livre Francais, 1945.

———. *Les Juifs d'Afrique du Nord.* Paris: Presses Universitaires de France, 1952.

Cohen, Erik. "The Black Panthers and Israeli Society." In *Israeli Society 1967-1973,* edited by Reuven Kehana and Simhah Kopstein. Jerusalem: Academon 1974 pp. 166-74.

Cohen, Haim J. *Yehudei Asia Veafrika Bamizrah Hatihon* [The Jews of Asia and Africa in the Middle-East]. Tel-Aviv: Hakibbutz Hameuhad Publishing House, 1972.

Cohen, Ofrah, ed. *Mizug Galuyot* [The fusion of exiles]. Jerusalem: Magnes Press, 1969 (Hebrew).

Committee of Investigation of Delinquent Youth in Israel. "Prakim Mitoh Hadoh" [Chapters from the report]. *Megamot* 7, no. 4 (October 1956): 377-89 (Hebrew).

Confino, Michael. "Nigudim Vetmurot Betsfon Afrika" [Conflicts and changes in Northern Africa]. *Mibifnim* 16, no. 2 (November 1953): 56-81 (Hebrew).

Curtis, Michael, and Chertoff, Mordecai. *Israel: Social Structures and Change.* New Brunswick, N.J.: Transaction Books, 1973.

De Nesry, Charles. *Le Juif de Tanger et le Maroc.* Tanger: Editions Internationales, 1956.

Deshen, Shlomoh. "Defusei Hishtanut Shel Masoret Datit: Beit Haknesset Haedati" [Patterns of change in religious tradition: the ethnic synagogue]. In *Mizug Galuyot,* edited by Ofrah Cohen. Jerusalem: The Magnes Press, 1969, pp. 66-73 (Hebrew).

———. *Immigrant Voters in Israel*. Manchester: Manchester University Press, 1970.

———. "Israeli Judaism: Introduction to the Major Patterns." *International Journal of Middle East Studies* 9 (February 1978), pp. 141-69.

———. "Political Ethnicity and Cultural Ethnicity in Israel during the 1960's." In *Urban Ethnicity*, ASA Monographs. London: N.Y.: Tavistock Publications, 1974, pp. 281-309.

———, and Shokeid, Moshe. *The Predicament of Homecoming*. Ithaca and London: Cornell University Press, 1974.

Deutsch, Akivah. "Dmut Haelitah Beparvar Teimani" [The image of elite in a Yemenite neighborhood]. *Megamot* 9 no. 4 (October 1958): 328-37 (Hebrew).

Editors. "Hakdamah" [Preface]. *Megamot* 23, nos. 3-4 (December 1977): 9-14 (Hebrew).

Eisenstadt, Shmuel with Curelaru Myriam. *The Forms of Sociology—Paradigms and Crisis*. New York: John Wiley & Sons, 1976.

Fuerstein, Reuven, and Rishel, M. "Yaldei Hamellah—Pigur Tarbuti Etsel Yeladim Marokaim Umashmauto Hahinuhit [The children of the Mellah—cultural backwardness among Moroccan children and its educational significance]. Jerusalem: Henrietta Szold Institute, The Jewish Agency, 1964 (Hebrew).

Geertz, Clifford. "The Integrative Revolution." In *Old Societies and New States*, edited by C. Geertz. New York: The Free Press, 1965, pp. 105-57.

Goitein, S. D. "Hahinuh Hayehudi Beeretz Teiman Ketipus Shel Hinuh Yehudi Mekori" [Jewish education in Yemen as a type of original Jewish education]. *Megamot* 2, no. 2 (January 1950): 152-80 (Hebrew).

Glazer, Nathan, and Moynihan, Daniel P. *Beyond the Melting Pot*. Cambridge, Mass.: The MIT Press, 1974.

———, eds. *Ethnicity*. Cambridge, Mass.: Harvard University Press, 1975.

Gordon, Milton. "Toward a General Theory of Racial and Ethnic Group Relations." In *Ethnicity*, edited by Nathan Glazer and Daniel P. Moynihan. Cambridge Mass.: Harvard University Press, 1975, pp. 84-110.

Greenberg, Harold. *Israeli Social Problems in Perspective*. Tel Aviv: Dekel Academic Press, 1979.

Halpern, Hayim, and Yaron, Dan. *Immigrant Cooperative Villages*. Rehovot: Department of Agro-Economics, the Hebrew University of Jerusalem, 1955.

Hendershot, G. E. "Ethnic Stratification." In *Racial Tensions and National Identity*, edited by E. Q. Campbell. Nashville: Vanderbilt University Press, 1972, pp. 57-61.

Hoetinck, H. "National Identity, Culture and Race in the Caribbeans" In *Racial Tensions and National Identity*, edited by E. Q. Campbell, Nashville: Vanderbilt University Press, 1972, pp. 17-44.

Horowitz, Dan, and Kimmerling, Baruch. "Some Social Implications of Military Service and the Reserve System in Israel." In *Israeli Society 1967-1973*, edited by Reuven Kehana and Simhah Kopstein. Jerusalem: Academon, 1974, pp. 118-181.

Horowitz, David L. "Ethnic Identity." In *Ethnicity*, edited by Nathan Glazer and Daniel P. Moynihan. Cambridge Mass.: Harvard University Press, 1975, pp. 111-40.

Inbar, Michael, and Adler, Haim. *Ethnic Integration in Israel*. New Brunswick N.J.: Transaction Books, 1977.

Kafih, Iahiah. *Hilhot Teiman, Haie Hayehudim Betsana Ubnoteah* [The ways of the Yemenites, the life of Jews in Sanaa and her daughters]. Jerusalem: Ben-Zvi Institute: Hebrew University, 1961 (Hebrew).

Katz, Elihu, and Zloczower, Abraham. "Hemshehiutam Shel Dfusim Edatiim Bador Hasheni (Teimanim)" [Continuity in ethnic patterns within the second generation (Yemenites)]. *Megamot* 9, no. 3 (June 1958): 187-200, (Hebrew).

Kehana, Reuven, and Kopstein, Simhah, eds. *Israeli Society 1967-1973*. Jerusalem: Academon, 1974.

Kimmerling, Baruch. "Anomia Veintegratsiah Bahevrah Haisraelit Uboltut Hasihsuh Haisraeli-Aravi" [Anomie and integration in Israeli society, and the salience of the Israeli-Arab conflict]. *Megamot* 19, no. 4 (September 1973): 349-73.

Klaff, Vivian. "Ethnic Segregation in Urban Israel." *Demography* 10, no. 2 (May 1973): 161-82.

Krausz, Ernest, ed. *Migration, Ethnicity and Community, Studies of Israeli Society*. Vol. 1. New Brunswick N.J. and London: Transaction Books, 1980.

Lenski, Gerhard. "Group Involvement, Religious Orientations and Economic Behavior" In *Racial and Ethnic Relations*, edited by B. E. Segal. New York: Crowell, 1972, pp. 154-68.

Levin, Josef, and Chen, Michael. "Behirot Sotsciometriot Bekitot Meuravot Mibehinah Edatit" [Sociometric Choices in Ethnically Heterogenous Classes]. *Megamot* 23, nos. 3-4 (December 1977): 189-208 (Hebrew).

Levy, Shulamit, and Guttman, Louis. *Indikatorim Hevratiim Leisrael:22 Beianuar-12 Bemers 1974* [Social indicators for Israel: January 22-March 12, 1974]. Jerusalem: Institute for Applied Social Research and Institute for Communication, The Hebrew University, 1974 (Hebrew).

Lipset, Seymour M. *The First New Nation*. New York: Anchor Books, 1967.

———. "The Israeli Dilemma." In *Israel: Social Structure and Change*, edited by Michael Curtis and Mordecai Chertoff. New Brunswick, N.J.: Transaction Books, 1973, pp. 349-62.

Lissak, Moshe. *"Degamei Ribud Vesheifot Mobiliut: Mekorat Hanaah Lemobiliut"* [Models of social stratification and aspirations to social mobility]. *Megamot* 15, no. 1 (January 1967): 66-82 (Hebrew).

———. *"Megamot Behishtalvut Haolim Bamaarah Haribudi Vehapoliti Shel Israel"* [Tendencies in the integration of immigrants in the stratification and political system of Israel]. *Mizug Galuyot*. Edited by Ofrah Cohen. Jerusalem: The Magnes Press, 1969 pp. 51-65 (Hebrew).

Lustick, Ian. *Arabs in the Jewish State*. Austin and London: University of Texas Press, 1980.

Marx, Emmanuel. "Alimut Ishit Beayarat Olim" [Individual violence in an immigrant town]. *Megamot*, 17, no. 1 (January 1970): 61-77 (Hebrew).

Marx, Karl. "Le 18 Brumaire de Louis Bonaparte." In *Les Luttes de Classes en France 1848-1850; Le 18 Brumaire de Louis Bonaparte*. Paris: Editions Sociales, 1949, pp. 115-276.

Mason, Philip. *Patterns of Dominance*. London: Oxford University Press, 1970.

Memmi, Albert. *Netsiv Hamelah* [The statute of salt]. Tel Aviv: Am Oved, 1960 (Hebrew).

Minkowitz, Moshe. *Mihamulah Leagudah* [From lineage to association]. Jerusalem: Kaplan School, The Hebrew University, 1967 (Hebrew).

Myrdal, Gunnar. *An American Dilemma*. New York, Toronto, London: McGraw-Hill, 1962.

Nakhleh, Khalil. "Cultural Determinants of Collective Identity: The Case of the Arabs in Israel." In *Problems of Collective Identity and Legitimization in Israeli Society*, edited by Reuven Kehana and Simhah Kopstein. Jerusalem: Academon, 1980, pp. 359-68.

Nordlinger, Eric. *Conflict Regulation in Divided Societies* Cambridge, Mass.: Harvard University Press, 1972.

Orans, Martin. "Caste and Race Conflict in Cross-Cultural Perspective." In *Race, Change and Urban Society*, edited by Peter Orleans and William E. Russell. Beverly Hills, California: Sage Publications, 1971, pp. 83-150.

Parkin, Frank. "Strategies of Social Closure in Class Formation." In *The Social Analysis of Class Structure*, edited by Frank Parkin. London: N.Y. Tavistock Publications, 1974, pp. 1-19.

Parsons, Talcott. "Some Theoretical Considerations on the Nature and Trends of Change of Ethnicity." In *Ethnicity*, edited by Nathan Glazer and Daniel P. Moynihan. Cambridge Mass.: Harvard University Press, 1975, pp. 53-83.

Patterson, Orlando. "Context and Choices in Ethnic Allegiance." In *Ethnicity* edited by Nathan Glazer and Daniel P. Moynihan. Cambridge, Mass.: Harvard University Press, 1975, pp. 305-49.

Paz, S. *Dimui Atsmi, Zehut Vehizdahut* [Self-image, identity and identification]. Jerusalem: Department of Education, The Hebrew University of Jerusalem, 1971 (Hebrew).

Peres, Yochanan. "Politika Veedatiut Beshalosh Shhunot Oni" [Politics and Ethnicity in Three Slums]. In *Israeli Society 1967-1973*, edited by Reuven Kehana and Simhah Kopstein. Jerusalem: Academon, 1974, pp. 175-99 (Hebrew).

————. *Yahasei Edot Beisrael* [Ethnic relations in Israel]. Tel Aviv: Sifriat Hapoalim, 1977 (Hebrew).

Ratshavi, Yehudah. "Zhor Leavraham, Zihronotav Shel R'Avraham Alnadaf Zt'l—Letoldot Hakehilah Hateimanit Birushalayim" [In Memory of Abraham— The Diary of Rabbi Avraham Alnadaf—A History of the Yemenite Community in Jerusalem]. In *Prakim Betoldot Hayishuv Hayehudi Birushalayim* [Chapters in the history of the Jewish settlement in Jerusalem]. vol. 2. Edited by Menahem Friedman, Ben Zion Yehoshua, and Josef Tobi. Jerusalem: Yad Ben-Zvi, 1976 pp. 144-91 (Hebrew).

Remba, Oded. "Income Inequality in Israel: Ethnic Aspects." In *Israel: Social Structure and Change*, edited by Michael Curtis and Mordecai Chertoff. New Brunswick N.J.: Transaction Books, 1973, pp. 199-214.

Rekhess, Eli. *A Survey of Israeli-Arab Graduates form Institutions of Higher Learning in Israel (1961-1971)*. Tel Aviv: Shiloah Institute, Tel Aviv University, 1974.

Riger, Hagit "Lebayot Hahitarut Shel Noar Teimani Baaretz" [The problem of integration of Yemenite youth in the country]. *Megamot* 12, no. 3 (April 1952): 244-84 (Hebrew).

Rose, Arnold. "Minorities." *The International Encyclopedia for Social Sciences*, vol. 10, edited by David L. Sills. USA: Crowell, Collier and Macmillan Inc.: 1968, pp. 365-71.

Rosenfeld, Henry. "Eer Olim, Kiryat Shmoneh" [An immigrant town, Kiryat Shmonah]. *Mibifnim* 20, nos. 1-2 (May 1958): 87-95 (Hebrew).

Rotenschtreich, Nathan. "Sikum" [Conclusions]. In *Mizug Galuyot*, edited by Ofrah Cohen. Jerusalem: The Magnes Press, 1969, pp. 188-91 (Hebrew).

Roumani, Maurice M. *From Immigrant to Citizen*. The Hague: Foundation for the Study of Plural Societies, 1979.

Saisset, Pierre. *Heures Juives au Maroc* Paris: Reider, 1930.

Schiff, Zeev, and Haber, Eitan. *Leksikon Lebithon Israel* [Israel, army and defense, a dictionary]. Tel Aviv: Zmora, Bitan, Modan Publishers, 1976 (Hebrew).

Shapira, Dvorah. "Habayot Hasotsialiot Beshikun Olim Vetafkidah Shel Ovedet Sotsialit" [Social Problems in an immigrant neighborhood and the role of the social worker]. *Megamot 7*, no. 3 (July 1956): 286-95 (Hebrew).

Shapira, Ovadiah. *Moshavei Olim Beisrael* [Cooperative settlements of new immigrants in Israel]. Jerusalem: The Jewish Agency, 1972 (Hebrew).

Shapira, Rinah, and Hadad, M. "Shlitah Bemashavim Vehithabrut Hevratit" [Commanding Resources and social integration]. *Megamot 23*, nos. 3-4 (December 1977): 161-73 (Hebrew).

Shapiro, Yonathan. *Hademokratiah Beisrael* [Democracy in Israel] Ramat-Gan: Massadah, 1977.

Shelah, Hanan. "Dfusim Shel Nisuim Bein Edatiim Beisrael Bashanim 1952-1968" [Patterns of marriage among ethnic groups in Israel—1952-1968]. In *Israeli Society, 1969-1973*, edited by Reuven Kehana and Simhah Kopstein. Jerusalem: Academon 1974, pp. 333-59.

Shibutani, Tamotsu, and Kwan Kiani. *Ethnic Stratification, A Comparative Approach*. London: MacMillan, 1965.

Shild, Ozer. "On the Meaning of Military Service in Israel." In *Israel: Social Structure and Change*, edited by Michael Curtis and Mordecai Chertoff. New Brunswick, N.J.: Transaction Books, 1973, pp. 419-32.

Shils, Edward. *The Torment of Secrecy*. London: Heinemann, 1956.

———. "Centre and Periphery." In essays presented to Michael Polanyi, *The Logic of Personal Knowledge*. London: Routledge and Kegan Paul, 1961, pp. 117-30.

Shokeid, Moshe. "The Decline of Personal Endowment of Atlas Mountain Religious Leaders in Israel." *Anthropological Quarterly 52*, no. 4 (October 1979): 186-96.

———. "Immigration and Factionalism: An Analysis of Factions in Rural Israeli Communities of Immigrants." *British Journal of Sociology 19*, no. 4 (December 1968): 385-406.

Shuval, Judith. "Value Orientations of Immigrants in Israel." *Sociometry 26* (June 1963): 247-57.

———. *Bayot Hevratiot Bearei Pituah* [Social Problems in Development Towns]. Jerusalem: The Institute for Social Applied Research, 1959 (Hebrew).

Simpson, George, and Yinger, Milton. *Racial and Cultural Minorities*. New York: Harper and Row, 1958.

Smooha, Sammy. *Israel: Pluralism and Conflict*. London and Henley: Routledge and Kegan Paul, 1978.

———. "Mediniut Kayemet Vealternativit Klapei Haaravim Beisrael" [Existing and Alternative Policy Towards the Arabs in Israel]. *Megamot 26*, no. 1 (September 1980): 7-36 (Hebrew).

Stock, Ernest. *From Conflict to Understanding, Relations Between Jews and Arabs in Israel Since 1948*. New York: Institute of Human Relations Press, 1968.

Tahon, H. *Edot Beisrael* [Jewish Groups in Israel]. Jerusalem: Reuven Mass. 1957 (Hebrew).

Tobi, Yosef. "Letoldot Hayahasim Bein Hateimanim Vehasfaradim Birushalayim Bashanim Tarma'b-Tarsa't" [The history of Yemenite-Sephardic relations in Jerusalem from Tarmab to Tarsat]. In *Prakim Betoldot Hayishuv Hayehudi Birushalayim* [Chapters in the history of the Jewish settlement in Jerusalem], edited by Menahem Friedman, Ben Zion Yehoshua, Yosef Tobi. Jerusalem: Yad Ben-Zvi 1976, pp. 192-215 (Hebrew).

Tsadok, Moshe. *Yehudei Teiman, Toldoteinhem Veorhot Haiyehem* [Yemenite Jews, their history and ways of life]. Tel Aviv: Am Oved, 1967 (Hebrew).

Van den Berghe, Pierre. *Race and Racism*. New York: John Wiley, 1967.

———. *Race and Ethnicity*. New York: Basic Books, 1970.

Weingrod, Alex. *Israel: Group Relations in a New Society*. London: Pall Mall Press, 1965.

———. *Reluctant Pioneers—Village Development in Israel*. Ithaca, N.Y.: Cornell University Press, 1966.

———. "Recent Trends in Israeli Ethnicity." *Ethnic and Racial Studies* 2, no. 1 (January, 1979): 55-65.

Zamir, Rinah. "Beer Sheva 1958-1959—Tahalihim Hevratiim Beeer Pituah" [Beer Sheba 1958-1959—Social Processes in a Development Town]. In *Mivneh Hevrati Shel Israel* [Social Structure of Israel], edited by Shumel N. Eisenstadt, Haim Adler, Rivkah Bar-Yossef, and Reuven Kehana. Jerusalem: Academon, 1966, pp. 335-65 (Hebrew).

Znaniecki, Florian. *Modern Nationalities: A Sociological Study*. Westport, Connecticut: Greenwood Press Publishers, 1973.

Zureik, Elia T. *The Palestinians in Israel, A Study in Internal Colonialism*. London, Boston & Henley: Routledge and Kegan Paul, 1979.

Index

ABOUT THE AUTHOR

ELIEZER BEN-RAFAEL is a Senior Lecturer in the Department of Sociology and Anthropology at the University of Tel-Aviv, Israel. He is the author of *Social Aspects of Guerilla and Anti-Guerilla Warfare* (with M. Lissak) and *Le Nouveau Kibbutz* (with M. Konopnicki and P. Rombaud).